PRIMATE FIELD STUDIES

MW00836788

Series Titles:

The Spectral Tarsier

Sharon L. Gursky, Texas A&M University

Strategies of Sex and Survival in Hamadryas Baboons: Through a Female Lens

Larissa Swedell, Queens College, The City University of New York

The Behavioral Ecology of Callimicos and Tamarins in Northwestern Bolivia

Leila M. Porter, The University of Washington

The Socioecology of Adult Female Patas Monkeys and Vervets

Jill D. Pruetz, Iowa State University

Apes of the Impenetrable Forest: The Behavioral Ecology of Sympatric Chimpanzees and Gorillas

Craig B. Stanford, University of Southern California

A Natural History of the Brown Mouse Lemur

Sylvia Atsalis, Lincoln Park Zoo

Forthcoming:

The Gibbons of Khao Yai

Thad Q. Bartlett, The University of Texas at San Antonio

PRIMATE FIELD STUDIES

Many of us who conduct field studies on wild primates have witnessed a decline in the venues available to publish monographic treatments of our work. As researchers we have few choices other than to publish short technical articles on discrete aspects of our work in professional journals. Also in vogue are popular expositions, often written by nonscientists. To counter this trend, we have begun this series. **Primate Field Studies** is a venue both for publishing the full complement of findings of long-term studies and for making our work accessible to a wider readership. Interested readers need not wait for atomized parts of long-term studies to be published in widely scattered journals; students need not navigate the technical literature to bring together a body of scholarship better served by being offered as a cohesive whole. We are interested in developing monographs based on single- or multi-species studies. If you wish to develop a monograph, we encourage you to contact one of the series editors.

About the Editors:

Robert W. Sussman (Ph.D. Duke University) is currently Professor of Anthropology and Environmental Science at Washington University, St. Louis, Missouri, and past Editor-in-Chief of *American Anthropologist*, the flagship journal of the American Anthropological Association. His research focuses on the ecology, behavior, evolution, and conservation of nonhuman and human primates, and he has worked in Costa Rica, Guyana, Panama, Madagascar, and Mauritius. He is the author of numerous scientific publications, including *Biological Basis of Human Behavior*, Prentice Hall (1999), *Primate Ecology and Social Structure* (two volumes), Pearson Custom Publishing (2003), and *The Origin and Nature of Sociality*, Aldine de Gruyter (2004).

Natalie Vasey (Ph.D. Washington University) is currently Assistant Professor of Anthropology at Portland State University in Portland, Oregon. Her work explores the behavioral ecology, life history adaptations, and evolution of primates, with a focus on the endangered and recently extinct primates of Madagascar. She has presented her research at international venues and published in leading scientific journals. She is dedicated to educating students and the public-at-large about the lifestyles and conservation status of our closest relatives in the Animal Kingdom.

A Natural History of the Brown Mouse Lemur

Sylvia Atsalis, Ph.D.
Lincoln Park Zoo

PEARSON
Prentice Hall

Upper Saddle River, New Jersey 07458

Library of Congress Cataloging-in-Publication Data

Atsalis, Sylvia.

A natural history of the brown mouse lemur / Sylvia Atsalis.
   p.   cm. — (Primate field studies)
Includes bibliographical references and index.
   ISBN-13: 978-0-13-243271-9
   ISBN-10: 0-13-243271-4
   1. Brown mouse lemur.   I. Title.

QL737.P933A87 2008
599.8'3—dc22   2007032033

Publisher: Nancy Roberts
Editorial Assistant: Lee Peterson
Full Service Production Liaison: Joanne Hakim
Marketing Director: Brandy Dawson
Marketing Manager: Lindsey Prudhomme
Operations Specialist: Benjamin Smith
Creative Director: Jayne Conte
Cover Design: Kiwi Design
Cover Photos: Sylvia Atsalis
Manager, Cover Visual Research & Permissions: Karen Sanatar
Director, Image Resource Center: Melinda Patelli
Manager, Rights and Permissions: Zina Arabia
Manager, Visual Research: Beth Brenzel
Photo Coordinator: Joanne Dippel
Full-Service Project Management: Dennis Troutman/Stratford Publishing Services
Composition: TexTech International
Printer/Binder: RR Donnelley & Sons Company

Credits and acknowledgments borrowed from other sources and reproduced, with
permission, in this textbook appear on appropriate page within text.

Pearson Education LTD., London
Pearson Education Singapore, Pte. Ltd
Pearson Education, Canada, Ltd
Pearson Education–Japan
Pearson Education Australia PTY, Limited

Pearson Education North Asia Ltd
Pearson Educación de Mexico, S.A. de C.V.
Pearson Education Malaysia, Pte. Ltd
Pearson Education, Upper Saddle River,
   New Jersey

10 9 8 7 6 5 4 3 2 1
ISBN 13: 978-0-13-243271-9
ISBN 10: 0-13-243271-4

Dedicated to Eric C. Johnstone and in memory of John Atsalis and Warren Kinzey, for their generosity and inspiration

Contents

List of Figures   xi
List of Tables   xv
Preface   xvii

1   Mouse Lemurs: The World's Smallest Primates   1

The Cheirogaleidae   3
Researching the Brown Mouse Lemur   7
Mouse Lemur Species   10
Mouse Lemur Distribution   12
Distinctive Features of the Cheirogaleidae   16

2   Researching the Brown Mouse Lemur   21

Description of the Study Site   21
Rainfall and Temperature Patterns   23
Phenological Monitoring   24
Flowering and Fruiting Patterns   25
Insect Availability   30
Live-Trapping Mouse Lemurs   35
Observing Mouse Lemurs   38

3   **Diet and Feeding Ecology**   **41**

The Diet of Mouse Lemurs   41

Investigating Diet in the Brown Mouse Lemur   44

Use of Plants and Prey   47

Frugivory   47

Bakerella, the Fruit of Preference   51

Beetles, the Prey of Preference   55

Other Organic Matter Found in Fecal Samples   56

Fruit: Availability and Consumption   56

Phytochemical Analysis of Fruits Eaten   60

Animal Prey: Availability and Consumption   60

Observations of Mouse Lemurs Feeding   63

Mouse Lemurs and Mistletoes   65

Mouse Lemurs and Beetles   72

Comparing the Diets of Mouse Lemur Species   73

What Can Mouse Lemurs Tell Us about
Primate Origins   75

Fecal Sampling as a Way to Study Diet   77

Suggested Directions for Future Studies   78

Summary   79

4   **Seasonal Changes in Body Mass and Activity Levels**   **81**

How Small Mammals Respond to Climatic
and Resource Fluctuations   81

Seasonal Fluctuations in the Cheirogaleidae   83

Investigating Seasonal Fluctuations in the Brown
Mouse Lemur   87

Fattening and Hibernation   91

Population Fluctuations in Body Mass,
Tail Circumference, and Activity Levels   96

Differences in Seasonal Response at RNP   100

Comparing Seasonal Responses of Mouse
Lemur Species   107

Emerging from Hibernation   108
Sleeping Nests   110
The Effects of Trapping   112
Suggested Directions for Future Studies   112
Summary   113

5   The Social Life of the Brown Mouse Lemur   115

Sociality in Nocturnal Strepsirrhines   115
Investigating Social Organization in the Brown
Mouse Lemur   121
Social Interactions of the Brown Mouse Lemur   124
The Solitary Mouse Lemur   126
Understanding Spatial Distribution Through Trap Data   129
Changes in Population Composition   131
Seasonal Fluctuations in Trap Sex Ratio   135
Migration Patterns and Population Continuity   138
Population Residents   142
Scramble and Contest Competition   143
Suggested Directions for Future Studies   145
Summary   147

6   Reproduction in the Brown Mouse Lemurs   149

Reproductive Patterns of Mouse Lemurs   149
Assessing Reproductive Condition in the Brown
Mouse Lemur   154
Testicular Enlargement, Estrous Cycles, Gestation,
and Births   156
Reproductive Seasonality   161
The Advantages of Estrous Synchrony   163
Postpartum Estrus   165
Atypical Estrus   166
Male Reproductive Patterns   167

Young Mouse Lemurs   169
Female Reproductive Potential   171
Summary   173

**7   The Annual Cycle of the Brown Mouse Lemur:
An Overview   175**

A Year in the Life of the Brown Mouse Lemur   175
Local Ecologies   181
Mouse Lemurs as Small Mammals   183
The Future   185

References   187
Index   223

List of Figures

Figure 1–1 Map of Madagascar Showing the
Current Known Distribution of Mouse Lemurs   14

Figure 2–1 Monthly Rainfall and Temperature
Fluctuations in Talatakely, RNP   24

Figure 2–2 Monthly Percentage of 888 Trees and
Shrubs Bearing Buds and Flowers Sampled
in Four Plots in Talatakely, RNP   27

Figure 2–3 Monthly Percentage of 888 Trees
and Shrubs Bearing Fruit Sampled in Four
Plots in Talatakely, RNP   27

Figure 2–4 Monthly Percentage of 161 Vernacular
Species Bearing Buds and Flowers Sampled
in Four Plots in Talatakely, RNP   28

Figure 2–5 Monthly Percentage of 161 Vernacular
Species Bearing Fruit Sampled in Four Plots
in Talakely, RNP   28

Figure 2–6 Fresh Insect Mass (g) and Number of
Insects Collected Semimonthly in Talatakely, RNP   32

Figure 2–7 Monthly Number of Insects Collected
Compared with Monthly Rainfall and Flowering
Patterns of Trees and Shrubs in Four Plots in
Talatakely, RNP   32

Figure 2–8 Monthly Percentage of Insect Orders
Captured During Sampling in Talatakely, RNP   34

Figure 2–9 Total Number of Various Taxa of Insects
Captured Monthly from July 1993 to May 1994 During

Sampling in Talatakely, RNP and the Number
of Nights That Each Taxon Was Captured 35

Figure 3–1 Monthly Percentage of *Microcebus Rufus*
Fecal Samples Containing Remains from Fruit Only
or Fruit and Insects or Insects Only 47

Figure 3–2 Percentage of *Microcebus Rufus* Fecal Samples
Containing Insect and Spider Remains ($n = 115$) 55

Figure 3–3 Monthly Measures of Fruit Presence in
Microcebus Rufus Fecal Samples in Talatakely, RNP 57

Figure 3–4 A Comparison of *Bakerella* Plants Bearing
Fruit with the Presence of *Bakerella* in Fecal Samples
of *Microcebus Rufus* 58

Figure 3–5 Monthly Percentage of Plants Bearing Fruit
That Were Food Resources for *Microcebus Rufus* in
Talatakely, RNP 59

Figure 3–6 Monthly Measures for the Presence of Prey
Items in Fecal Samples of *Microcebus Rufus* 62

Figure 4–1 Seasonal Fluctuations in Body Mass (g) and
Tail Circumference (cm) in One Brown Mouse Lemur
Male (M2) 94

Figure 4–2 Percentage Deviation of Monthly Average
Body Mass (g) and Tail Circumference (cm) Values
from Population Averages (43.5 g and 2.7 cm
Respectively) in Adult Brown Mouse Lemur Males
in Talatakely, RNP 100

Figure 4–3 Percentage Deviation of Monthly Average
Body Mass (g) and Tail Circumference (cm) Values
from Population Averages (42 g and 2.7 cm
Respectively) in Adult Brown Mouse Lemur
Females in Talatakely, RNP 101

Figure 4–4 Monthly Frequency of Four Body Mass (g)
Classes in Brown Mouse Lemur Males as the
Percentage of All Males Trapped Each Month
in Talatakely, RNP 101

Figure 4–5 Monthly Frequency of Four Body Mass (g)
Classes in Brown Mouse Lemur Females as the
Percentage of All Females Trapped Each Month
in Talatakely, RNP 102

Figure 5–1 Distribution of the Number of Brown
Mouse Lemurs Captured at Trap Sites from
February 1993 to May 1994, in Talatakely, RNP 130

Figure 5–2 Distribution of the Number of Male and
Female Brown Mouse Lemurs Captured at Trap Sites
from February 1993 to May 1994 in Talatakely, RNP   131

Figure 5–3 Percentage of Male and Female Brown Mouse
Lemurs Captured and the Number of Different Traps
That They Entered from February 1993 to May 1994
in Talatakely, RNP   132

Figure 5–4 Percentage of Male and Female Brown Mouse
Lemurs Captured and the Number of Times They
Entered Traps from February 1993 to May 1994
in Talatakely, RNP   132

Figure 5–5 Trap Results for Brown Mouse Lemurs
Captured Between February 1993 and May 1994
in Talatakely, RNP   133

Figure 5–6 Average Number of Individual Brown
Mouse Lemur Males (ANM) and Average Number
of Individual Brown Mouse Lemur Females (ANF)
Captured per Night in Each of Four Periods from
February 1993 to May 1994 in Talatakely, RNP   134

Figure 5–7 Number of Individual Brown Mouse Lemur
Male and Female Trap Captures Before the Onset (July
and August) and During the Main Part (September
Through December) of the Breeding Season in
Talatakely, RNP   136

Figure 5–8 Spatial Distribution of Resident Brown Mouse
Lemur Males (M16 etc.) and Resident Brown Mouse
Lemur Females (F10 etc.) Based on Locations of Trap
Capture in Talatakely, RNP   143

Figure 6–1 The Reproductive Pattern of *Microcebus Rufus*
Females in Talatakely, RNP   157

Figure 6–2 Fluctuations in Male Brown Mouse Lemur
Monthly Average Testicular Width (mm) and Testicular
Volume (mm^3)   158

Figure 7–1 Rainfall, Temperature, and Resource
Seasonality in Association with the Reproductive
Schedule, and Other Milestones in the Annual Life
Cycle of *Microcebus Rufus* at Talatakely, Ranomafana
National Park, Madagascar   179

List of Tables

Table 3–1 Fruits Identified as Food Sources for Brown
    Mouse Lemurs   48

Table 3–2 Percentage of 240 Fecal Samples That
    Contained Specific Fruits Eaten by Brown Mouse
    Lemurs (Total Sampled, 334)   50

Table 3–3 Measurements of Fruits Identified as Food
    Sources for Brown Mouse Lemurs   52

Table 3–4 Monthly Presence of All Fruits (Based on
    Seed Presence) in 334 Fecal Samples of Brown
    Mouse Lemurs   53

Table 3–5 Phytochemical Analysis of Select Fruits Eaten
    by Brown Mouse Lemurs and Two Nonfood Fruits
    for Comparison   61

Table 4–1 Mass (g) and Tail Circumference (cm)
    of Male and Female *Microcebus Rufus* in Talatakely, RNP   89

Table 4–2 Monthly Mean Body Mass (g) and Tail
    Circumference (cm) Fluctuations in Male and
    Female Brown Mouse Lemurs That Fattened and
    Hibernated in RNP   92

Table 4–3 Mean Body Mass and Tail Circumference
    Values for Male and Female Brown Mouse Lemurs
    in RNP Before and after Hibernation   93

Table 4–4 Partial Data Available Demonstrating
    Seasonal Fluctuations in Monthly Mean Body
    Mass (g) and Tail Circumference (cm) Fluctuations
    in Male and Female Brown Mouse Lemurs in RNP   95

Table 4–5 Male and Female Brown Mouse Lemurs That
Did Not Experience Seasonal Fluctuations in Monthly
Mean Body Mass (g) and Tail Circumference (cm)
in the Dry Season in RNP   97

Table 4–6 Population-Level Body Mass and Tail
Circumference Values for Male and Female Brown
Mouse Lemurs for Two Seasonal Periods in RNP   98

Table 5–1 Summary of Trap Results for *Microcebus Rufus*
in Ranomafana National Park   130

Table 6–1 Summary of Results from Studies on
Reproductive and Mating Patterns of Various
Mouse Lemur Species   150

Table 6–2 Sequence of Reproductive Events and
Changes in Body Mass of Select Females During
the Mating Season   159

Table 6–3 Changes in Body Mass of Gestating Females   160

Preface

Students of primate behavior often begin their research already devoted to a particular species. Gorillas, chimpanzees and bonobos are common interests, but I have also known colleagues with a fondness for capuchins, colobus, or baboons. If there was any predilection on my part, it was a penchant for the unusual, and a tendency for taking up a challenge. I did not start out loving mouse lemurs. When I began my studies in biological anthropology, my intention was to study the evolution of social behavior. Typically, a study of this nature involves focusing on species that live in social groups in which social interactions are common and visible. Yet, I ended up spending many months following animals that were often not much wider than the leaves behind which they hid, and to whose social interactions I rarely was privy.

In Ranomafana National Park (RNP), mouse lemurs followed the rhythms of the forest. With the rains came the seasonal banquet of fruits and insects. Mouse lemurs gorged themselves into rotund spheres. I called them *little bulls*, their necks were so puffy with fat. As the rains slackened, fat mouse lemurs sank into a deep sleep, until the shortening of the night whispered that it was time to mate. Testicles, normally shrunken, inflated to the size of small walnuts, and the sealed sexual skin of the females split bloody open to receive eager mates. There was boisterous chatter among the boughs and branches, and wild chases. A few months later, all was quiet as the forest transformed into a nursery where mouse lemur nests were filled with many, tiny, scrawny, grey infants. Within two months, the young, already grown and sporting the bright reddish-brown fur of adults, were initiated into the life cycle. In the rainforest, I discovered, trees and mouse lemurs kept flawless time.

There were other lessons, too, that I learned from the Malagasy forest and its people; to be patient, to know that to be still in observation may be more valuable than to measure, define, and determine. More importantly,

I learned that the jungle's trees and the mouse lemurs kept flawless time . . . without me.

I remembered the lessons of the rainforest when I was desperate to escape the claustrophobia of drenched vegetation, when cyclones destroyed the rickety bridges that crossed the rivers surrounding the study area, our contacts to provisions and humanity. Yet I was rarely alone in the forest, although most fellow researchers and friends would leave eventually, while I remained to finish my long-term research project. The night before their departure there would be festivities and extra food, and parting gifts of old t-shirts, worn-out socks, an extra pair of field pants, moldy books, a few good batteries. I took the old t-shirts with gratitude, and when I left, I passed them on to my field guides. I have a picture of the youngest, Le Jean, wearing the one with a funny crayola likeness of the Eiffel Tower. Next to him stands another trusted guide, Jean-Marie, his father, wrapped to the neck with what looks like a gingham tablecloth, a traditional Malagasy dress. I will never forget these and the other RNP guides, who were instrumental to the completion of my dissertation research. They always wore so proudly the full regalia of raingear that I had brought for them.

Since my stay at RNP, the research station has been dramatically modernized, but at the time, amenities were simple. We lived in tents, water was carried from the Namorona River that ran adjacent to the site, we relied on candles and flashlights for light, food was cooked over a gas ring, or for larger meals, in a huge soot-covered kettle over burning wood, and bathing was often done by warming a little water in a kettle. I am glad to have known forest life in its basic essentials.

For the experience of living in Madagascar, the satisfaction of completing a challenging doctoral thesis, and the opportunity to write this monograph, I have a cadre of people to thank. Among them, I maintain feelings of immense gratitude towards my late doctoral advisor, Warren Kinzey, who, even while facing an abrupt decline in his health, stood by me, a rock of support. I also thank my second advisor, Eric Delson, for his always judicious insights. He continues to be a source of support and I am grateful for his periodic advice. My advisory committee, John Oates, Sara Stinson, Patricia Wright, and Bob Sussman, offered invaluable comments for improvements on the dissertation and much needed encouragement when the times got tough.

Bob Sussman and Natalie Vasey should be congratulated for envisioning the brilliant idea of this series of monographs, and I thank Bob Martin and other anonymous reviewers for comments that greatly improved this volume.

While in Madagascar, as well as before and after, I am forever grateful for the camaraderie, support, and research help offered so generously by Dan and Liz Turk, Louise Martin, Chia Tan, Ny Yamashita, Susan Foxman, Liz Balko, Julien Stark, Jörg Ganzhorn, Jutta Schmid, Peter Kappeler,

Annie Singer, Amy Gabrion, Sarah Willis, Eleanor Sterling, Leanne Nash, Hilary Morland, Martine Perret, Petter Walsh, Joe and Katie Gonder, Marian Dagosto, Brian Shea, Matt Ravosa, Larry Cochard, Kashka Kubdzela, Lorna Profant, Wendy Dirks, and Steve Lindquist. For support while writing my dissertation and later this monograph, I also thank my family, Anna, Gus and Mary Atsalis, as well as Todd Schaner, and Nancy and John Johnstone.

The Malagasy Government, the Department of Water and Forests, Benjamin Andrianamihaja, and the staff of Ranomafana National Park, made my research possible. The cabin managers, Jeanette and Aimée, made the cabin cozy and functional, while my Malagasy colleagues, Jean-Claude and Tina provided their unconditional friendship. Without the tireless work of my team of field guides, my research would have been much more restricted in scope; it is impossible to be thankful enough for the efforts of Raliva Pierre, Jean-Marie, Rakotoniaina Jean, Ratalata François, Rajeriarison Emile, and the late Rakotonirina Georges.

My friend and colleague Larissa Swedell informed me of the monograph field series and answered many questions. Richard Cambell provided invaluable statistical advice. Librarian and friend, Courtney Lavery, provided invaluable reference services (and a patient ear) that expedited exponentially the writing of the monograph. Kara Nuss was instrumental in completing the onerous task of compiling the reference list. Comments from Sue Margulis and Mark Domke improved the manuscript. I thank The Chicago Zoological Society (Brookfield Zoo) and Lincoln Park Zoo for logistical support. The research was made possible by generous support of the National Science Foundation, the National Geographic Society, Wenner-Gren Anthropological Association, and Sigma Xi.

Lastly, I thank my late father, John Atsalis, for teaching me to hold nature, beauty, and truth in the highest esteem, and my husband, Eric Johnstone, who sustains me daily with his magnanimous spirit, his generous support, his patience, and his clever wit that keeps me laughing—without him the writing of this monograph would not have been possible.

A Natural History
of the Brown Mouse
Lemur

1

Mouse Lemurs: The World's Smallest Primates

Mammals can be spectacular in many ways, perhaps none more strikingly so than in the large sizes they can reach. The African bush elephant, the largest living land mammal, can weigh an impressive seven tons and stands a massive twelve-feet high. Large, conspicuous mammals attract both public and research interest. They are often elevated to flagship status and can be impressive ambassadors for national conservation efforts. Yet most mammals lack impressiveness of size. The great majority measure less than one foot, and their inconspicuousness is often compounded by cryptic and nocturnal habits. Even among primates, which typically are neither small nor nocturnal, there are species that combine these traits. Mouse lemurs, which weigh approximately 25–110 g, are the world's smallest living primates (Atsalis et al., 1996; Zimmermann et al., 1998; Rasoloarison et al., 2000; Yoder et al., 2000). Small size and nocturnal activity make these and other nocturnal primates fascinating but also a challenge to study. Indeed, for most of primate research history, the study of nocturnal species has been relatively sporadic. In the past, each published paper was a major contribution to our understanding of a lifestyle uncommon within the visually dominated diurnal primate world but not uncommon among mammals at large (e.g., Charles-Dominique, 1971, 1972; Martin, 1973; Petter, 1977, 1978; Charles-Dominique and Petter, 1980; Hladik et al., 1980; Pagès, 1980; Clark, 1985; Harcourt and Nash, 1986a). More recently, noteworthy research findings have advanced considerably our understanding of nocturnal primate behavior and ecology. The application of new or refined technology, such as radiotelemetry, microchips,

Microcebus rufus, the brown mouse lemur in Ranomafana National Park

and genetic analyses, has led to research breakthroughs. The pioneering and curious spirit of research biologists has been the driving force behind our growing understanding of the nocturnal primate world in all its diversity, but underlying the goals and aspirations of scientific research may be a sense of urgency as habitat destruction threatens wildlife worldwide.

Are nocturnal primates destined to go "from obscurity to extinction," as Martin (1995) so succinctly wondered? Perhaps this sad fate will be avoided because even as extinction threatens many primates, long-term studies on nocturnal species are leading the way to transforming our understanding of the order. Advances in our knowledge of nocturnal primates are especially significant on the island of Madagascar, where approximately 60% of primate species are nocturnal. Nevertheless, the fear that the world may lose species to extinction—not only nocturnal lemurs but also other species that comprise Madagascar's rich natural world—before we discover or become familiar with them is a realistic one. The island's central plateaus are largely devoid of forest, possibly as a result of anthropogenic activities since occupation took place approximately two thousand years ago (Wright and Rakotoarisoa, 2003). Today, although approximately 90% of the island's animals live in forests (Dufils, 2003), only small pockets of forests remain hugging the coastal line (Smith, 1997).

In recent years, the island has drawn the interest of biologists keen to discover its unique flora and fauna. Madagascar may be poor in diversity of diurnal mammals (Goodman et al., 2003) and birds (Hawkins and Goodman, 2003), but it is rich in reptiles (Raxworthy, 2003) and amphibians (Glaw and Vences, 2003). Notably, 84% of all land vertebrates there are endemic (Goodman and Benstead, 2005). For those interested in primate behavior, Madagascar boasts intriguing attractions: the country ranks among the highest in the world in primate diversity (Mittermeier et al., 1994); all primates on the island are found nowhere else; and the majority of them, like most of Madagascar's mammals, are nocturnal (Martin, 1972a). Lemurs are the best-known animals of Madagascar's wildlife, attracting worldwide scientific and ecotourist attention to the island's unique biodiversity. Lemurs are used as indicators of ecological monitoring, and their presence has been an important factor behind the creation of numerous protected areas on the island (Durbin, 1999). The distinctiveness of Madagascar's flora and fauna, particularly the lemurs, was one of the deciding factors that attracted me to do my doctoral research there. Many other researchers have been similarly captivated, and the wealth of recent research on the island has been excellently compiled and summarized in an ambitious reference tome, *The Natural History of Madagascar* (Goodman and Benstead, 2003).

In Madagascar, I became part of a cohort of scientists eager to understand the lives of nocturnal primates. My study is now one of many that paint a broad picture of previously unsuspected variety and complexity within the world of nocturnal primates. Many colleagues old and new continue to make important contributions to nocturnal primate ecology and social behavior. In this monograph, I pay tribute to their continued efforts while presenting my own research on the brown mouse lemur *Microcebus rufus*, in Ranomafana National Park (RNP), a block of lush rainforest in the southeastern part of the island. During the seventeen months of my field study, I collected data on many aspects of the brown mouse lemur's biology. Some aspects were studied more comprehensively than others, but in total the research focused on establishing the important events that mark the annual life cycle of mouse lemurs at RNP. In this chapter, I present some initial background information on mouse lemurs and the family to which they belong, the Cheirogaleidae. Some of these varied topics will be developed further in chapters to follow. My hope is that the readers of this volume will find mouse lemurs as exciting as I did when I first stepped into the rainforest of Ranomafana's national park.

THE CHEIROGALEIDAE

Mouse lemurs are strepsirrhines—that is, they belong to the suborder of primates called the Strepsirrhini, which also includes the other Malagasy lemurs, the galagos (bushbabies) of sub-Saharan Africa, and the lorises of sub-Saharan Africa and Southeast Asia. The Strepsirrhini are characterized by the development of a tooth comb in which the anterior lower teeth are elongated, slender, and procumbent (Rasmussen and Nekaris, 1998). [An exception to this feature is the aye-aye, *Daubentonia madagascariensis*, which may have lost the trait as its teeth specialized in a different way (Ankel-Simons, 1996).] Extant strepsirrhine primates also possess a grooming claw instead of a nail on the second pedal digit (Schwartz and Tattersall, 1985).

Primates in the suborder Strepsirrhini are characterized by a moist, naked rhinarium similar to the wet noses of cats and dogs—in that sense, there exist both primate and nonprimate *strepsirrhine* mammals. In contrast, members of the other primate suborder, the Haplorhini (monkeys, apes, and humans) possess a dry, hairy upper lip. [Prosimian is another taxonomic grouping used to designate lemurs, lorises, galagos, as well as tarsiers and all early primates (Fleagle, 1998), but in this volume I mostly use Strepsirrhini, and Haplorhini, to refer to the principal primate taxa.] The strepsirrhine rhinarium is linked through the split upper lip to a membrane of the oral cavity, the vomeronasal or Jacobson's organ, where airborne odor molecules such as pheromones are processed (Rouquier et al., 2000; Liman and Innan, 2003). Primate strepsirrhines share this trait, indicative of a well-developed olfactory system, with many nonprimate mammals (carnivores, insectivores, rodents, bats, and more).

Yet another trait shared by strepsirrhine mammals is the tapetum lucidum. Located behind the retina of many diurnal and nocturnal strepsirrhines, the tapetum lucidum is a reflecting membranous layer that enhances the eye's ability to register light by increasing retinal sensitivity in low-light conditions (Pariente, 1979; Martin, 1994). The tapetum lucidum has played a prominent role in discussions regarding ancestral primate adaptations. Accepted wisdom viewed the membrane as an adaptation specifically for the nocturnal lifestyle, and because it is found in diurnal strepsirrhine primates as well as nocturnal ones, it was held that all strepsirrhines were descendent from a nocturnal ancestor (Martin, 1994). Recent evidence has cast doubt on this scenario. Tan et al. (2005) discovered, through comparative genetic analysis of opsin genes (involved with color vision), that ancestral primates may have been cathemeral or even diurnal. The researchers proposed that different groups of primates shifted to nocturnal activity at different times in evolutionary history and as they did so, nocturnal features were strengthened whereas diurnal ones were lost or relaxed. Today, the presence of the tapetum lucidum in nocturnal primates is a lucky perk for the researcher as the membrane reflects brightly when subjects are observed by flashlight. The yellow-orange glow is considerably helpful in locating animals in the dark and can be especially useful, as I discovered, when observing animals in thick forest.

Among the strepsirrhines, mouse lemurs, genus *Microcebus*, belong to the family Cheirogaleidae, a group of small-bodied (<500 g), arboreal, primarily quadrupedally locomoting, nocturnal lemurs that includes: *Cheirogaleus* (dwarf lemurs), *Mirza* (giant mouse lemurs), *Phaner* (fork-crowned lemurs), and the monotypic *Allocebus trichotis* (hairy-eared dwarf lemur), the latter long thought to be extinct but rediscovered (Meier and Albignac, 1991; Groves, 2005). Among the Cheirogaleidae, chromosomal studies show that there are cytogenetic differences between *Phaner* and the other species (Rumpler et al., 1994), whereas molecular research indicates that *Allocebus, Mirza,* and *Microcebus* are more closely related to each other than to *Cheirogaleus* (i.e., they form a clade or monophyletic group of species) (Pastorini et al., 2001). Lastly, *Mirza* and *Microcebus* may be more closely related to each other than to the other members of the family (Rumpler et al., 1994).

Cheirogaleids display features that are relatively unusual among primates but are common among other small mammals. Species of *Cheirogaleus* and *Microcebus* and possibly *Allocebus trichotis* are the only primates known to enter periods of hypothermia and lethargy, either daily or seasonal, the latter after accumulating body fat. As will be discussed in later chapters, these behaviors represent adaptations for coping with stressful environmental conditions. Another unusual, for primates, feature is that cheirogaleids commonly produce litters that consist of two to four offspring.

Patience and persistence, mandatory requirements for the nocturnal primate researcher, have yielded a plethora of information on diet, life history, and reproduction although the most exciting discoveries concern cheirogaleid sociality. Members of the family were generally thought to be nongregarious, usually foraging alone at night and not found active within cohesive social groups. We are aware now that cheirogaleids do not lack a social life and that they typically form well-defined but dispersed social networks of rich diversity. Even their daytime sleeping associations constitute an important element of their social life.

Cheirogaleus medius, the lesser dwarf lemur, a species that among primates has the unique ability to hibernate annually for seven months (Dausmann et al., 2004), has been found to form permanent pair bonds while at the same time engaging in extra pair couplings during the reproductive period (Müller 1998, 1999a,b,c; Fietz, 1999a,b; Fietz et al., 2000; see Fietz, 2003a for a review). *Mirza coquereli,* Coquerel's mouse lemur, at Kirindy Forest (a site near Morondava on the west coast, where research on several cheirogaleids is ongoing) lives in matrilinear clusters in which members actively defend borders (Kappeler, 1997a, 2003; Kappeler et al., 2002). *Phaner furcifer,* the Masoala fork-crowned lemur, an exudate specialist, spends the majority of the night alone but maintains vocal contact with its mate. The pair engages in conflicts with other pairs over access to exudate trees (Schülke, 2003). Little information on *Allocebus trichotis* exists, but even for this species, it is known that several individuals sleep together in tree holes (Rakotoarison et al., 1997).

Mouse lemurs are found throughout Madagascar although to date much of the research has taken place in the dry, deciduous forests of Madagascar's west coast. Madagascar is in the southern hemisphere and the seasons are inverse. Thus, the problem that confronts lemurs in dry forests, is survival during the dry season, or the austral winter, when food resources are scarce. Over thirty years ago, seminal field research primarily on the grey mouse lemur, *Microcebus murinus*, laid the foundations for understanding mouse lemur natural history, establishing this species as an omnivore, with seasonal shifts in diet, activity levels, body weight, and body temperature (Martin, 1972b, 1973; Pagès, 1978, 1980; Charles-Dominique and Petter, 1980; Hladik et al., 1980; Barre et al., 1988; Pagès-Feuillade, 1988). Seasonal behaviors were also observed in captivity (e.g., Petter-Rousseaux, 1974, 1980; Petter-Rousseaux and Hladik, 1980; Aujard et al., 1998; Génin and Perret, 2000) and found to be linked to changes in photoperiod affecting the pituitary gland (Petter-Rousseaux, 1970, 1974, 1980; Martin, 1972c; Perret, 1972; Perret and Aujard, 2001). Other cheirogaleids of dry forests were found to maintain dietary specializations, seasonal patterns in food intake, body fat accumulation, and the ability to enter daily or seasonal periods of lethargy. These were considered to be adaptations to the highly seasonal conditions of food availability in the forests of the west coast (Petter-Rousseaux, 1980; Petter-Rousseaux and Hladik, 1980; Schmid, 1996; Fietz, 2003b; Kappeler, 2003). The diet of the grey mouse lemur typified omnivory, encompassing fruit, insects, flowers, buds, gums, nectars, plant and insect secretions, small vertebrates, and some leaves (Martin, 1972b, 1973; Hladik et al., 1980; Barre et al., 1988; Corbin and Schmid, 1995; Génin, 2001).

The ability to enter a hypothermic state is a particularly fascinating aspect of mouse lemur biology. This phenomenon is commonly associated with species that live in northern climates, including many rodents such as chipmunks (*Tamias*), ground squirrels (*Spermophilus*), prairie dogs (*Cynomys*), marmots (*Marmota*), and hamsters (*Cricetus*) (French, 1988). Bats also undergo daily and seasonal periods of hypothermia (e.g., Altringham, 1996). Like bats, mouse lemurs experience daily *torpor* and seasonal prolonged *hibernation* (Ortmann et al., 1996, 1997; Schmid et al., 2000). Research at Kirindy on the physiology of torpor has revealed that, during the wet season, mouse lemurs accumulated body fat that was metabolized during the resource-poor dry season, when animals reduced body temperatures and activity, resting in their nests for days at a time (Ortmann et al., 1996, 1997; Schmid, 1996, 2000). Sexual differences were discovered in these behaviors, with females fattening more than males (Pagès-Feuillade, 1988) and hibernating for long periods whereas males stayed mostly active (Fietz, 1998; Schmid and Kappeler, 1998). Mating too, was found to be highly seasonal in mouse lemurs (e.g., Fietz, 1999c; Radespiel, 2000), like that of many other Malagasy primates (e.g., van Horn and Eaton, 1979; Rasmussen, 1985; Lewis and Kappeler, 2005), with the onset of sexual activity resulting in changes in vulval appearance and spectacular increases in testicular size (Martin, 1972b; Glatston, 1979; van Horn and Eaton, 1979; Perret, 1990).

The social organization of mouse lemurs has been the subject of many studies, which will be described in detail in Chapter 5. Results from the first attempts to study mouse lemur social organization suggested that they lived in localised "populaton nuclei" within which a few males had home ranges that encompassed those of several females, with surplus males driven to the periphery of the nucleus (Martin, 1972b, 1973). More recently, trap and radiotracking studies revealed considerable overlap of home ranges of both sexes, more than previously thought for what were considered to be solitary and possibly territorial species (Pagès-Feuillade, 1988; Radespiel, 2000; Schwab, 2000; Kappeler, 2003). Mouse lemurs have been found to sleep alone or in groups, in tree holes or in nests that they constructed by themselves (Martin, 1973; Kappeler, 1998). Daytime sleeping associations undergo seasonal changes in composition; outside of the breeding season, males tended to sleep alone and females in small groups, whereas pairs were found together during the mating season (e.g., Martin, 1972b, 1973; Pagès-Feuillade, 1988; Radespiel et al., 1998).

For detailed information on mouse lemurs as well as other cheirogaleids and lemurs, the reader may wish to peruse the excellent *All the World's Primates* (Rowe, 2008), a complete reference volume with professional photography and a digital database.

RESEARCHING THE BROWN MOUSE LEMUR

Weighing an average of 42 g, the brown mouse lemur is among the smallest of mouse lemurs (Schmid and Kappeler, 1994; Atsalis et al., 1996). The field study described here was the first long-term study on the species. Research under rainforest conditions poses its own set of challenges, but it was with great anticipation that I began my project. Given what was known of the congeneric and predominantly dry forest dweller, *M. murinus*, I was particularly interested in the potential influence of the rainforest environment on mouse lemur behavior. By focusing on the rainforest, where seasonal climatic variations presumably were less pronounced, I set about to answer the questions: what kind of environmental stresses do brown mouse lemurs face in the rainforest, and how do they cope with their environment?

I knew from the experience of other researchers who had studied nocturnal species, such as the aye-aye (Sterling, 1993a), that radiotracking a small solitary primate in the rainforest would be a challenge. I expected

View from "belle-view" lookout in Ranomafana National Park.

that the brown mouse lemur's diminutive size would be an obstacle to locating and following them in dense foliage and hilly terrain. I had already been warned that using live traps was not a reliable method for capturing mouse lemurs at RNP (Harcourt, personal communication, 1992). Indeed, Harcourt (1987) had managed to capture some males but very few females, whereas another researcher had struggled to catch even a minimal number of individuals (Harste, personal communication, 1993). Therefore, in addition to live traps routinely used to study small mammals, I came armed with other equipment suitable for studying nocturnal species, such as ultra-lightweight radiocollars for tracking and solar panels to refuel the many rechargeable flashlight batteries that I would need to conduct nightly walks in search of mouse lemur activity. Should my attempts at live-trapping prove unproductive, at least I could try to follow mouse lemurs on their perambulations through the forest and get a picture of their habits and foraging range. In the end, it was the live traps that allowed intimate observation of mouse lemurs and gave me many clues to their behavior.

While in Madagascar, I visited and collaborated with researchers at Kirindy who were experimenting with a technology new for nocturnal primate identification: transponder tags. Uniquely programmed with a special code, the tags are microchips that are placed subcutaneously by trained staff; the emitted signal is picked up by a scanning wand, allowing for permanent, quick, and easy identification of the captured animal

The research cabin at Talatakely in Ranomafana National Park.

(Nietfeld et al., 1994). Although at RNP I relied on tiny ear notches for identification, a technique traditional to mammal studies (e.g., Nietfeld et al., 1994), which worked well with mouse lemurs, today transponders are being used successfully at RNP to investigate predator response (Deppe, 2005) and reproduction (Blanco, 2007) in brown mouse lemurs.

My research at RNP centered on an investigation of diet, seasonal fluctuations in body fat and activity levels, reproductive patterns, and aspects of social organization. In terms of diet, the degree of insectivory in mouse lemurs was a main point of inquiry. Accepted theory was that small primates should focus on nutritionally concentrated foods such as insects (Hladik, 1979; Clutton-Brock and Harvey, 1983; Coe, 1984; Kay, 1984; Richard, 1985). Fruit was known to figure importantly in the diet of the grey mouse lemur (Martin, 1972b, 1973; Hladik et al., 1980), but there was some evidence to support the idea that insects were the preferred food of brown mouse lemurs (Harste, 1993; Harste et al., 1997). Compared with *M. murinus*, the mouth and tooth morphology of *M. rufus* is characteristic of insectivores (Martin, 1995). Nevertheless, no systematic field research on diet had been conducted. It also remained to be documented whether brown mouse lemurs underwent the distinct seasonal variations in body weight and activity levels, common among dry forest cheirogaleids. Prior to the present study, there were some indications, though no firm evidence, that body weight and annual activity did not fluctuate in *M. rufus* to the same degree as in *M. murinus* (Martin, 1972b; Ganzhorn, 1988).

The potential lack, or smaller degree, of fluctuations in the brown mouse lemur accorded with accepted notions on climate in the eastern rainforest regions of Madagascar, which was considered to be less seasonal than in the west (Donque, 1972). In fact, seasonal periods of resource scarcity had been found to occur in Ranomafana (Overdorff, 1991; Hemingway, 1995), raising the need for re-evaluation of what was accepted regarding mouse lemur behavior.

MOUSE LEMUR SPECIES

Madagascar can be roughly divided into three ecological zones that influence the distribution patterns of lemurs and other species: the humid east coast, the dry west coast, and the arid south (Martin, 1972a; Tattersall, 1982). Initially, mouse lemurs were classified as one species, *M. murinus*, with two distinct forms: a long-eared grey form, found predominantly on the west coast and a short-eared red (rufous or brown) form found throughout the east coast rainforests (Petter, 1962; Petter et al., 1977). When the two forms were recognized to be sympatric in southeastern Madagascar, they were elevated to species level; the red form on the east coast became *Microcebus rufus*, whereas the predominantly west coast–dwelling grey form became *Microcebus murinus* (Tattersall, 1982).

Within the past decade, the number of recognized cheirogaleid species has more than doubled. This extraordinary increase in recognized diversity of nocturnal primates has occurred partly as a result of intensified research efforts and partly through the application of new taxonomic tools including reliable molecular methods and identification of species-specific vocalizations (Groeneveld et al., 2006; Honess et al., 2006; Olivieri et al., 2006). Thus, over the years, the taxonomy of mouse lemurs has been refined with many new species recognized and described. Another red form was noted to occur sympatrically with *M. murinus* on the west coast (Petter, 1962; Petter et al., 1977; Schmid and Kappeler, 1994). It was thought to be a rediscovery of a previously described species named *M. myoxinus* (Peters, 1852). This red species of the west coast differed from *M. rufus* of the east coast. Averaging 30 g, it was discovered to be the smallest living primate (Schmid and Kappeler, 1994; Atsalis et al., 1996). Later, comparative morphometric and genetic studies showed the tiny mouse lemur to be not *M. myoxinus,* but a totally new species, now renamed *M. berthae* (Rasoloarison et al., 2000; Yoder et al., 2000). This clarification now made *M. berthae* the smallest living primate. Then, yet another red form, *M. ravelobensis,* was described (Zimmermann et al., 1998; Pastorini et al., 2001). Additional mouse lemur species continue to be proposed with regularity, and the taxonomy of western (Rasoloarison et al., 2000; Yoder et al., 2000) and eastern species (Louis et al., 2006) has been further clarified.

Based on results from the latest morphometric, genetic, and behavioral analyses, researchers have suggested the presence of twelve mouse lemur species (Schmid and Kappeler, 1994; Zimmermann et al., 1998; Rasoloarison et al., 2000; Kappeler and Rasoloarison, 2003; Kappeler et al., 2005; Louis et al., 2006) listed here as follows:. *M. berthae* (Berthe's mouse lemur), *M. griseorufus* (the red and grey mouse lemur), *M. jollyae* (Jolly's mouse lemur), *M. lehilahytsara* (Goodman's mouse lemur), *M. mittermeieri* (Mittermeier's mouse lemur), *M. murinus* (grey mouse lemur), *M. myoxinus* (pygmy mouse lemur), *M. ravelobensis* (golden-brown mouse lemur), *M. rufus* (brown mouse lemur), *M. sambiranensis* (Sambirano mouse lemur), *M. simmonsi* (Simmons's mouse lemur), and *M. tavaratra* (northern rufous mouse lemur). At the time of writing this book, additional proposed mouse lemur species remained to be described in more detail (Louis et al., 2006).

Some scholars consider the recognition of so many new species exaggerated (Tattersall, 2007). Although there is ample evidence to recognize some new species, for others quantitative analyses are weak (Tattersall, 2007). The implication is that, in some cases, the proposed distinctions among mouse lemurs of different localities may represent nothing more than intraspecific variation (Tattersall, 2007). Even critics, however, accept that a good part of the new mouse lemur taxonomy is justified given the available information (Tattersall, 2007).

Dramatic advances have been made in our knowledge of the cheirogaleids, and the discovery of many new species of mouse lemur figures importantly in this improved understanding. The energizing complexity of *Microcebus* parallels the situation among other nocturnal primate groups, in which many new cryptic species have been found as data on genetics, behavior, and vocalizations accumulate (Bearder, 1999; Nekaris and Bearder, 2007). Among the other cheirogaleids, the genus *Cheirogaleus* contains several more species than the two, *C. major* and *C. medius*, widely recognized until recently (Groves, 2000). At least one of the new species, *C. crossleyi*, is found in more geographic locations than previously thought (Hapke et al., 2005). In addition, fresh research has led to the discovery of a new species of *Mirza*, previously considered to be a single species genus (Kappeler et al., 2005). Not surprising, given the cryptic nocturnal habits of cheirogaleids (and other nocturnal strepsirrhines), their biodiversity, particularly that of mouse lemurs, has not always been obvious.

Mouse lemur species differ in body mass and other measurements (Schmid and Kappeler, 1994; Atsalis et al., 1996; Rasoloarison et al., 2000). In addition, they are characterized by marked differences in certain DNA sequences that have led to the differentiation of species and identification of new ones (Leipoldt et al., 1998; Yoder et al., 2000; Louis et al., 2006). The degree of DNA-sequence differentiation points to an unexpectedly ancient separation of several species, a finding that is surprising given that forty years ago, only a single species was recognized for all of Madagascar

(Martin, personal communication, 2006). As field research diligently continues, additional species may be recognized and our understanding of their geographic distribution improved. Indeed, some researchers emphasize that further analyses of mitochondrial DNA (mtDNA) sequences from mouse lemur populations across Madagascar may reveal additional diversity in both eastern and western species (Yoder et al., 2000).

Ranomafana's mouse lemur species is sometimes referred to as the red mouse lemur or the eastern rufous mouse lemur (Groves, 2005), but in keeping with the naming convention at RNP, I refer to M. *rufus* as the brown mouse lemur. The practice of referring to M. *rufus* simply as the "rufous" mouse lemur may not be advisable because as Tattersall (1982) explains this designation has been used for both eastern and western species because of similar pelage coloration. To avoid undue confusion, in this book most mouse lemur species will be referred to only by their scientific names. Only for M. *murinus*, the most commonly studied species, and M. *rufus*, the subject of this book, will both scientific and common names be used.

MOUSE LEMUR DISTRIBUTION

Traditionally, the central highlands of Madagascar were considered to be the main physical barrier to gene flow, a barrier between the east and west of the island, contributing to lemur geographic distribution and marking their taxonomic differences (Martin, 1972a). Studies using mtDNA in mouse lemurs have questioned the view that taxonomic boundaries follow the east coast (rainforest)–west coast (dry forest) divide, proposing instead that the evolutionary relationship between the various species of mouse lemurs may be the result of a north–south division (Yoder et al., 2000; Yoder 2003). Nevertheless, even though molecular data have confirmed at least two north–south divides of the island on the west coast, with rivers acting as physical barriers (Pastorini et al., 2003), the central highlands underlying the east–west divide is still considered to be the primary geographic subdivision of the island (Martin, 1972a, 1995; Louis et al., 2006). Other researchers, however, view the central highlands less of a barrier and more as a crossroad between east and west, offering routes for species exchange and dispersal through intermittently forested passages (Godfrey et al., 1999). This perspective may explain, for example, the close relationship proposed between M. *myoxinus*, currently inhabiting án area in the west coast, and the brown mouse lemur found in the east coast (Schmid and Kappler, 1994).

Mouse lemurs inhabit a wide range of Madagascar's forested habitats (Mittermeier et al., 1994; Rowe, 1996). M. *rufus* was thought to occur in rainforests throughout the eastern coast (Harcourt and Thornback, 1990). With new species discovered in the east coast, M. *rufus* has been confirmed

Adjacent to the camp site, the Namorona River cuts through Ranomafana National Park.

in RNP (and possibly further north in Mantadia National Park near Andasibe; Louis et al., 2006) (Figure 1–1). *M. simmonsi* is known from Betampona Special Reserve, the Tampolo Forest, and Zahamena National Park, all located in the eastern part of the island (Louis et al., 2006). *M. mittermeieri* is known only from the reserve of Anjanaharibe-Sud in northeastern Madagascar (Louis et al., 2006). *M. jollyae* is currently known from Mananjary and Kianjavato in central-eastern Madagascar, near RNP (Louis et al., 2006). *M. lehilahytsara* has been proposed as a new species found in Andasibe and the adjacent Mantadia National Park (Kappeler et al., 2005), but agreement remains to be reached on this taxonomic designation (Louis et al., 2006; Tattersall, 2007). *M. murinus* is thought to be a wide-ranging species, inhabiting mostly dry deciduous forests of a western and southern distribution (Tattersall, 1982; Kappeler and Rasoloarison, 2003; Louis et al., 2006). Among other locations, *M. murinus* is found in the southern tip of Madagascar, in Madena where it occupies small patches of evergreen forest (Tattersall, 1982; Louis et al., 2006). *M. murinus* is also found in sympatry with *M. berthae* in the Kirindy Forest (Rasoloarison et al., 2000; Yoder et al., 2000) and with *M. ravelobensis* in Ampijoroa Forestry Reserve in the dry deciduous forest of the Ankarafantiska Nature Reserve (Zimmermann et al., 1998). Other west coast mouse lemur species have more restricted geographic ranges. *M. griseorufus* is located in the southwestern location of Beza Mahafaly

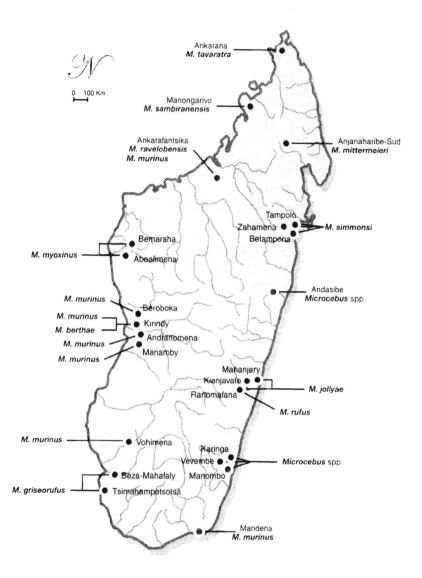

Figure 1–1 Map of Madagascar showing the current known distribution of mouse lemurs, *Microcebus* (based on Rasoloarison et al., 2000; Yoder et al., 2000; and Louis et al., 2006). *Microcebus* spp. represents populations whose taxonomic status is under review.

and Tsimanampetsotsa. This species is thought to occur sympatrically with *M. murinus* in the Ihazoara Valley area (located a few kilometers from Beza Mahafaly) (Rasoloarison et al., 2000). Finally, *M. myoxinus, M. tavaratra,* and *M. sambiranensis* also occur in narrow ranges on the west coast of Madagascar (Rasoloarison et al., 2000; Yoder et al., 2002; Louis et al., 2006). Yoder et al. (2002) have confirmed that reproductive isolation acts to keep the evolutionary boundary between sympatric populations. Ongoing investigations are being conducted to clarify the phylogeny and distribution of mouse lemur populations across Madagascar.

M. murinus is a good model for the study of species geographic variation because the species is so wide-ranging, found from the evergreen litoral rainforest of the southern tip of Madagascar up to at least the dry deciduous forests of the National Park of Ankarafantsika in the north (Lahann et al., 2006). Indeed researchers have discovered significant ecogeographic variation in life-history traits of the grey mouse lemur including the fact that population body mass increased with decreasing average temperatures across regions (Lahann et al., 2006). This seems to imply that adapting to local environmental conditions is very important for mouse lemur survival (Lahann et al., 2006). On the other hand, the limited geographic range characteristic of many of the other mouse lemur species is related to the high diversity of lemur species in Madagascar (Martin, 2000). The recognition of so many new cryptic species enhances the exceptional primate diversity for which Madagascar is already known compared to other geographic regions with primates (Tattersall, 2007). The remarkable adaptive radiation on the island has been attributed to high levels of local plant diversity, as well as to the existence of numerous physical barriers that inhibit gene flow. But whereas mouse lemurs were thought to be the most adaptable of Malagasy primates, even showing a proclivity for living in dense vegetation and near the edges of forest fragments (Lehman et al., 2006), produced as a result of anthropogenic disturbance, the important conservation implication of the newly discovered localized diversity is that fragmentation and loss of habitat—an ongoing problem in Madagascar—can potentially lead to local extinctions of those species with limited geographic range (Martin, 1995, 2000; Schwab and Ganzhorn, 2004). Even in captivity, where large populations of *M. murinus* are maintained, there is a problem with loss of genetic diversity (Neveu et al., 1998). Therefore, implementing conservation measures in the wild and improving husbandry management in captivity are both more relevant than ever for mouse lemurs, the taxon of lemurs thought to be the most abundant and therefore the least vulnerable to extinction pressures.

Madagascar is located 400 km east of the southern coast of Africa. Madagascar's current position with respect to Africa dates to 120 million years ago. Interestingly, when Madagascar separated from Africa, it was attached to the Indian subcontinent, which split from the island and moved forward to collide with Asia 88 million years ago (Rabinowitz et al., 1983; Storey, 1995; Krause et al., 1997). Therefore, Malagasy strepsirrhines evolved in isolation from other primate relatives, but because primates are estimated to have evolved after the separation of Madagascar from the other continents, approximately 81 million years ago (Tavaré et al., 2002), the puzzle remains as to how they arrived on Madagascar. The possibility that the ancestral lemurs came to Madagascar from India has been suggested (Gingerich, 1975) although Africa is more commonly held to be their place of origin (Yoder et al., 1996). Rafting on drifting vegetation from Africa has been proposed to explain primate presence on the island (Martin, 1972a; Kappeler, 2000). Given that members of the Cheirogaleidae are able to reduce metabolic rates and lower body temperatures during periods of seasonal inactivity and that they tend to sleep in aggregations that enhance energy savings, it is possible to imagine groups of small, inactive primates surviving a long raft journey to Madagascar. Chromosomal and molecular evidence strongly suggests that all Malagasy primates have a common ancestry (i.e., they are monophyletic), the result of a single migration from Africa (Dutrillaux and Rumpler, 1995; Yoder et al., 1996, 2000; Yoder, 2003).

DISTINCTIVE FEATURES OF THE CHEIROGALEIDAE

Small size, nongregarious social organization, and a strictly nocturnal lifestyle form a triptych of influences on cheirogaleid ecology and behavior. This combination of features was thought to distinguish cheirogaleids from their diurnal, group-living, large-bodied lemur and other primate relatives. However, with recent contributions to our understanding of nocturnal social life, our perception of how cheirogaleids behave has changed radically. In general, nocturnal strepsirrhines are no longer considered to be uniform in their nongregarious social habits. Although they may forage primarily in solitude, they have well-developed social networks. Within these social networks, previously unsuspected complexity and diversity have been discovered in the degree of home range overlap and direct contact between individuals as well as in their nesting associations (e.g., Pagès, 1980; Clark, 1985; Harcourt and Nash, 1986a; Nash and Harcourt, 1986; Barre et al., 1988; Pagès-Feuillade, 1988; Sterling and Richard, 1995; Fietz, 2003b; Sterling, 2003; Weidt et al., 2004; Dammhahn and Kappeler, 2005). Results from accumulated research suggest that most nocturnal strepsirrhines live either in dispersed multi-male, multi-female networks or in pair-bonded relationships (Müller and Thalmann, 2000; Martin, 2002). Additional studies on other nocturnal primates from Africa and Asia continue to enrich our understanding of social variability (Pullen et al., 2000; Nekaris, 2003).

Overall, diversity in the social lives of nocturnal primates may parallel the diversity found in diurnal group-living primates (Tattersall and Sussman, 1989; Richard and Dewar, 1991; Kappeler, 1995; Müller and Thalmann, 2000), differing only in the ways by which sociality is mediated among individuals (Clark, 1985; Sterling and Richard, 1995). Nocturnal primates often communicate and maintain social relationships through vocalizations, indirectly through olfactory cues that persist in space and time, and through their daytime sleeping associations (Bearder, 1987). Researchers are focusing on understanding the ways that nocturnal primates maintain their social ties by studying olfactory and auditory communication, and by investigating the interrelationships among social factors, chemocommunication and physiology (Perret, 1992, 1995; Zimmermann and Lerch, 1993). Mouse lemurs use their well-developed olfactory apparatus (Schilling, 1979) for social spacing and interactions during mating. Urine washing is considered to be a main form of communication among mouse lemurs because they do not possess specialized scent glands (Perret, 1992). The deposition of urine on substrates may serve to maintain spacing in the forest (Schilling, 1980), and scent-marking is high during the mating period and highest in the period just before females enter estrus (Lebec, 1984). In general, the special features of nocturnal primate communication and how they influence the ways that nocturnal primates maintain social networks call for considerable more research.

Traits that characterize nocturnal strepsirrhines, such as small size, nocturnality, and, in some, the ability to become dormant, are often observed among nonprimate mammalian species studied in temperate climates (Halle and Stenseth, 2000), but how these traits affect nocturnal strepsirrhine life histories requires further investigation. As an example, rather than being a primitive quality, the *broadening* of thermoregulatory capacity characteristic of those cheirogaleids that enter hibernation is considered to be an ecological adaptation related to food availability (Müller, 1985; McNab, 1986; Genoud, 2002). And yet, how thermoregulation relates to resource availability and to the specific dietary needs of small primates remains open for exploration. Moreover, small body size is typically associated with higher metabolic rates, which in turn are related to increased reproductive rates and shortened lifespans (Bourlière, 1975; Schmidt-Nielsen, 1984). However, some nocturnal strepsirrhines exhibit relatively low metabolic rates, in some cases below expected values based on body size alone (Kurland and Pearson, 1986; Ross, 1992). This is true for the lorises whose basal metabolic rates are 30–60% lower than expected for mammals of their size (Müller, 1985). Genoud (2002), however, offers the interesting point that high metabolic rates are generally lacking in primates as a group and that low basal rates can be found even among diurnal primates. This finding implies that low basal metabolic rates and nocturnality are not linked exclusively, even though some of the lower metabolic rates and the ability to enter daily and seasonal periods of lethargy have been found only among nocturnal strepsirrhines (Müller, 1985), including mouse lemurs (Perret, 1998).

Debate also surrounds the role of body size on life history in nocturnal strepsirrhines. Researchers question whether body size is the primary influencing factor (Rasmussen and Izard, 1988). Some suggest that life history is related to differences in body size through maternal reproductive investment (Kappeler, 1995); yet others consider that body size may act on life history traits through differential mortality (Western, 1979; McNab, 1980; Promislow and Harvey, 1990; Kappeler, 1995). In support of this idea is the extreme vulnerability to predation that is faced by mouse lemurs and other small-bodied mammals (Bourlière, 1975; Clutton-Brock and Harvey, 1977a; Wright, 1985; Goodman et al., 1993; Goodman, 2003; Musto et al., 2005). In turn, by promoting cryptic behavior, predation may be an important influence on ranging and nesting patterns. In this light, nongregarious social organization characteristic of many nocturnal strepsirrhines can be considered an extreme form of cryptic behavior (Charles-Dominique, 1975, 1977, 1978).

Much more remains to be investigated regarding the influence of small body size, nocturnality, and nongregarious social organization on the ecology and behavior of small nocturnal primates. One significant question concerns the possible resemblance of extant nocturnal primates to a model of the ancestral primate. Among lemurs, cheirogaleids have been proposed as potential models of the ancestral form (Purvis, 1995), and it has been argued that the common ancestor of living primates may have been a primate not unlike the mouse lemur (Martin, 1972a, 1995). The combination of nocturnality, solitary foraging habits, small size, litter production, nest building, and the ability to enter torpor are traits that mouse lemurs have in common with other small mammals implying that they are ancient features, possibly shared by the earliest primates (Charles-Dominique and Martin, 1970; Martin, 1972a, 1995). Recently, doubts have been cast on the potential relevance of *Microcebus* as a paradigm for the ancestral primate. Some propose that ancestral primates may have been much smaller than mouse lemurs, likely close to 10–15 g (Gebo, 2004), whereas others have inferred that they were markedly larger, one kilogram or more (Soligo and Martin, 2006). Because body size influences how a species adapts within its environment, these two hypotheses would lead to different biologies and survival patterns. Whatever the case, from an evolutionary standpoint, the study of mouse lemur behavioral patterns may continue to offer insights into the links and commonalities between primates and other mammals.

To summarize, we know that mouse lemurs—diminutive, nocturnal Malagasy primates—are generally omnivorous animals that move through the forest quadrupedally, consuming fruits, insects, small vertebrates, sap, and gum. They can store fat and become dormant in response to seasonal food scarcity. Like many other nocturnal strepsirrhines, they form nongregarious social networks and males compete for females during the mating season. They give birth to litters, which are sheltered in the leaf nests or tree hollows that are also used for resting during periods of inactivity. This array of features offers many possibilities for exciting and rewarding research. As is common for a graduate student, prior to embarking on my adventure on Madagascar, I had set specific goals to focus the direction of my field study. While in the field, I maintained the initial goals, but I also seized many additional opportunities to expand the scope of the study. The result is a work akin to a natural history of the species because I was able to gather data on many key behaviors of mouse lemurs, beyond the scope of my initial hypotheses. The different facets of the study are addressed in separate chapters. At the end of chapters, I suggest areas of research that would enhance our understanding of the behavior and ecology of *M. rufus* and mouse lemurs in general. The final chapter weaves together information on diet, life history, spatial distribution, and reproduction offering a summary of the natural history of the brown mouse lemur in Ranomafana. A timeline illustrates how the various events in the annual life cycle of the species relate to each other and to seasonal climatic and resource changes. I hope that this book may provide the incentive for more young and seasoned researchers to undertake the special challenges involved with nocturnal primate field work.

2

Researching the Brown Mouse Lemur

DESCRIPTION OF THE STUDY SITE

Between January 1993 and June 1994, only short breaks interrupted my seventeen-month stay in the rainforest of Ranomafana National Park (RNP), where this study was carried out. As a student collecting data for doctoral research, I faced the usual financial and time constraints that impeded long-distance travel, so I made the decision to stay at the site for the duration of study. I soon discovered that by maintaining continued contact with mouse lemurs in their natural habitat, I gained invaluable insights into how the animals adjusted their behaviors under seasonally fluctuating resource availability and changing climatic conditions.

In Malgache, *rano* means water and *mafana* means hot. About a hundred years ago, hot springs were discovered in the valley, and the French created a spa around them. The area became known as the town of Ranomafana. Located in southeastern Madagascar (21°16'S and 47°20'E), the park adjacent to the town encompasses lowland to montane tropical moist forest that ranges in altitude from 500 to 1,500 m. The park, an integrated conservation and development project offering ecotourism and research opportunities, was inaugurated in 1991 (Wright, 1997). The forest belongs to that part of the eastern biogeographic region of Madagascar characterized by the highest species diversity and endemism in the country (Mittermeier et al., 1986). Characteristic of this richness are the twelve taxa of primates known to be found within RNP: *Avahi laniger* (the woolly lemur, family Indriidae),

Cheirogaleus major (the greater dwarf lemur, family Cheirogaleidae), *Microcebus rufus* (the brown mouse lemur, family Cheirogaleidae), *Daubentonia madagascariensis* (the aye-aye, family Daubentoniidae), *Lepilemur* sp. (the sportive lemur, family Lepilemuridae), *Eulemur fulvus rufus* (red-fronted brown lemur, family Lemuridae), *E. rubriventer* (red-bellied lemur, family Lemuridae), *Hapalemur aureus* (golden bamboo lemur, family Lemuridae), *H. griseus* (lesser bamboo lemur), *H. simus* (greater bamboo lemur, family Lemuridae), *Varecia variegata variegata* (black and white ruffed lemur, family Lemuridae), and *Propithecus diadema edwardsi* (Milne-Edwards' sifaka, family Indriidae). The first five listed are nocturnal. Many primate studies at RNP have focused on diurnal species (e.g., Dagosto, 1989; Overdorff, 1991, 1993, 1996; Glander et al., 1992; Wright, 1992, 1995; Merenlender, 1993; Meyers and Wright, 1993; Hemingway, 1995; White et al., 1995; Yamashita, 1996; Balko, 1997; Wright et al., 1997; Tan, 2000; Grassi, 2001; Durham, 2003). A few studies have concentrated on nocturnal ones (*M. rufus*—Harcourt, 1987; Harste, 1993; Harste et al., 1997; Atsalis, 1998; Deppe, 2005; Blanco, 2007; *C. major*—Wright and Martin, 1995; *A. laniger*—Harcourt, 1991; Roth, 1996).

Within RNP's 43,500 hectares, the Talatakely Research Station (at 1,100 m elevation), where at the time of my study the majority of research was carried out, was located near the main entrance to the park. [Today, the International Training Center for the Study of Biodiversity (*Centre ValBio*) has replaced the old research station. Inaugurated in 2003, the *Centre ValBio* is located adjacent to the park and provides research facilities and some living amenities for researchers.] A third of the park, including Talatakely, has been selectively logged, most recently in 1986 and 1987 (Wright, 1995). Consequently, at Talatakely, below the 18–35 m canopy, the thinning of the trees left an understory with many shrubs belonging to the Rubiaceae and the Myrsinaceae, as well as with bamboo and epiphytes, particularly mistletoes in the genus *Bakerella* (family Loranthaceae) (Turk, 1995). During the course of my study, I discovered that *Bakerella*, locally called "tongolahy," was a favorite food item for mouse lemurs at RNP (Chapter 3). Though mouse lemurs were found at all heights of the rainforest, the understory was useful for research purposes because the lower height significantly improved observation of mouse lemur activity and made it easier to find nests.

At RNP there were several possible predators of mouse lemurs: *Asio madagascariensis* (the Malagasy barn owl, a significant predator of the grey mouse lemur; Goodman et al., 1993), *Eutriorchis astur* (the Malagasy serpent eagle), *Polyboroides radiatus* (the Malagasy harrier hawk), and *Accipiter henstii* (Henst's goshawk). *Sanzinia madagascariensis* (the Malagasy boa) and the diurnal viverrid *Galidia elegans* (a mongoose-like carnivore) preyed on *Cheirogaleus major* (Wright and Martin, 1995) and also hunts mouse lemurs (Deppe, personal communication, 2007). Other nocturnal viverrids (*Cryptoprocta ferox, Fossa fossana, Galidictis fasciata,* and *Eupleres* sp.) were known to prey on larger-bodied lemurs (Wright et al., 1997; Wright, 1998).

To understand the feeding ecology of the brown mouse lemur, I compared food choices with resource availability as both fluctuated over the year. Previous studies on mouse lemurs suggested that the bulk of the diet would come from fruit and insects. Accordingly, I monitored plant phenological patterns and changes in insect abundance to determine resource availability, while simultaneously collecting fecal samples from live-trapped mouse lemurs to determine dietary composition. Because tropical phenological patterns vary depending on plant species diversity and water availability (Bullock and Magallanes, 1990), phenological patterns, reflecting abundance of available buds, flowers, and fruits, were compared with the diversity of plants having buds, flowers, and fruits, as well as with rainfall patterns. Select results from phenological monitoring are presented in this chapter and in Chapter 3, where mouse lemur diet is discussed in detail. For statistical analyses, both parametric and nonparametric statistics were used as appropriate (following Siegel and Castellan, 1988). Unless otherwise indicated, all tests were two-tailed with level of significance set at 0.05. The Bonferroni criterion was applied when several tests were carried out sequentially (Rice, 1989).

RAINFALL AND TEMPERATURE PATTERNS

Standard methods were used to collect weather data. A rain gauge was set in an open area near the research cabin; it was emptied daily or, in case of extreme rainfall, whenever full. Temperature was recorded from a thermometer placed in the shade. Following Hemingway (1995), I designated the dry season as the period that encompassed no more than one month of rainfall *exceeding* 200 mm. The wet season was designated as the period with no more than one month of *less than* 200 mm of rainfall. Given these criteria, the wet season occurred from December to March and the dry season from April to November (Figure 2–1). There was one exception, though, when in 1993 it rained over 200 mm for two consecutive months in the dry season.

Rainfall over one complete annual cycle averaged 4,485 mm. Rainfall over one complete wet season (December 1993–March 1994) totaled 3,150 mm, whereas during a complete dry season rainfall averaged 1,335 mm (April 1993–November 1993 and April 1994–November 1994). Temperatures were highest during the wet season (see Figure 2–1). The average monthly minimum temperature was 13.1°C (SD, ±2.5), and the average monthly maximum temperature was 22.5°C (SD, ±2.8).

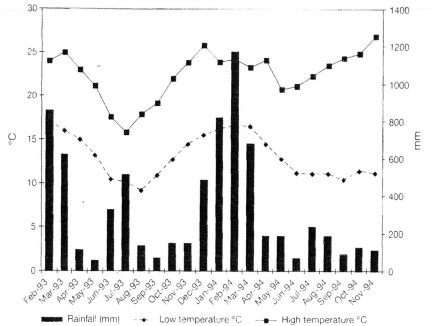

Figure 2–1 Monthly rainfall and temperature fluctuations in Talatakely, RNP. Cyclones occurred in March 1993, February 1994, and March 1994. The study site was evacuated for two weeks in March 1994; reported rainfall is underestimated for this month and overestimated for April 1994 when we returned to the study site. (Adapted from Atsalis, 1999a; used with permission from Springer Science and Business Media.)

PHENOLOGICAL MONITORING

By monitoring the phenology of a large number of trees, I gained an understanding of how plant resources fluctuated seasonally. Four parcels, each approximately 50 m × 10 m, were chosen to serve as botanical plots. Their locations were selected based on ease of accessibility and habitat differences within the Talatakely region, where mouse lemurs ranged. Two plots were situated in low, damp areas, whereas two were on drier hill ridges. In an effort to minimize the number of young, nonfruiting plants in our sample, only those with a diameter at breast height (DBH) of 3 cm or more were tagged for monitoring. As plants died or were felled by inclement weather, they were excluded from further monitoring. The data presented here are based on 888 trees and shrubs monitored for twenty-three consecutive months (excluding August 1993 when data were not collected), including seven months after my departure from RNP.

Two Ranomafana guides, Raliva Pierre and Rakotoniaina Le Jean, helped in the monthly phenological monitoring. Pierre, with whom I worked especially closely, was well versed in Malagasy botany. He provided the local names for almost all the plants we encountered. For formal plant identification, we relied on the expert help of Dan Turk, who was completing graduate work on the trees of RNP, and on a master list compiled previously through the collaboration of RNP guides and the Missouri Botanical Garden. Pierre easily recognized typical fruiting and flowering patterns, a knowledge acquired through long years of familiarity with the forest. We collected data during the first week of each month. On those days, Pierre and I, along with Le Jean, our young "botanist" in training, walked through each plot recording the presence of buds, flowers and fruits using a scale of 0 to 5. With these data, I determined the monthly percentage of individual plants that contained buds, flowers and fruit, as a measure of resource abundance. I also determined how many different kinds of plants contained buds, flowers and fruit, as a measure of resource diversity. Data from the four plots were analyzed separately and then consolidated. Because it never became entirely clear which stage of fruit ripeness mouse lemurs preferred, analyses included data on the presence of unripe fruit, ripe fruit, and both unripe and ripe fruit combined.

As the study progressed, we became familiar with fruits that mouse lemurs ate. To monitor the plants that bore these fruits, as they became known to us we set up a second schedule of phenological monitoring. My guides called it the *petite phenologie* (French for "small phenology"), and the term stayed. Each time we discovered a new kind of fruit eaten by mouse lemurs, we located and tagged five to ten mature sample members of the plant for monitoring. Using the same scoring system used in the botanical plots, we monitored these plants at the beginning and in the middle of each month. The phenology of these plants—known fruit resources for mouse lemurs—was compared with data from the botanical plots, which represented general, habitat-wide fruit resource availability. To the *petite phenologie*, I also added *Ficus* (figs, family Moraceae) because their seeds were similar to ones that remained unidentified in mouse lemur fecal samples. Local people, including RNP guides, informed me that mouse lemurs ate figs. Also, when fig fruits were offered to captured mouse lemurs during feeding trials, the animals sometimes ate them (Harste, 1993).

FLOWERING AND FRUITING PATTERNS

The DBH of trees and shrubs that we monitored within the botanical plots ranged from 3 to 74 cm. However, the DBH of approximately 76% of our sample was only between 4.5 and 10 cm. The height of plants reached between 2 and 24 m, and approximately 86% of plants sampled were less than 10 m in height. Monitored plants represented thirty-five families, fifty-four genera, and approximately ninety-two vernacular species (omitting some common subdivisions such as "madinidravina" or "vaventiravina," meaning small-leafed and large-leafed plants, respectively). The most abundant genus in terms of number of individual trees present (approximately 12% of trees sampled in the botanical plots) was *Psychotria*, and overall the family to which *Psychotria* belongs, Rubiaceae, was the most abundant in my sample (approximately 17% of trees sampled).

At RNP, the appearance of lushness was not made apparent through an abundance of flowers blooming simultaneously and fruits bursting with ripeness, but rather in the profusion of leafy matter and in the tangled masses of lianas, vines, and epiphytic plants. Indeed, during most months, phenological monitoring revealed that flowers and fruits were present in relatively low supply. For instance, the majority of individual plants bore only a small abundance of fruit at any given time, mostly within the range of 0.5–2.0 phenological score. In part, the low abundance may have reflected the presence of immature plants in the botanical plots. However, my results paralleled the phenological patterns recorded in other studies at RNP and elsewhere in Madagascar, in that the flower and fruit season was somewhat prolonged but production was generally low (e.g., Wright et al., 2005). Furthermore, at RNP, production may be irregular, asynchronous, or occurring in alternate-year cycles (e.g., Overdorff, 1993; Sterling, 1993a; Wright et al., 2005). For yearly flowering peaks, a strong correlation has been found between tropical plant phenologies and rainfall although the correlation can be weaker for rainforests than for dry forests (van Schaik et al., 1993). In Madagascar, studies in the dry forests confirmed that phenological patterns were closely correlated to rainfall patterns (Hladik et al., 1980; Sauther, 1992; Meyers, 1993; Sörg and Rohner, 1996). Similarly, RNP was characterized by seasonal variation in flower and fruit availability and abundance. Maximal flower production occurred during the rainy season (Figure 2–2), although overall there was no statistically significant correlation between flower production and monthly rainfall (r_s = .133, N = 21). During the first rainy season that we collected data, flower production was plentiful in February 1993 (9% of plants); during the second rainy season, production peaked in December 1993 (10% of plants).

Fruit production occurred year-round, with 6–19% of plants containing fruit in any given month (Figure 2–3). Generally, fruiting patterns were similar in amplitude over the two years of the study. As with flower production, monthly fruit production and rainfall were not significantly correlated (r_s = − .062, N = 21), but peak fruit production, which occurred at the end of the rainy season (March) and at the beginning of the dry season, followed peak flower production. As in other tropical forests (Frankie et al., 1974), the exact timing and amplitude of peak flower and fruit production varied somewhat from year to year perhaps because the same plants did not flower every year.

In terms of diversity, the number of vernacular species producing buds was high during some of the months of high precipitation, for instance in

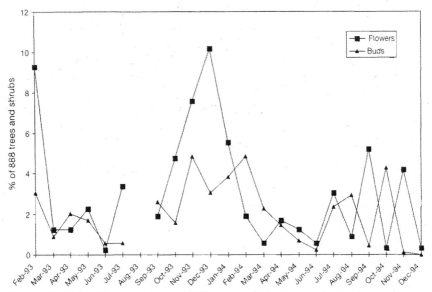

Figure 2–2 Monthly percentage of 888 trees and shrubs bearing buds and flowers sampled in four plots in Talatakely, RNP. Data were not collected in August 1993.

February 1993 (14%) and December 1993 (19%) (Figure 2–4). Naturally, these months were followed by spikes, albeit of smaller amplitude, in diversity of flower production in April 1993 (7%) and February 1994 (11%). The number of vernacular species in fruit varied from 15% to

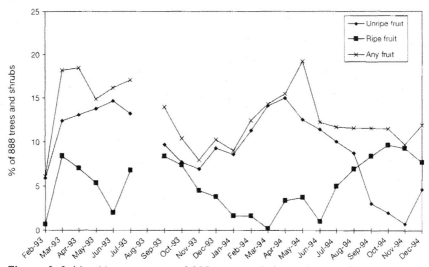

Figure 2–3 Monthly percentage of 888 trees and shrubs bearing fruit sampled in four plots in Talatakely, RNP. Data were not collected in August 1993. (From Atsalis, 1999a; used with permission from Springer Science and Business Media.)

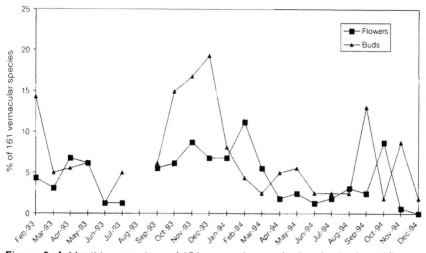

Figure 2–4 Monthly percentage of 161 vernacular species bearing buds and flowers sampled in four plots in Talatakely, RNP. Data were not collected in August 1993.

approximately 24% of plants (Figure 2–5). Some of the high peaks in available fruit diversity coincided with periods of high rainfall—22%, March 1993; 21%, July 1993; 23%, December 1993; 21%, February 1994—but overall there was no significant correlation between monthly precipitation and monthly diversity ($r_s = .189$, $N = 21$).

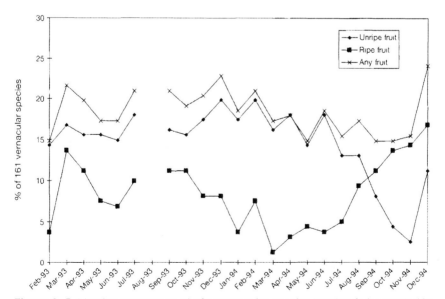

Figure 2–5 Monthly percentage of 161 vernacular species bearing fruit sampled in four plots in Talakely, RNP. Data were not collected in August 1993. (From Atsalis, 1999a; used with permission from Springer Science and Business Media.)

The relationship between peaks in diversity and peaks in abundance may depend on the relative density of the species in fruit; if a few common species are in fruit, then abundance, but not diversity, would show an increase. This observation may explain why in the same year the number of trees and shrubs in fruit (abundance) peaked in the dry season (May 1994; see Figure 2–3), but the number of vernacular species in fruit (diversity) increased at the height of the rainy season (December 1993; see Figure 2–5).

Whereas the phenological patterns in the botanical plots represent a general view of abundance and diversity, results from the *petite phenologie* are of special interest because they represent actual food availability for mouse lemurs. Through the *petite phenologie*, we monitored 176 trees, shrubs, lianas, and epiphytic plants. The sample represented twenty-eight vernacular species, eighteen known genera (two remained unknown) and fifteen families (see Table 3–1 for list of fruits eaten by mouse lemurs). Trees and shrubs in the sample were relatively short in stature and of small diameter. The average total height was 5.4 m (SD, ±3.0; range, 1.0–15.0 m); average height from the base of the tree to start of crown foliage, 4.0 m (SD, ±2.2; range, 0.75–12.0 m); and DBH , 8.4 cm (SD, ±9.0; range, 1.1–75.8 cm). The average height of trees and shrubs that acted as supports of the epiphytes and vines eaten by mouse lemurs was 9.6 m (SD, ±3.2; range, 1.0–16.5 cm), whereas the epiphytes and vines themselves were found at an average of 7 m (SD, ±4.0; range, 1.0–16.0 m). Generally, epiphytes and vines were found at all forest heights, but the low height of these specimens was chosen to facilitate data collection. The average height of the fig trees was 7.7 m (SD, ±2.8; range, 3.0–14.0 m). DBH of fig trees was 31.3 cm but the range of size was very broad (Range, 2.9–101.0 cm), and height from base to foliage was 4 m (SD, ±1.2; range, 2.0–5.5 m). Fruits of the figs "Voararano" and "Voara special" grew off the tree trunks at 0.25–10 m off the ground.

Here, I included data on trees and shrubs whose seeds were found in fecal samples for five months or more. These are seeds from the plants *Bakerella*, *Medinilla, Rhipsalis, Psychotria*, and *Viscum* (see Figure 3–5). I also included data from trees of *Ficus* because seeds that resembled those in figs were present in fecal samples each month of the study. Phenological samples of the genera *Medinilla, Rhipsalis*, and *Viscum* included only one vernacular species each. The sample of *Psychotria* contained three vernacular species, two identified as mouse lemur fruit sources. The sample of *Bakerella* contained several varieties (two subspecies of *Bakerella clavata*, the species *B. grisea*, and one other unknown species of *Bakerella*). With the exception of one variety (a subspecies of *B. clavata*), all of the other *Bakerella* samples were verified food sources for mouse lemurs. Four different vernacular species of fig (Malagasy names are Voararano, Famakilela madinidravina, Famakilela vaventiravina, and Voara special) were included. Fig fruits were produced throughout the year, though different varieties of fig produced fruit at different periods of the year. *Psychotria* and *Bakerella* exhibited fruiting patterns that were similar to each other: fruiting activity occurred year-round, with high availability in the wet season continuing into part of the dry season. The seeds of *Bakerella* were found in mouse lemur feces year-round, including October and November when *Bakerella* fruit were low in availability. Perhaps any absence of fruit on the *Bakerella* plants that we monitored was a function of the fruiting patterns of the specific taxa of *Bakerella* that we chose to monitor.

In contrast to the year-round availability of *Bakerella*, the availability of other epiphytes—*Viscum, Medinilla,* and *Rhipsalis*—was more seasonally restricted. When monitoring these epiphytes, we knew of and included only one vernacular species in the plant samples, which may explain the narrower fruiting window. The sample of *Bakerella* (and *Psychotria*), on the other hand, encompassed more than one vernacular species, likely making the fruiting period appear longer. *Viscum* was available for part of the dry season and all of the wet season in 1993. *Medinilla* exhibited a consistent pattern of high fruit availability during periods of high rainfall, and *Rhipsalis* was available throughout the dry season.

INSECT AVAILABILITY

Because insects were a potential food resource for mouse lemurs, my team of guides and I conducted monthly collection sessions as a way to measure their abundance in the forest. We collected insects from July 1993 to May 1994. With two exceptions, collection took place twice monthly at two different sites per night (i.e., four collection sessions per month), for twenty-one nights. Given the arboreal habits of mouse lemurs, I used a method that was appropriate for collecting diverse flying insects (modified from Smythe, 1982). Insects were attracted to the light from lamps fueled with petrol, night lights powered with solar energy, and black lights. They landed on a suspended white sheet and were captured in a jar that contained ether. We began collecting at nightfall and continued for four hours, after which we counted the total number of insects captured and recorded their total mass using a bag and a Pesola spring scale. Single monthly averages of body mass were computed for comparison with rainfall data and with monthly averages of values measuring insect consumption based on fecal analysis.

With the help of *Peterson's Field Guide* (Borror and White, 1970) and relying on the experience of one of the RNP guides, Emile Rajeriarison, the insects captured were identified to order and, when possible, to family level. The large number of insects present in the tropics and the many taxonomic problems associated with identifying them pose significant challenges when attempting a detailed inventory of tropical insects (Claridge, 1986). Little information on tropical insects exists to help in identification beyond the ordinal level, and although data on Malagasy invertebrates are increasing they are still scanty (Paulian and Viette, 2003). For instance, only recently was an effort launched at RNP to identify the many species of true dung

The author with insect collection set-up: a plain sheet and lights to attract insects during collection sessions for monitoring resource availability in RNP

beetles present (Hanski 2004). Without the aid of an authoritative reference guide for Malagasy tropical insects at the time of our study, we considered identification beyond the ordinal level to be tentative. *Peterson's Field Guide* (Borror and White, 1970) used an older classification with two orders, the Hemiptera (considered equivalent to the taxonomic name of Heteroptera) and the Homoptera. Later classifications, such as the one in Borror et al. (1981) and used by Julian Stark to identify the chitin remains in the feces that I brought back to the United States, rank the Heteroptera (the true bugs) and the Homoptera (cicadas, leafhoppers, etc.) as suborders of the order Hemiptera (commonly called *bugs*). Additionally, the designation Orthopteroid was used by Julian Stark, as a superordinal taxon representing the older concept of Orthoptera (containing crickets, mantises, grasshoppers, cockroaches, and walking sticks). I used Stark's taxonomic designations in this volume.

In the twenty-one nights of data collection, we captured 9,975 insects, weighing 271 g. The number of insects captured and their fresh mass were significantly correlated ($r_s = .827, N = 11$) (Figure 2–6). The correlation between monthly insect abundance (mass) and rainfall approached significance ($r_s = .636, N = 10$, excluding July 1993 for which only partial data existed) whereas monthly *number* of insects captured was not correlated with rainfall ($r_s = .297, N = 10$, excluding July 1993 for which only partial data existed). Generally, however, high peaks in insect availability took place with the approach of, as well as during the rainy season (Figure 2–7).

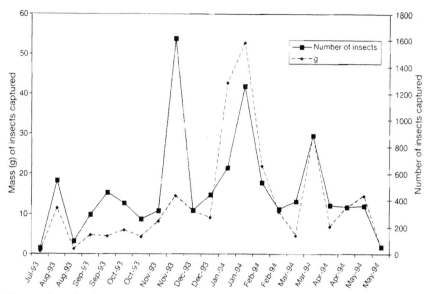

Figure 2–6 Fresh insect mass (g) and number of insects collected semimonthly in Talatakely, RNP Values represent data combined from two collection sites per night except for July 1993 (only one collection, only one night), December 1993 (one site/night), March 1994 (one site the first night). Low values in July and December may be a consequence of fewer collection sessions (Adapted from Atsalis, 1999a; used with permission from Springer Science and Business Media.)

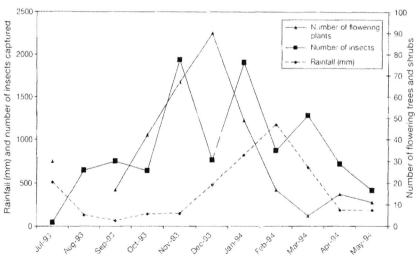

Figure 2–7 Monthly number of insects collected compared with monthly rainfall and flowering patterns of trees and shrubs in four plots in Talatakely, RNP Insect values represent data combined from two collection sites per night for two nights monthly, except for July 1993 (only one collection, only one night), December 1993 (one site/night). March 1994 (one site the first night). Low values in July and December may be a consequence of fewer collection sessions. Phenological data were not collected in August 1993.

This pattern may be expected because insects are generally less active in periods of low temperatures, (in Madagascar that would be in the dry season), as was discovered in other tropical sites where insects were collected (Bordignon, 2006). December was low in insect presence, most likely because we collected at a single site per collection night, but November and January were characterized by a large number of captured insects. Months of high insect availability were sometimes associated with an increased number of trees in flower (see Figure 2–7).

We identified fourteen insect orders. The number of different orders captured per month fluctuated between seven and twelve (Figure 2–8). We noted the least variety in July, the first month of data collection, possibly because this was when we conducted the fewest collection sessions. Peaks in abundance varied for each order and for some groups the variation was more dramatic than for others (see Figure 2–8). Members of the order Lepidoptera were the most frequently captured (Figure 2–9). Among Coleoptera (beetles), we recognized members of the superorders Curculionoidea (snout beetles and weevils) and Elateroidea (click beetles). Many of the insects identified as Homoptera were plant- and leaf-hoppers. We also identified aquatic insects of the family Corixidae (or water boatmen). Aquatic insects in the Coleoptera and Diptera were also detected.

By and large, the relationship between the number of insects captured per month and their fresh mass depended upon the specific orders of insects prevalent at the time of capture (see Figures 2–6 and 2–8). In November, the

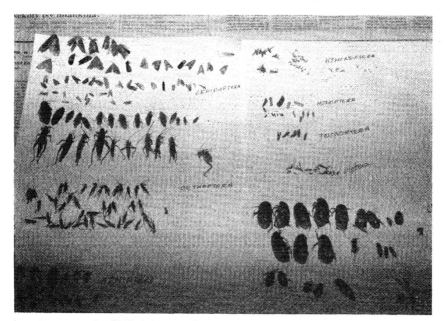

Insects captured in RNP during a collection session.

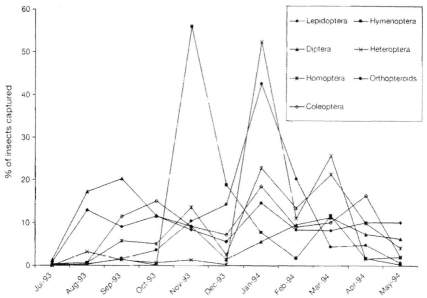

Figure 2–8 Monthly percentage of insect orders captured during sampling in. Talatakely, RNP. Only most frequently captured orders are shown. Values are from two collection sites per night except for July 1993 (only one collection, only one night), December 1993 (one site/night), March 1994 (one site the first night). Low values in July and December may be a consequence of fewer collection sessions. The superorder Orthopteroids replaces the order Orthoptera. Heteroptera and Homoptera are suborders of the order Hemiptera.

last month of the dry season, ants accounted for the peak in the number of insects captured. The greatest insect mass was observed in January, the first month of the rainy season, when we captured many large insects belonging to the order Hemiptera (shown in the Figure as suborders Heteroptera and Homoptera), and to the superorder of Orthopteroids. In this month, during the second collection night, a large number of these insects (498 of 1,258) belonged to the suborder Heteroptera. We tentatively identified the bugs as belonging to one of two families: Nabidae (440 of 498 insects captured) and Pentatomidae (58 of 498). Nabidae, or damsel bugs, are common predaceous insects that occur in low vegetation, whereas the Pentatomidae, commonly known as "stink bugs," are found worldwide. They produce strong defense odors from their thoracic glands (Borror and White, 1970; McGavin, 2002). March was another peak month, both in number and fresh mass of insects captured during the second night. As in January, the peak was associated with an increase in damsel bugs (259 of 885 insects captured). The difference between the two nights in March may have been the result of collecting at only one site during the first night and to the large number of ants (light in mass) captured (197 of 394 insects).

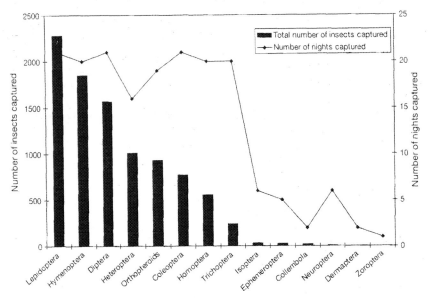

Figure 2–9 Total number of various taxa of insects captured monthly from July 1993 to May 1994 during sampling in Talatakely, RNP and the number of nights that each taxon was captured. The superorder Orthopteroids replaces the order Orthoptera. Heteroptera and Homoptera are suborders of the order Hemiptera. Insect values represent data combined from two collection sites per night for two nights monthly, except for July 1993 (only one collection, only one night), December 1993 (one site/ night), March 1994 (one site the first night).

LIVE-TRAPPING MOUSE LEMURS

At the time of this study, Talatakely had an area of over 5 km² of mapped trails. Live-trapping, a method of capture traditionally used by small-mammal biologists, was ideally suited for studying the tiny mouse lemur but previous investigators at RNP had not always been successful in capturing mouse lemurs and other cheirogaleids. As I discovered, the reason behind poor capture rates was not in the trap method but in the timing, because mouse lemurs avoided traps in December and January (Chapters 4, 5, and 6).

With the help of RNP guides Jean Marie and Ratalata Francois, fifty-four Sherman live traps (22.2 cm × 6.6 cm × 6.6 cm) were set in the main trap area (MTA) approximating a grid. A few traps were set outside of the MTA closer to the research cabin. Analyses were conducted using data from all traps unless otherwise indicated. Traps were set 50 m apart following distance markers situated along the lines of the established trail system. I chose the 50 m distance because it was mentioned as the home-range diameter of *Microcebus* by Martin (1972b), whose work was the most authoritative guide to mouse lemur behavior at the time of my research. The trap area encompassed roughly 27 ha of comparatively undisturbed forested areas on ridge tops and valleys. I avoided high-traffic tourist trails, the more degraded areas of Talatakely, such as those near the research cabin, and bamboo patches. Traps were placed a few meters above ground in trees located just off the trails. Traps were kept closed in the daytime and baited with banana in the early evening to be checked later for mouse lemurs, on average nine nights per month (for 147 nights). Traps were brought to the research cabin for mouse lemurs to be weighed and measured, and then released at the site of capture. Live-trapping is used throughout Madagascar by many

RNP guide Le Jean setting a Sherman live-trap for mouse lemurs.

researchers to study mouse lemurs. Likely because mouse lemurs can enter shallow torpor, adverse effects from live-trapping have not been reported.

Individuals were sexed upon their initial capture. Males were identified as M1, M2, etc., and females as F1, F2, etc. The tiny ear notches, taken to identify animals, were preserved and later used by Yoder et al. (2002) and by Heckman (2005) to conduct genetic analyses. Metric data were taken using simple tools, including calipers and a flexible tape measure. Body mass was recorded using a 100 g Pesola spring scale. We also took basic measurements of the ears, head, body, and tail and noted overall body condition as well as the individual's level of activity (lethargic/energetic). Body mass and tail circumference were taken each time an individual was captured, as these were expected to change seasonally. Female reproductive condition was evaluated based on the condition of the nipples and the vulval area and through abdominal palpation to check for pregnancy (details in Chapter 6). Male testicular size was measured with calipers (details in Chapter 6).

Traps with mouse lemurs were washed prior to returning them in the forest, and all traps were washed weekly. Approximately five fecal samples per week were selected randomly from marked mouse lemurs. The samples were temporarily preserved in 70% alcohol until we had the time to examine them. A dissecting magnifying scope available at the site helped to magnify the contents for easier identification of remains.

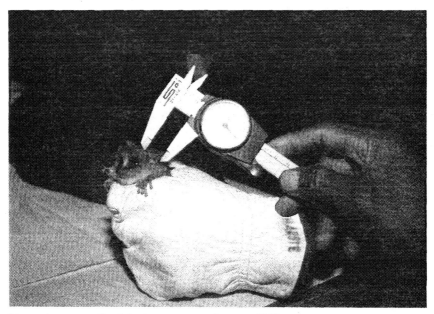

Measuring ear width of the brown mouse lemur in RNP

OBSERVING MOUSE LEMURS

Over the course of the study period, RNP guides, visiting student volunteers, and I radiotracked four mouse lemurs at different times, for 116 hours, during which we recorded 478 observations. Using ordinary cable ties, the animals were fitted with transmitters that weighed 4–5 g and had a peak current of 1.3, a pulse rate of 30 or 35, and a pulse width of 15 or 19 ms. I used a Telonics TR-4 receiver and a two-element RA 14 flexible antenna to locate and track the animals. Our transmitters were expected to be 100% waterproof and to have a three-month lifespan.

We radiotracked between dusk and 2 A.M., but the duration of each radiotracking session depended on weather conditions and our ability to locate the radiocollared individual. When a mouse lemur was located, we recorded behavior and location on a continuous basis. The number of hours spent radiotracking were calculated from the moment of detection of the first radio signal to the time we last heard the signal prior to terminating the radiotracking session. The time between these points included periods when the animal was out of sight and when the radio signal was lost. Because feeding and other behavioral observations of radiocollared individuals constituted a small proportion of total radiotracking time, they are reported as anecdotal observations.

The cost of radiotracking equipment was high, and I expected that tracking efforts would yield information more consistently than proved to be the case. Apart from the usual problem of lack of animal visibility, both the radiotransmitters and the receiver suffered from water damage and malfunctioned. I did not have adequate insulation to protect the equipment from the high humidity and rainfall. The receiver functioned moderately well when weather conditions were dry or if allowed to dry sufficiently following exposure to moisture, but it never achieved the expected 100 m reception distance. In addition, expectations of a three-month lifespan for each radiotransmitter were quickly dashed as some transmitters malfunctioned as early as a week following attachment. These problems discouraged me from continuing to radiotrack. Instead, I concentrated on live-trapping as the main method of collecting important information on mouse lemurs. That said, radiotracking did provide interesting insights, which will be described in chapters to follow.

Accompanied by RNP guides, I also conducted seventy-five nocturnal walks spaced over the course of the study period. Nocturnal walks were another way to observe mouse lemurs in their habitat and to gain information on behavior and diet. A typical walk, at an average pace of 700–800 m/hr, lasted between two to three hours. Nocturnal walks were made on one of three predesignated routes located along Talatakely's already established trail system. Selected routes covered between 1,000 and 2,000 m. The walks took place whenever the opportunity arose and weather permitted. As a team of two, we began either at dusk or at midnight and continued until we reached the end of the predesignated route or until rain forced us to stop. We did not use red-light filters and night vision scopes. We recorded location and behavioral data for any nocturnal primate sighted, and for mouse lemurs, we recorded observations continuously as long as animals remained in view. Nocturnal walks provided many insights into feeding behavior especially in the ways that mouse lemurs captured insects. To locate and observe animals, we used high power binoculars (7 × 42), headlamps, and flashlights. The latter were powered by rechargeable batteries fueled by solar power via portable solar panels. In this way, I kept the environmental and financial costs of the project's energy needs low.

3

Diet and Feeding Ecology

THE DIET OF MOUSE LEMURS

What did a diminutive, nocturnal, solitary forager eat while rambling in the thickness of a tropical rainforest? Because lack of visibility was a significant obstacle to direct observation of animals feeding, investigating diet and feeding ecology was bound to be a challenge. In the early days of nocturnal primate studies, when attitudes even among behavioral ecologists made certain methods of data collection acceptable, diet was sometimes studied by killing animals and inspecting gut contents. For many obvious reasons this method was less than ideal, and today this casual permissiveness with animal life is, thankfully, no longer acceptable. A different noninvasive method was to collect the feces of animals in an attempt to decipher the composition of diet from the digested and expelled remains. At RNP, the indispensable tool in revealing the dietary secrets of mouse lemurs was live-trapping because the floors of the traps held the vital evidence, telltale *fecal clues* of the night's feeding foray: seeds, scraps of fruit skins, and the dismembered body parts of insects and spiders. The most complete studies of nocturnal mammals, such as bats and lorises, have been done in noninvasive ways, through long hours spent following animals in the night as well as by sifting through fecal remains (e.g., Whitaker, 1988; Nekaris and Rasmussen, 2001; Bordignon, 2006). At RNP, insects eaten were recognized through fragments of exoskeleton in the feces, whereas the seeds in the feces were identified by seeking a match with fruiting trees among the many in the forest. Often, this was a daunting task, akin to searching for a needle in the proverbial haystack. Consequently, many fruits eaten by brown mouse lemurs at RNP remained unidentified, and yet, the results of the research described in this chapter remain among the few good inventories of diet for any cheirogaleid species.

Given their diminutive size, I was curious to investigate how body size in mouse lemurs would affect the kind of food resources that these animals sought in order to meet their protein and energy requirement. Body size affects the kind of food resources an animal is able to use, especially when it comes to meeting protein requirements. Species that rely on insects for protein tend to be relatively small whereas those that rely on leaves tend to be larger, the accepted view being that primates below 500 g include a high proportion of insects in their diet (Kay, 1984). Protein in insects, in contrast to that found in leaves, is more easily digestible by small mammals because breaking down plant cellulose requires the action of symbiotic bacteria, a slow process of digestion, and a long gut, which can be accommodated only by a larger body size (Fleagle, 1988). Insects, on the other hand, are rich in carbohydrates, fats, and essential minerals, satisfying the nutritional needs and high metabolic requirements of a small mammal (Clutton-Brock and Harvey, 1977b; Hladik, 1979; Coe, 1984; Fleagle, 1984; Kay, 1984; Ripley, 1984; Richard, 1985). Based on these body size/diet requirements, it was argued that small primates should rely on animal matter as their primary source of protein (Gaulin, 1979; Hladik, 1979, 1981; Clutton-Brock and Harvey, 1983; Kay, 1984). Mouse lemurs, being the smallest of all primates, were hypothesized to be the most insectivorous, a view reinforced by comparing them to highly insectivorous galagos (Charles-Dominique, 1972; Harcourt, 1986; Harcourt and Nash, 1986a; Harcourt and Bearder, 1989). Whether mouse lemurs met some of their protein needs from insects was not in question; rather I aimed to shed light on the degree of insectivory of brown mouse lemurs at RNP and the degree of flexibility in their dietary choices.

Although there are exceptions, the diet of most small mammals is characterized by variety and includes both plant and animal matter (Bourlière, 1975; Eisenberg, 1981; Cork, 1994). With few exceptions, the only overall trend found in mammalian diets as body mass becomes smaller is a decrease in consumption of high-fiber (particularly high-cellulose) foods (Cork, 1994). Therefore, to satisfy their protein and energy needs, small nocturnal primates should feed on high-energy foods, adopting a varied diet that follows the temporal fluctuations in the natural abundance of resources. For instance, gum (a complex polymerized sugar exudate produced in response to damage to the tree trunk) is a potentially high-energy food exploited by many small primates, such as lemurs, galagos, lorises, and the tiniest anthropoids, the marmosets and tamarins (Bearder and Martin, 1980; Power, 1996). Strepsirrhines feed on gum by scraping it off trees using the specialized toothcomb, which is composed of the procumbent lower incisors and canines (Bearder, 1999). Galagos may supplement gums with insects, or they may mix fruit with insects (Bearder, 1999). Among the Cheirogaleidae, *Phaner* is a gum specialist, supplementing the diet with insects (Charles-Dominique and Petter, 1980; Schülke, 2003). Other cheirogaleids, such as *Mirza* and *Cheirogaleus*, secure mixed diets composed of plant and animal matter (Hladik et al., 1980; Wright and Martin, 1995). In contrast to these and other species that maintain diverse diets, some small nocturnal primates are indeed mostly insectivorous. The Mysore slender loris is one example; 96% of feeding observations were on animal prey, predominantly ants armed with chemical defenses (Nekaris and Rasmussen, 2003). Even more extreme are the various species of *Tarsius* studied, which have been found to feed entirely on prey items, mostly insects, with no reports of plant foods eaten (e.g., Niemitz, 1984; Tremble et al., 1993).

Data from short-term field studies hinted that *Microcebus* was not an extreme insectivore, maintaining instead a great deal of dietary diversity (Martin, 1972b; Tattersall and Sussman, 1989). In fact, *M. murinus* is said to consume an omnivorous diet comprised mostly of fruits, insects, and gums. The diet also includes flowers, buds, sap (the circulating fluid in a tree), nectars, plant and insect secretions, occasionally small vertebrates (chameleons and tree-frogs), and even some leaves (Martin, 1972b, 1973; Hladik et al., 1980; Barre et al., 1988; Corbin and Schmid, 1995; Reimann et al., 2003; Dammhahn and Kappeler, 2006; Radespiel et al., 2006). In addition, *M. murinus* was found to specialize on local plant foods, particularly berries (Martin, 1972b), with insects selected more opportunistically based on peaks of availability (Martin, 1972b; Hladik et al., 1980). Hladik et al. (1980) concluded that fruits were the staple diet of *M. murinus*, complemented with animal matter, mostly beetles. Indeed, a high level of frugivory was confirmed for this species in a recent study in Madena's littoral rainforest during which 63% of feeding observations on grey mouse lemurs were on fruit (Lahann, 2007).

Gums and sugary secretions produced by the larvae of Homoptera have been found to be of particular importance to mouse lemurs studied in dry forests. *M. murinus* was discovered feeding on gums in 75–80% of feeding episodes (Génin, 2001). Several other studies confirmed that the secretions of homopteran larvae were an important food resource in the dry season not only for *M. murinus*, but also for *M. ravelobensis* and *M. berthae* (Corbin and Schmid, 1995; Reimann et al., 2003; Dammhahn and Kappeler, 2006; Radespiel et al., 2006). These secretions, produced by colonies of larvae, fall onto branches below, drying into a crystalline form that mouse lemurs lick (Corbin and Schmid, 1995). Insect secretions are high in sugar and low in protein, so that animal matter such as the beetles and spiders that supplemented the diet of these species probably served as sources of protein (Dammhahn and Kappeler, 2006; Radespiel et al., 2006).

For *M. rufus*, available data suggested a diet that included insects but also a high proportion of fruit (Martin, 1972b; Harcourt, 1987; Ganzhorn, 1988, 1989a,b; Wright and Martin, 1995). Insects were proposed as preferred dietary items during certain periods of the year (Harste et al., 1997). As with the dry forest species, the full complement of foods eaten by *M. rufus* could not be revealed through short-term research because the foods that primates need and use are not evenly distributed and available throughout the year. Long-term studies that encompass both wet and dry seasons are necessary in order to compile the full complement of foods eaten, and to understand how dietary choices change seasonally depending on availability. Given that Ranomafana is characterized by relative scarcity in fruit and insect abundance during the dry season (Overdorff, 1991; Meyers and Wright, 1993; Hemingway, 1995; Wright, 1997), I expected to find that mouse lemurs changed their feeding habits to accommodate fluctuations in available resources. Therefore, my objectives were to investigate the importance of fruit versus insects in the diet, to identify preferred dietary items, and to explore seasonal food choices over an annual cycle.

INVESTIGATING DIET IN THE BROWN MOUSE LEMUR

Observations of mouse lemurs seen in the act of feeding were rare because of their small size, the low light levels in the forest, the thickness of the vegetation, and the high levels of precipitation. Thus, the key to effective data collection through direct observation was persistence, allowing feeding observations to accumulate through repeated nocturnal walks in the forest, and while radiotracking. In fact, most of the information on diet in this study came from fecal analysis of live-trapped animals. I determined the preferred food items of the brown mouse lemur by evaluating the frequency of their appearance in the feces. Food choices were assessed by comparing actual fruit and insects consumed to the amount of fruit and insects available as recorded through phenological monitoring and insect surveys.

Fecal samples from 111 known individuals—66 male and 45 female—were collected. Overall, 51% of individuals sampled provided only one sample each. Only 22% of known males and 16% of known females contributed more than three each. On average twenty samples were collected per month (range 9–34). Of the 334 fecal samples collected, 266 contained some evidence of fruit (seeds, skins, or pith), 240 contained some type of fruit seed, and 254 contained evidence of insects and, more rarely, spiders. Seeds were grouped within each sample according to similarity, then counted and measured. Seeds of species belonging to the same genus usually could not be distinguished from one another and were counted as one fruit type. To identify the fruits eaten, seeds in the feces were compared with those of fruiting plants in the forest. Following a match, we collected fruits from the plant to determine their color, average mass, length, width, and typical number of seeds. Unidentified seeds were numbered as "unidentified fruit" (U.F.1, etc.). Other unidentified seeds that were sufficiently similar to belong to the same fruit were placed in a single group numbered as an "unidentified fruit category" (U.F. category 1, etc.). By lumping together seeds that were similar in appearance, I avoided overestimating the number of fruits that mouse lemurs potentially ate.

Chitin is the key component of insect exoskeletons and made up most of the prey remains in the fecal samples. I examined and quantified insect remains using a magnifying scope, but for more accurate identification, chitin remains from a random subsample of 115 fecal samples collected between April 1993 and May 1994 were stored to be checked later by Julian Stark, an expert entomologist at the American Museum of Natural History in New York City. By reconstructing insect parts, Stark also estimated the minimum number of prey items in each sample.

To assess whether mouse lemurs were frugivorous or insectivorous, I compared three dietary categories—fecal samples containing only fruit, only insect, and both fruit and insects—to their frequency counts using a loglinear model (likelihood-ratio chi-square test). Data from consecutive two-month intervals were combined to obtain expected cell frequencies large enough to make use of this model. Multiple samples from the same individual were treated as independent observations.

I also devised various measures to quantify the quantity and diversity of fruits and insects eaten. When the volume or mass of fruits and insects are known, it is possible to directly compare ingested biomass of fruit with ingested biomass of insect matter (Korschgen, 1969; Whitaker, 1988). However, whereas data on the mass and size of fruits eaten by mouse lemurs were available, I did not have the corresponding information for the insects that they consumed. Therefore, I followed the example of researchers who studied ape diets. Instead of directly comparing quantities of different food categories eaten, I used various measures described below to monitor feeding patterns over the course of the study period.

- *MNI-F, or minimum number of individual fruit per fecal sample.* The MNI-F measured the amount of fruit contained in a fecal sample based on the number of seeds present. If the seeds could be identified as belonging to a particular fruit, then the actual number of fruits eaten by the mouse lemur was estimated based on the number of seeds contained in a typical fruit. If a known fruit species contained a variable number of seeds, for example, one or two, it was assumed that the minimum number of fruits had been eaten. When the typical fruit contained many seeds (e.g., figs), or the seeds remained unidentified, or only skins and pith were found, fruit presence in the sample was recorded as one fruit.

- *NFT, or number of fruit types per fecal sample.* NFT measured diversity of fruits found in each sample. A similar measure was used to quantify seasonal fluctuations in fruit intake in the diet of apes (Tutin et al., 1991; Tutin and Fernandez, 1993; Yamagiwa et al., 1993; Remis, 1994). Seeds grouped together according to similarity were counted as one vernacular species. The presence of skins without seeds was counted as one vernacular species.
- *TFT, or total number of different fruit types.* TFT measured diversity of fruits sampled monthly across all fecal samples. A similar measure was used for apes (Tutin and Fernandez, 1993; Yamagiwa et al., 1993). TFT was based on the collective NFT values for each month. Small body size limits the amount of fruit ingested per night and the distance ranged per night so that fewer types of fruiting trees can be visited by each individual. Food passing through the gut is fairly rapid in the mouse lemur, averaging 4 hours (Harste, 1993), so that the following morning's remains may represent only a sample of the previous night's feeding activity. Therefore, it was necessary to determine TFT because individual fecal samples could not represent adequately the diversity of fruits eaten by the population.
- *VS, or volumetric score per sample.* I estimated the quantity of chitin in a fecal sample by using a volumetric score of 1–3, which was based on how much space of a microscope slide was covered by insect parts. A similar scoring system was used for apes and galagos (Harcourt and Nash, 1986a; Tutin and Fernandez, 1993; Yamagiwa et al., 1993).
- *MNI-I, or minimum number of individual invertebrates found per sample.* The MNI-I was determined by reconstructing the number of prey items from the remains of body parts present in each of 115 samples examined by an expert entomologist in the United States.
- Diversity of insects eaten was measured via the monthly number of insect orders identified in the 115 fecal samples. This measure of diversity is less fine-tuned than the NFT value used for fruit because an order is a broader grouping than a vernacular taxon.

Biochemical analyses were performed on a selection of fruits commonly eaten by *M. rufus*. *Pittosporum* and *Dypsis*, not eaten by mouse lemurs, were chosen as controls. To prepare for biochemical analyses at a later date, we collected fruits, removed the seeds (except for figs which had too many seeds to remove) and dried the cut-up flesh and skin. The fruit was dried through a combination of the sun's heat, and a heating oven at 60°F. Eventually, the samples were analyzed in the laboratory of Jörg Ganzhorn at Hamburg University, Germany, where phytochemical analyses were conducted to determine the amount of total nitrogen, fat, fiber (acid detergent fiber), protein, condensed tannin, and sugar in each sample. Protein concentrations were calculated by using two methods: one that provided a standard but crude estimate of protein content (by multiplying total nitrogen from the Kjeldahl by the factor of 6.25), the other by directly extracting protein from the powdered plant material (using NaOH, then measuring the protein concentrations in the extract as equivalents to bovine serum albumin; BioRad technique). Condensed tannins were measured as equivalents to Quebracho tannin, and these are relative units.

USE OF PLANTS AND PREY

Frugivory

Of 334 fecal samples collected, 207 contained the remains of both fruit and insects, 73 contained only fruit remains (skins, pulp or seeds), and 48 contained only insect remains. The proportion of fecal samples in each of the three dietary categories changed significantly during the study period (chi-square test likelihood ratio $\chi^2 = 49.89$, $p < .001$) (Figure 3-1). Of the three categories, the "insect only" category exhibited the greatest fluctuation, decreasing to zero in December 1993, January 1994, February 1994, March 1994 and May 1994, whereas the "fruit only" category showed a more consistent presence.

The MNI-F for each fecal sample ranged from 0 to 36 fruits. On average 4.5 fruits were found in each fecal sample but the majority contained only a single fruit. The NFT for each sample ranged between 0 and 6 fruit types,

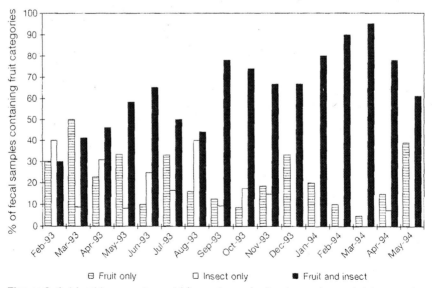

Figure 3-1 Monthly percentage of *Microcebus rufus* fecal samples containing remains from fruit only, fruit and insects, or only insects. (From Atsalis, 1999a; used with permission from Springer Science and Business Media.)

averaging 1.3. Eighty-eight percent of fecal samples contained only 1 or 2 types of fruit, whereas the remaining 12% contained between 3 and 6. In other words, fecal sampling indicated that, individually, when mouse lemurs ate fruit, they consumed between 1 and 6 different kinds of fruits per night. Obviously this is a minimum number because given rapid gut passage, animals may have voided before entering the trap. TFT per month ranged from 3 to 15, averaging 7.6 different fruit varieties. I found no correlation between TFT and monthly number of collected samples (Spearman rank correlation $r_s = .131$, $N = 16$), suggesting that collecting additional fecal samples would not have increased the fruit varieties found monthly through fecal sampling.

In total, twenty-four different kinds of fruit were identified in the diet of the brown mouse lemur at RNP, the majority detected exclusively through fecal sampling (Table 3–1). Of 240 fecal samples with fruit seeds, approximately

Table 3–1 Fruits Identified as Food Sources for Brown Mouse Lemurs

Taxonomic Name	*Family*	*Vernacular Name*[a]	*Plant Type*	*Method of Detection* *Fecal Sample*	*Through Direct Observation*
Alberta humblotii[b]	Rubiaceae	Fatsikiahitra Madinidravina	Shrub	Yes	No
Anthocleista amplexicaulis	Loganiaceae	Dendemivavy	Tree	Yes	Yes
Aphloia theaeformis	Flacourtiaceae	Fandramanana Lavaravina	Tree	No	Yes
Bakerella sp.	Loranthaceae	Tongolahy Fotsy	Epiphytic semi-parasite	Yes	Yes
Bakerella clavata subsp. 1	Loranthaceae	Tongolahy Madinidravina L.F.	Epiphytic semi-parasite	Yes	No
Bakerella grisea	Loranthaceae	Tongolahy Vaventiravina L.F.	Epiphytic semi-parasite	Yes	Yes
Cissus sp.	Vitaceae	Vahirano Madinidravina	Liane	Yes	No
Ficus sp.	Moraceae	Vahihafa	Scrambling Shrub	No	Yes
Gaertnera sp.	Rubiaceae	Bararata Vaventiravina	Tree	Yes	Yes
Harungana madagascariensis	Clusiaceae	Harongana	Shrub to medium-sized tree	Yes	No
Ilex mitis	Aquifoliaceae	Hazondrano	Tree	Yes	No
Maesa lanceolata	Myrsinaceae	Voarafy	Shrub to small tree	Yes	No
Medinilla sp.[c]	Melastomataceae	Kalamasimbarika	Epiphyte	Yes	No

Table 3-1 Continued

Nuxia sp.[d]	Loganiaceae	Lambinanala	Tree	Yes	No
Oncostemum botryoides	Myrsinaceae	Kalafana Madinidravina	Tree	No	Yes
Psidium cattleianum	Myrtaceae	Goavy Gasy	Shrub	Yes	Yes
Psychotria sp.	Rubiaceae	Voanananala Madinidravina L.F.	Shrub	Yes	No
Psychotria sp.	Rubiaceae	Voanananala Madinidravina R.F. #1	Shrub	Yes	No
Psychotria sp.	Rubiaceae	Voanananala Madinidravina R.F. #2	Shrub	Yes	No
Psychotria sp.	Rubiaceae	Voanananala Vaventiravina R.F.	Shrub	No	Yes
Rhipsalis baccifera	Cactaceae	Voatsilelolelo	Epiphyte	Yes	No
Viscum sp.	Viscaceae	Tongolahy Maitso	Epiphytic semi-parasite	Yes	No
Unknown	Menispermaceae	Hazotana	Liane	Yes	No
Unknown	Rubiaceae	Voanananamboa	Shrub	Yes	No

[a]Madinidravina—small-leafed; Vaventiravina—large-leafed; Lavaravina—large, round-leafed; L.F.—long-leafed; R.F.—round-leafed.

[b]Or Cavaco (Dan Turk, personal communication, 1993).

[c]Tentative identification.

[d]May be misidentified; fruit of Nuxia are small, dry, and capsular, possibly not edible by mouse lemurs (Dan Turk, personal communication, 1993).

Source: From Atsalis, 1999a; used with permission from Springer Science and Business Media.

44% had at least one kind of fruit seed that remained unidentified indicating that the number and diversity of fruits consumed by mouse lemurs was underestimated in this study. Close inspection of the differences of these unidentified seeds led me to estimate that mouse lemurs in our sample consumed an additional 40–52 different kinds of fruits. Fruits identified belonged to seventeen genera and, including two unidentified ones, to fourteen families. Seven of the fruits identified came from epiphytes or lianas. Discussions with Ranomafana's guides revealed that some of the fruits (Aphloia, Bakerella, Gaertnera, Psidium and Harungana) were eaten by other lemurs and by birds.

There was wide disparity in the frequency with which different fruit seeds were present in the feces (Table 3–2). Bakerella seeds predominated in the sample pool. Medinilla, the second in seed presence, was found in only one-sixth of the number of samples in which Bakerella was found.

Table 3–2 Percentage of 240 Fecal Samples that Contained Specific Fruits Eaten by Brown Mouse Lemurs (Total Sampled, 334)

Fruit in the Fecal Sample	% of Samples with Fruit Seeds	Number of Months
Bakerella	57.9	16
Medinilla	9.6	6
Viscum	9.2	7
Rhipsalis baccifera	7.5	5
Psychotria	6.7	6
Gaertnera	3.8	3
Nuxia	2.9	2
Psidium cattleianum	2.1	4
Cissus	1.7	4
Maesa lanceolata	1.3	1
Alberta humblotii	1.3	2
Anthocleista amplexicaulis	0.8	2
Ilex mitis	0.8	1
Hazotana	0.4	1
Harungana madagascariensis	0.4	1
Voananamboa	0.4	1

Values in the last column refer to the number of months the fruit was detected in samples.

Source: Adapted from Table III in Atsalis, 1999a; used with permission from Springer Science and Business Media.

Seeds from the tree species sampled that had the highest basal area, *Weinmannia bojeriana,* were never present in fecal samples (although flower parts were).

To determine the typical size and color of fruits preferred by mouse lemurs, I collected and measured, when possible, fresh samples of fruits. The majority of fruits contained 1–2 seeds (67%), but two fruits averaged 70 seeds/fruit. *Alberta humblotii* had the longest seeds eaten by mouse lemurs, averaging 8.3 mm. Other seeds swallowed by mouse lemurs were about half the length, or less (Table 3–3). In terms of mass and size of fruit, *Psidium cattleaianum,* averaging 7600 mg and 23 mm length (for ripe fruit), and *Anthocleista amplexicaulis,* averaging 4000 mg and 26 mm length (for ripe fruit) were the largest ones eaten. Overall, fruits eaten were of diverse size: 31% were as large as those eaten by large-bodied diurnal lemur species (Dew and Wright, 1998), averaging greater than 9–10 mm in length. However, the dimensions of fruits and seeds ingested by the brown mouse lemur at RNP are within the range of those recently reported for *M. murinus* (see Table 2 in Lahann, 2007), although it appears that some of the fruits eaten by brown mouse lemurs were larger (see Table 3 in Lahann, 2007). Lastly, in Ranomafana all fruits eaten by brown mouse lemurs but one were

Buds, flowers. and young fruit of the mistletoe *Bakerella*. Fruit from this epiphytic plant were a favorite food item for the brown mouse lemur in RNP.

green in color when unripe ($N = 16$). The color of ripe fruit varied: 40% were reddish; 27%, white; 20%, yellow; and 13% were green ($N = 15$).

Bakerella, the Fruit of Preference

Bakerella is an epiphytic plant endemic to Madagascar. It was the predominant fruit in the diet of the brown mouse lemur at RNP. The seeds of tongolahy, the local name for the plant, appeared in approximately 42% of the total number of fecal samples. Seeds were present in fecal samples in every month of the study period (Table 3–4).

Bakerella species are mistletoes, flowering plants that belong to the wide-ranging family Loranthaceae. Some members such as the holly have important associations with human traditions (Calder, 1983). Mistletoes directly derive all or most of their nutrition from other flowering plants during most or all of their life cycle. All have haustoria, modified roots through which plants connect to the host plant (Nickrent, 2002). Like *Bakerella,* most types are hemiparasitical (i.e., partial parasites), in that they are capable of photosynthesis but draw water and nutrients from the host's xylem through their haustoria (Richards, 1952; Nickrent, 2002). The fruit of *Bakerella* is a one-seeded berry that does not actually contain a true seed but rather an embryo surrounded by starchy endosperm (Godschalk, 1983a; Mabberley, 1987). The seed is enveloped in a white viscin layer, which itself is surrounded by

Table 3-3 Measurements of Fruits Identified as Food Sources for Brown Mouse Lemurs

Fruit Measurement	Number of Seeds Per Fruit	Seed Length (mm)	Seed Width (mm)	Unripe Fruit Length (mm)	Unripe Fruit Width (mm)	Ripe Fruit Length (mm)	Ripe Fruit Width (mm)	Unripe Fruit Mass (mg)	Ripe Fruit Mass (mg)
Mean	11	4.7	2.8	8.7	7	11	9	870	1300
Median	2	2.5	2.3	7.6	6	9.3	7.7	180	320
Range	1.0–70	1.3–8.3	0.3–5.8	4.6–24.9	3.4–14.3	5.7–25.7	4.2–23.1	30–6600	100–7600
Number of different fruits sampled	24	16	16	14	14	13	13	14	11
Sample size range[a]	2–80	5–50	5–50	1–78	1–78	10–51	10–51	8–100	10–51

[a] The sample size varied for each fruit. Shown here is the range of number of fruits measured over all species.

Table 3–4 Monthly Presence of All Fruits (Based on Seed Presence) in 334 Fecal Samples of Brown Mouse Lemurs

February 1993	*Bakerella,* Hazotana, *Rhipsalis*
March 1993	*Bakerella,* Hazondrano, *Medinilla,* U.F.2, U.F.3, U.F. Category 4, U.F.5, U.F.6, Voanananala, Voarafy
April 1993	*Bakerella, Medinilla, Psidium, Rhipsalis,* U.F.2, U.F. Category 4, Voanananala
May 1993	*Bakerella, Cissus,* Harongana, U.F. Category 1, U.F.2, U.F. Category 4, *Viscum,* Voanananala
June 1993	*Bakerella, Cissus,* U.F. Category 1, U.F.2, U.F. Category 4, U.F.7, *Viscum,* Voanananala
July 1993	*Bakerella,* U.F.2, U.F. Category 4, U.F.8, *Viscum*
August 1993	*Bakerella, Psidium,* U.F.2, U.F. Category 4, U.F. Category 9, *Viscum*
September 1993	*Bakerella,* Lambinanala, U.F.2, U.F.8, U.F.10, U.F. Category 11, U.F. Category 4, *Viscum,* Voananamboa
October 1993	*Bakerella,* Lambinanala, U.F.11, U.F. Category 4, *Viscum*
November 1993	*Bakerella,* Fatsikiahitra Madinidravina, U.F.11, *Viscum*
December 1993	*Bakerella,* Dendemivavy, Fatsikiahitra Madinidravina, *Medinilla,* U.F.11, U.F.12
January 1994	*Bakerella,* Dendemivavy, U.F.11, U.F.12, U.F.13, U.F.14, U.F.15, U.F.17
February 1994	*Bakerella, Gaertnera, Medinilla, Rhipsalis,* U.F.15, U.F.16, U.F.17, U.F. Category 18, U.F.19, U.F.20, U.F.21
April 1994	*Bakerella, Cissus, Gaertnera, Medinilla, Psidium, Rhipsalis,* U.F.17, U.F. Category 18, U.F.2, U.F.22, U.F. Category 27, U.F.28, U.F.29, U.F.30, Voanananala
May 1994	*Bakerella, Cissus, Psidium,* U.F. Category 4, Voanananala

U.F.—Unidentified fruit; A "Category" includes unidentified fruit seeds that may or may not belong to one fruit.

Source: From Atsalis, 1999a; used with permission from Springer Science and Business Media.

a fleshy viscous nutritious skin of mesocarp (Godschalk, 1983a; Polhill and Wiens, 1998). The viscin layer is a specialized structure, not found in non-parasitic plants. Its stickiness attaches the seed to the host when it is deposited (Godschalk, 1983a). Unlike other plant seeds, I suspected that the stickiness associated with *Bakerella* made it difficult for a mouse lemur to spit out or manually remove the seed, thereby providing a more reliable record of fruit consumption through fecal sampling. To compare, *Psidium* (guava), a fruit reported by RNP guides to be popular with this population of mouse lemurs, had a juicy pulp with many large and heavy seeds that could be spit out prior to swallowing, probably accounting for their low frequency in the feces. Indeed, one captured mouse lemur ate the fruit flesh of guava without ingesting the seeds. Thus, at least for some fruit species, the number of seeds present in fecal samples may be a low estimate of fruit actually consumed.

Clusters of unripe fruit of *Bakerella* mistletoe, a favorite fruit of brown mouse lemurs in RNP

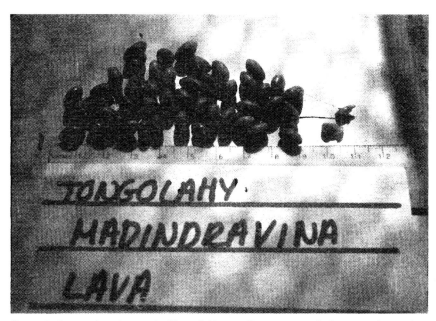

Bakerella fruit and sticky seeds. The stickiness allows the seed of this epiphytic plant to attach to host plants

Ranomafana guides and I identified six different varieties of *Bakerella* in the study area. Through fecal analysis and direct observation, we knew that mouse lemurs fed on at least three of these. We judged the number of varieties ingested by differences in the external morphology of the seeds found in the feces. Berries voided were easily identifiable as whole seeds of *Bakerella*, but because of the subtlety of seed differences it is likely that more varieties than we were able to distinguish were actually being eaten.

Beetles, the Prey of Preference

The value for MNI-I per fecal sample ranged from 1 to 12 different prey items, averaging 2.2. As with fruit, the majority of samples contained remains from only one prey item although when results from all the samples were taken together, insects belonging to nine different orders were identified (Figure 3–2). Caterpillars were placed in a separate category from adult Lepidoptera because of the different habitats that they occupy. The "Unidentified Invertebrates" category contains material that could not be identified to class. In sixteen fecal samples, the remains of Hymenoptera (ants etc.) could not be distinguished from Heteroptera (true bugs) and were placed in the "Unidentified Insects" category.

Fifty-six percent of the samples checked contained only one of the categories listed in the figure, whereas close to 96% contained up to three of the

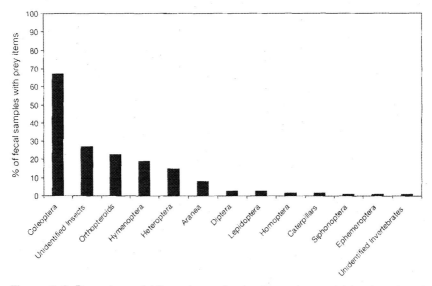

Figure 3–2 Percentage of *Microcebus rufus* fecal samples containing insect and spider remains (*n* = 115). The "Unidentified Insect" category contains 16 samples in which Hymenoptera could not be distinguished from Heteroptera. The "Unidentified Invertebrates" category contains remains that could not be identified to class level. (Adapted from Table IV in Atsalis, 1999a; used with permission from Springer Science and Business Media.)

categories listed. Insects in the order Coleoptera (beetles) predominated in the feces of the brown mouse lemur at RNP. Sixty-seven percent of fecal samples examined contained beetles, many of which had multiple specimens. Specifically, in the 115 samples examined, 250 insect identifications were made of which 121 were beetles. As with *Bakerella*, the order Coleoptera was the only one present in the fecal samples for all months that insect remains were examined. Beetles were found in over 50% of the fecal samples for nine out of twelve months sampled.

Other Organic Matter Found in Fecal Samples

Woody filaments, tiny pieces of bark and twig (sometimes with leaf), and moss were occasionally present in the feces and may have been ingested in the process of obtaining gum or sap; on one occasion, we had noted a mouse lemur licking exposed cambium, possibly for access to gum or sap. Filaments and anthers of *Weinmannia bojeriana* and flower parts from other unidentified species were also detected. Other items found were moth scales, fragments of the egg case of a praying mantis, a soft invertebrate, possibly an earthworm, and insect eggs, larvae or pupae, the latter most likely ingested with fruit. Intact ants, which may have been ingested coincidently with fruit, were also detected. Mouse lemur fur, likely the result of grooming, was found regularly in the fecal samples.

Fruit: Availability and Consumption

Measures of fruit resource abundance (see Figure 2–3) and available diversity (see Figure 2–5) were not significantly correlated with general measures of fruit quantity and diversity present in the diet (Figure 3–3). Specifically, there were no significant correlations between the monthly number of plants in fruit in the botanical plots and monthly averages of MNI-F ($r_s = .411$, $N = 15$, all fruit included-ripe and unripe) and NFT ($r_s = .336$, $N = 15$, all fruit included-ripe and unripe). As for fruit diversity, there were no statistically significant correlations between monthly number of vernacular species of trees and shrubs in fruit in the botanical plots and monthly values of NFT (unripe fruit, $r_s = .357$; ripe fruit, $r_s = -.144$; all fruit, ripe or unripe, $r_s = .224$, $N = 13$) and TFT (unripe fruit, $r_s = .288$; ripe fruit, $r_s = -.115$; all fruit, $r_s = .339$, $N = 13$). These results suggest that the feeding patterns of brown mouse lemurs at RNP did not always follow the habitat-wide patterns of fruit availability. Rather, brown mouse lemurs had specific fruit preferences, as discussed earlier. Mouse lemurs, however, increased their intake of fruit at the end of the rainy season around February and March, when fruit availability was also relatively high. At this time, the measures of NFT, TFT, and MNI-F exhibited monthly increases (see Figure 3–3). (February 1993 is an exception probably because of observer inexperience associated with first month of data collection in the

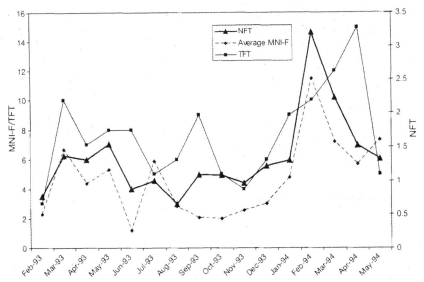

Figure 3–3 Monthly measures of fruit presence in *Microcebus rufus* fecal samples in Talatakely, RNP. Left *y*-axis is the monthly average MNI-F (minimum number of individual fruits found in each fecal sample) and the monthly TFT (total number of different fruit types sampled, found monthly in all fecal samples combined). Right *y*-axis is the monthly average NFT (number of fruit types found in each fecal sample). (Adapted from Table VII in Atsalis, 1999a; used with permission from Springer Science and Business Media.)

study.) This period of high fruit abundance and increased fruit consumption coincided with important events in the brown mouse lemur life cycle: mouse lemurs began accumulating body fat prior to hibernating during the dry season and young mouse lemurs, offspring of the most recent reproductive period, began to feed independently (Chapter 4).

Although brown mouse lemurs depended on *Bakerella* as a main source of food, there was significant monthly variation in the presence of this fruit in the fecal samples (Kruskal-Wallace Test = 74.75, $p < .001$, $N = 334$). Specifically, *Bakerella* occurred in 11% of fecal samples in December 1993, but reached 70% in February 1994 (Figure 3–4). The monthly average number of *Bakerella* seeds found in fecal samples was highly correlated with monthly average MNI-F ($r_s = .915$, $p < .01$, $N = 16$) indicating that *Bakerella* influenced seed representation in the feces. The presence of *Bakerella* in the fecal samples, however, was relatively low for all months of the dry season with the exception of July 1993, when increased rainfall may have caused increased fruit maturation (see Figure 2–1 for rainfall patterns). It is particularly interesting that in July, despite an overall increase in the variety of fruit available in the forest (see Figure 2–5), only the consumption of *Bakerella* increased. This observation is supported by the increased value for monthly average MNI-F in this month (see Figure 3–3), likely as a result of intake of *Bakerella* (see Figure 3–4), as that fruit's abundance was increased in the forest.

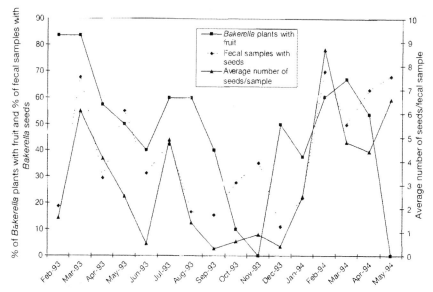

Figure 3–4 A comparison of *Bakerella* plants bearing fruit with the presence of *Bakerella* in fecal samples of *Microcebus rufus*. Left *y*-axis is the monthly percentage of *Bakerella* plants bearing fruit (unripe) and the monthly percentage of fecal samples containing *Bakerella* seeds. Right *y*-axis is the average number of *Bakerella* seeds per fecal sample. (Adapted from Table VI in Atsalis, 1999a; used with permission from Springer Science and Business Media.)

The values for MNI-F and NFT also peaked in February 1994 with several new kinds of fruit seeds appearing in the fecal samples, among them *Rhipsalis* and *Medinilla*, both epiphytes (see Table 3–4). Given mouse lemur preference for the epiphytic *Bakerella* and *Viscum*, it appears that, overall, the fruits of epiphytes were favored food sources. Epiphytes are generally sensitive to dry weather conditions, but two sequential cyclones may have promoted epiphytic abundance in February and March, when mouse lemurs consumed them. Lastly, high rainfall in February and March may have resulted in the high percentage of fruiting plants present in April 1994. During this month, mouse lemurs ate a highly diverse diet of fruits; TFT had its highest peak when five new fruits, which remained unidentified, joined the dietary repertoire (see Table 3–4).

Results from the *petite phenologie* were not correlated with those from the plot phenologies (r_s = .236, N = 20; only values for unripe fruit were used as those for ripe fruit in the *petite phenologies* were low). And even when I conducted separate comparisons between specific families or genera of the *petite phenologie* and the data from botanical plots, the results were the same. Only in the case of *Psychotria* (family Rubiaceae) was there a positive correlation (r_s = .877, $p <$ .01, N = 14) (Figure 3–5) and in the case of *Viscum*, a negative one (r_s = −.726, $p <$ .05, N = 9). *Viscum* appeared in

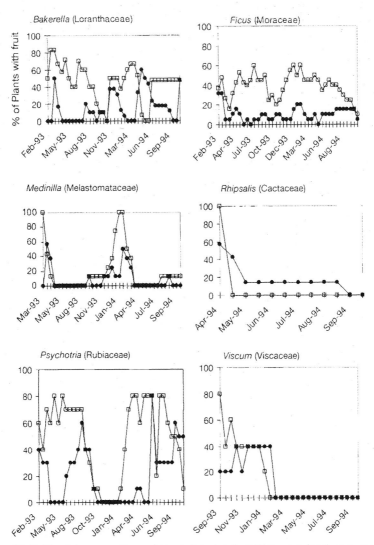

Figure 3–5 Monthly percentage of plants bearing fruit that were food resources for *Microcebus rufus* in Talatakely, RNP. Only the top five plants that were part of the diet are shown. Plants sampled semimonthly (*Bakerella* sampled once in July 1993, February 1994, and October 1994; *Psychotria* sampled once in February 1993, July 1993, October 1994; *Medinilla* sampled only once in July 1993, October 1994; *Rhipsalis* sampled once in April 1994, October 1994). Ripe fruit shown by closed circles, unripe fruit by open squares. Data from *Ficus* trees (family Moraceae) also presented; the seeds were similar to ones that remained unidentified in fecal samples. Phenological samples of the genera *Medinilla*, *Rhipsalis*, and *Viscum* included only one vernacular species each, the sample of *Psychotria* included three vernacular species, the sample of *Bakerella* included several varieties: two subspecies of *Bakerella clavata*, the species *Bakerella grisea*, and one other unknown species of *Bakerella*. *Ficus* included four different vernacular species of fig. (From Atsalis, 1999a; used with permission from Springer Science and Business Media.)

the feces between May and November overlapping some of the months of the dry season when general fruit abundance was relatively low (see Chapter 2). Fruits of *Viscum* were abundant for part of that period suggesting that this fruit was a resource that sustained mouse lemurs in times of scarcity.

Phytochemical Analysis of Fruits Eaten

The most notable result from phytochemical analysis was the relatively high fat content discovered for *Bakerella* (Table 3–5). The high fat content may explain the strong preference for *Bakerella* by mouse lemurs. Although all *Bakerella* samples were high in lipid content, the wide differences among them may have been related to varying levels of fruit ripeness. Among other fruits, only *Harungana* had high fat (but low sugar) content. *Alberta, Psidium,* and *Psychotria,* which were available and were eaten during more seasonally restricted periods than was *Bakerella,* had relatively higher sugar and lower fat content than did *Bakerella.* Both BioRad and Kjeldahl techniques, used to measure protein content, demonsrated that *Psychotria* contained high levels of protein. *Bakerella* sp. 2 was high only when measured using the BioRad technique, and *Bakerella clavata* sp. 2 was high only with the Kjeldahl technique. The two methods used to measure protein content were not correlated (Ganzhorn, personal communication, 1996). The Kjeldahl technique uses a conversion factor that assumes that all the nitrogen is found in protein (Herbst, 1986), but a more accurate protein estimate requires conversion factors appropriate for each particular food types being examined (Milton and Dintzis, 1981).

   Among the samples analyzed, *Dypsis nodifera,* a fruit not eaten by *Microcebus,* had very high levels of tannin. Although some *Bakerella* samples were also relatively high in tannin, the amount was less than half of what was contained in *Dypsis nodifera.* Likely, brown mouse lemurs avoided fruit with high tannin levels, an observation supported by Ganzhorn (1988, 1989b). In Ganzhorn's research, which explored the relationship of primates to secondary plant chemicals, *M. rufus* was one of a small sample of primates that seemed to avoid both tannins and alkaloids in fruits eaten. Other closely related lemurs, such as *Cheirogaleus major,* did not. Whether or not these differences are related to differential ability for detoxification remains to be determined.

Animal Prey: Availability and Consumption

Fecal analysis indicated that mouse lemurs ate animal prey, mostly insects, but also other prey items such as spiders, year-round. The data suggested that mouse lemurs may not have eaten insects based on their habitat-wide abundance as none of the values that I used to measure monthly insect

Table 3–5 Phytochemical Analysis of Select Fruits Eaten by Brown Mouse Lemurs and Two Nonfood Fruits for Comparison

Species	Family	Ripeness	% Nitrogen (Kjeldahl)	% Protein (Kjeldahl)	% Fat	% Fiber	Extractable Protein (BioRad)	Condensed Tannin[a]	%Sugar	Protein–Fiber Ratio
Alberta humblotii	Rubiaceae	ripe	0.55	3.6	0.65	28.47	5.55	0	59.8	0.19
Psidium cattleianum	Myrtaceae	ripe	0.47	3.03	1.68	25.03	1.14	2.95	38.5	0.05
Psidium cattleianum	Myrtaceae	unripe	0.5	3.23	0.91	37.41	2.72	7.41	22.9	0.07
Harungana madagascariensis	Clusiaceae	unknown	1.07	6.94	4.73		4.2	4.91	4.4	
Bakerella sp. 1	Loranthaceae	unripe	0.82	5.32	5.73	27.26	5.47	36.16	22.1	0.20
Bakerella sp. 2	Loranthaceae	unknown	0.64	4.18	9.57	61.13	8.22	20.34	9.7	0.13
Bakerella clavata sp. 1	Loranthaceae	ripe	0.98	6.36	14.72	27.42	3.31	4.71	6.7	0.12
Bakerella clavata sp. 2	Loranthaceae	ripe	1.13	7.34	26.57	53.3	2.92	0.59	2.4	0.05
Bakerella grisea	Loranthaceae	ripe	0.73	4.78	13.53	29.94	5.4	18.23	8.5	0.18
Psychotria sp.	Rubiaceae	unripe	1.67	10.86	1.06	34	10.54	33.53	36.9	0.31
Pittosporum verticillatum[b]	Pittosporaceae	ripe	1.9	12.38	0.52	28.75	4.49	1.81	40.7	0.16
Dypsis nodifera[b]	Palmae	unknown	0.84	5.44	1.12	35.91	8.68	86.23	32.4	0.24

[a]Reported tannin values may be higher than values from other laboratories.

[b]These are not Microcebus fruit sources.

Source: From Atsalis, 1999a; used with permission from Springer Science and Business Media.

presence in mouse lemur feces were correlated with monthly insect presence in the forest (VS and fresh mass of insects collected, $r_s = .109$, $N = 11$; MNI-I and number of insects collected, $r_s = .455$, $N = 10$; number of insect orders in the feces and number of insect orders captured, $r_s = .492$, $N = 11$). However, when focusing on beetles specifically, I found that these insects were consumed according to their availablity; the monthly average number of beetles found per fecal sample was significantly correlated with the monthly average number captured during our collection sessions as described in Chapter 2 ($r_s = .847$, $p < .01$, $N = 11$).

As reflected by MNI-I fluctuations (Figure 3–6), insects were eaten in relatively low quantities during certain months when insect abundance was relatively high in terms of total numbers: November 1993, January 1994, and March 1994 (see Figure 2–6), the latter marking the end of the rainy season. Whereas some primates may consume animal prey in association with high fruit availability (Di Fiore, 2003), the findings at RNP suggested the opposite was true for mouse lemurs. Mouse lemurs appeared to consume increased quantities of insects in the dry season (see Figure 3–6) when fruit availability (see Figure 2–3) and fruit consumption were low (see Figure 3–3). Mouse lemurs at the end of the rainy season were gorging on fruit but not consistently on insects—consumption of both fruit and

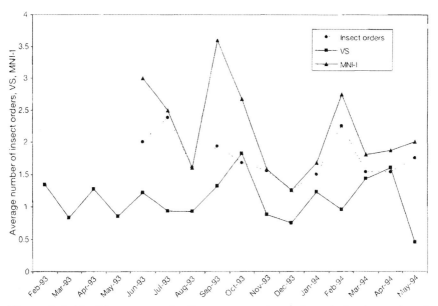

Figure 3–6 Monthly measures for the presence of prey items in fecal samples of *Microcebus rufus*. Shown are the average number of insect orders identified, the average VS (chitin in feces measured by a volumetric score of 1–3), and average MNI-I (minimum number of individual invertebrates found per sample). (Adapted from Table VII in Atsalis, 1999a; used with permission from Springer Science and Business Media.)

insects was elevated only in February. Thus, it seems that brown mouse lemurs at RNP increased their consumption of insects more commonly when fruit availability was low.

Moreover, it is possible that the specific insects responsible for the habitat-wide increases at the end of the rainy season were not preferred dietary items (see Figure 2–8). For instance, the toxicity of ants does not pose a problem for the loris, which consumes them abundantly (Nekaris and Rasmussen, 2001), but may deter mouse lemurs from eating them even when they are found in large quantities, as in the month of November. Crickets (family Gryllidae, Orthopteroids) were plentiful in January yet were identified only once in the fecal samples. The increase in insect availability in March was the result of an abundance of ants, and one heteropteran family, the Pentatomidae (see Figure 2–8). Commonly known as "stink bugs," they were bountiful, but they never turned up in mouse lemur feces, possibly because of their toxicity (Borror and White, 1970). Lastly, while trail censusing, mouse lemurs were twice seen feeding on Lepidoptera. These insects are easily detected in the feces of small mammals via the presence of scales (Whitaker, 1988; Bordignon, 2006), and, at RNP, they were the most frequently sampled order in monthly collection sessions. Fecal analysis provides evidence that moths are consumed regularly by other small mammals such as bats (Fenton et al., 1998), but in brown mouse lemurs at RNP they were found in only three fecal samples.

Overall, fecal sampling showed that mouse lemurs did not consume the full range of insect orders present in the forest as reflected through our monthly insect collection sessions; whereas eight of the fourteen orders identified during monthly insect sampling were captured regularly, only three orders were sampled on average each month in mouse lemur feces. However, the range of prey diversity in the diet may have been broader if more samples had been collected, because the number of insect orders were positively correlated with number of samples collected ($r_s = .794, p < .01, N = 12$). In addition, the methods that my guides and I used targeted the capture of flying insects because of the generally arboreal habits of mouse lemurs. Our techniques did not sample terrestrial species or those that frequent the upper heights of the forest, both potential resources for mouse lemurs.

OBSERVATIONS OF MOUSE LEMURS FEEDING

At RNP, a small area was reserved for attracting mouse lemurs for the benefit of tourists. Here, tourist guides occasionally skewered banana onto shrub branches and mouse lemurs availed of the fruit by scraping it with their toothcombs. We also saw mouse lemurs feeding during our nocturnal walks. Mouse lemurs were observed feeding on 42 of 342 sightings: eighteen on fruit, twenty-two on insects, one on sap or gum, and one remained undetermined. Not surprisingly, perhaps, mouse lemurs were most frequently seen consuming *Bakerella* (thirteen of eighteen feeding observations).

We discovered that when a mouse lemur alternated between resting and abruptly darting back and forth, it was hunting for insects. The animals searched energetically among leaves or thick tangles of lianas and vines or in bamboo thickets. Once finished they would usually return to their original location to wait or rest. Sometimes, mouse lemurs held their bodies frozen in a flag-like position with hindfeet (or both sets of limbs) holding tightly onto the support, body extended into mid-air. This position, called *cantilevering*, has been described for other cheirogaleids (Gebo, 1987). While suspended, brown mouse lemurs at RNP appeared intently watchful and their ears were cocked, suggesting that they were seeking prey, perhaps tuning into the sound of insects. Mouse lemurs are known to have relatively large ears for primates (Gebo, 2004; citing Hill, 1953), and Martin (1972b) has noted that the mobile ears are used to detect insects, which was evident from our observations at RNP.

On several other occasions, we saw mouse lemurs clutching large insects, which protruded from each end of a clenched forehand. Once, we observed a mouse lemur catching a beetle that was 3 cm long. On a different occasion, a mouse lemur closely inspected a millipede, later measured to be 11 cm long and 2 cm wide. Given that the average body length of a male mouse lemur is approximately 19 cm, from occiput to tip of tail, excluding the head (Atsalis et al., 1996), the millipede would have been a formidable prey item. The mouse lemur abandoned the capture effort when the millipede reared the front of its body up in defense. In test trials, one female spent four hours conquering and consuming a large scarab beetle that measured 4.5 cm in length and 2.5 cm in width (Harste, 1993).

Whereas mouse lemurs were not easily intimidated by large insects, they also took an interest in smaller ones that flew near them. Mouse lemurs tracked insects by following them with their heads and eyes, but they were rarely seen attempting to capture isolated flying prey. Perhaps, the energetic cost of pursuing a single flying insect was too high. In contrast, mouse lemurs were attracted to flying insects when they occurred in larger numbers. While radiotracking Male 22, we had ample opportunity to observe mouse lemurs feeding on flying insects. Plant flowering activity was at its highest between October 1993 and January 1994, peaking in December (see Figure 2–2). In the early part of October, my guides and I radiotracked Male 22 for seven nights. During four of those nights, Male 22 remained within the flowering crowns of two adjacent *Dombeya hilsenbergii* trees, a species that was fairly abundant in the forest and that flowered synchronously. *Dombeya* is characterized by a cyme type of flower in which a cluster of many small flowers constitutes a single inflorescence (Turk, 1995). The flowers attracted a large number of Diptera, Lepidoptera, and Coleoptera, which flew over the crowns in a cloud. Both mouse lemurs (Male 22 and others) and dwarf lemurs congregated on the crowns of the two trees. Seated on the ground at a distance of 16–18 m, my assistants and I recorded our nightly observations. As mouse lemurs fed, they also engaged in fierce competitive interactions. Competition among mouse lemurs and between mouse lemurs and dwarf lemurs involved chases, cuffing, and direct full-body contact. Because of the physical altercations, more than once a mouse lemur lost footing and fell, possibly to the ground approximately 18 m below. The breeding season may have intensified the competition among individuals, the crowns of the trees serving as an arena for males competing for females in addition to competing for food. But what kind of food? The flowering crowns were food reservoirs abundant with flying insects, but they also contained nectar. Pollen, too, may have been sought after. Pollen is a complex carbohydrate that is difficult to digest by small mammals, but it is high in protein compared with other plant tissues (Harborne, 1972; Howell, 1974). In contrast, nectar is a simple sugar easily broken down through digestion. Mouse lemurs sometimes approached flowers and seemed to taste something in the flower, which could have been nectar. At other times, the animals were seen engaging in an up-and-down head motion as though licking the flower, sometimes for a minute or more. The same flowers were visited repeatedly and successively suggesting that mouse lemurs were pursuing insects as well as feeding on nectar. A swarm of insects took flight above the mouse lemurs as they darted forward. While resting, mouse lemurs were seen tracking— as judged by their facial position—the flight of the surrounding cloud of flying insects. We watched as they would suddenly swipe at insects in the air and direct their forehand to the mouth. As the quantity of flowers decreased, from 90% of crown cover to 20% over the course of the week, mouse lemurs and dwarf lemurs continued to visit the crowns of *Dombeya* to capture insects until the flowers disappeared. As the presence of flowers waned, resulting in diminishing returns from plant food, Male 22 concentrated more on the capture of insects; on the final day of radiotracking, we observed seven insect catches by Male 22, compared with three the day before and none the two previous days.

MOUSE LEMURS AND MISTLETOES

Not surprisingly, results from this study demonstrated that mouse lemurs, like most other primates, have omnivorous tendencies; as Harding (1981) once noted, diversity rather than specialization is typical of the order Primates. Nevertheless, classifying mouse lemurs as omnivores reflects their feeding habits only in the broadest sense. Gross categorizations have limited value even as simple descriptive tools because they do not address the complexity of evolutionary adaptations that underlie dietary habits

(Harding 1981; Kay, 1984; Garber, 1987; Rosenberger, 1992). This conclusion is regularly reinforced through long-term field studies. For instance, Sterling's (1993a) study on the nocturnal aye-aye revealed that this lemur's unique morphological specializations—a long, spindly, middle finger that rotates 360° around the metacarpal joint and evergrowing incisors—were used not only to extract insect larvae hidden in tree trunks (Petter, 1977), as had been known traditionally, but also to harvest seeds and fungi. And, so it was with my study on the brown mouse lemur during which continued monitoring of diet revealed it to be a highly frugivorous species and therefore much like most other tropical small mammals (Fleming, 1975).

In Ranomafana, brown mouse lemurs relied on fruit as a major source of energy. Another significant finding of the study was that brown mouse lemurs favored the fruits of the mistletoe *Bakerella*. *Bakerella* was a dietary staple for mouse lemurs; the fruit was consumed in large quantities year-round, possibly because of the high fat content. In addition, *Bakerella* seemed to act as a keystone resource because it was consumed when other fruit species were low in abundance. In general, fruits are known to be high in sugars, but only a few are unusually high in protein and lipids (Foster and McDiarmid, 1983; Waterman, 1984). Lipid content greater than 10% of dry mass characterizes only one-quarter of all fleshy fruits (Stiles, 1993) including mistletoes in the family Loranthaceae (Walsberg, 1975; Foster and McDiarmid, 1983). Another mistletoe, *Viscum*, also figured importantly in the diet during the dry season when resource abundance in the forest was low. Like *Bakerella*, *Viscum* may have been a keystone resource for this mouse lemur population.

Mistletoes are considered to be highly nutritious specialized fruits that are dispersed by specialized frugivores (McKey, 1975; Howe and Estabrook, 1977; Godschalk, 1983b). Walsberg (1975) argues that the fruits of some mistletoes are sufficiently nutritious to sustain a specialist frugivore when other foods are lacking. However, there are differences in lipid content among mistletoes, with loranthoids (e.g., *Bakerella*) reported to have higher values than those of vicoids (e.g., *Viscum*) (Godschalk, 1983b). Fruit in the family Viscaceae are carbohydrate rich (Martínez del Rio, 1994), but, comparatively, *Bakerella*, with its high fat content, was probably the more important energy source because lipids have twice the energy content of carbohydrates (Paine, 1971).

The regular consumption of *Bakerella* by mouse lemurs suggests that the high fat content sustains Ranomafana's mouse lemurs during periods of food scarcity. The specific composition of dietary nutrients, particularly the composition of lipids, can have important survival and reproductive implications. The importance of particular lipids in the diet was documented for hibernating ground squirrels (*Spermophilus*), for which intake of dietary polyunsaturated fatty acids prior to hibernation resulted in lengthened topor bouts, lowered T_b (core body temperature) values, and decreased metabolic rates (Geiser and Kenagy, 1993; Florant, 1998). The quality of the fat ingested was significant; a diet of sunflower oil produced considerably more physiological response than did sheep fat. Free-ranging ground squirrels, too, increased their intake of foods high in essential fatty acids (seeds and nuts) prior to hibernation (Florant, 1998). With more energy saved, animals were more likely to survive hibernation, emerging with enough energy reserves to begin mating activities. Thus, at RNP the intake of *Bakerella* with its relatively high lipid content may aid in the accumulation of prehibernation fat stores and may influence the duration and depth of hibernation.

The specific lipid composition of mouse lemur diet may also carry important implications for the reproductive fitness of this tiny hibernating lemur. However, whereas consuming lipids may be advantageous for some hibernating small mammals (Florant et al., 1993), for one cheirogaleid species, *C. medius*, high-lipid fruits were not compulsory (Fietz and Ganzhorn, 1999). Instead, this species feasted on fruits high in sugar prior to doubling body mass in preparation for hibernation. The researchers suggested that increased intake of dietary unsaturated fatty acids may not be necessary in tropical species since they do not experience very low body temperatures during hibernation (Fietz and Ganzhorn, 1999; Fietz et al., 2001). Hibernating temperatures in small mammals of the temperate zone can hover around 1°C or lower, with hibernators experiencing different temperature ranges depending on their size and the environment. For instance, marmots hibernate at body temperatures ranging from 5–10°C, whereas other rodents lower their body temperatures to 1–6°C (French, 1992; Vaughan et al., 2000). Mouse lemurs and dwarf lemurs do not usually experience such low temperatures though body temperatures as low as 6.8°C and 9.3°C, respectively, have been reported (Schmid 1996; Dausmann et al., 2004). However, the smaller size of mouse lemurs (averaging 30–70 g) compared with dwarf lemurs (up to 600 g for *C. medius* and *C. major*) may impose different hibernation challenges, which require the former to take in more lipids than the larger species.

Ultimately, the nutritional value of mistletoe fruits and how well animals absorb their nutrients may also depend on the digestive efficiency of the animal (Waslberg, 1975; Worthington, 1989; Stiles, 1993). Birds rely on the high energy content of mistletoe fruits, supplementing protein needs with insects—as do brown mouse lemurs—but birds are known to reject the tough rind-like epicarp of mistletoe fruit (Polhill and Wiens, 1998). It may be that mouse lemurs do the same because the skins of *Bakerella* were not usually detected in fecal samples. Like birds, they may favor the thin fleshy skin that surrounds the mistletoe berry's viscous mesocarp, which is apparently very high in nutrients (Polhill and Wiens, 1998). Observations also suggested that some birds have a way of regurgitating a mistletoe's excess fibrous material, found in the fleshy layer of the fruit (Godschalk,

1983b). An investigation of rate and efficiency of mistletoe processing by captured mouse lemurs would shed light on how well animals process mistletoe berries to meet their caloric requirements. Studies of this nature have been done for birds, revealing large differences in how species reach their energetic needs (Walsberg, 1975).

Besides the nutritional characteristics of mistletoes, other factors make them suitable food sources for mouse lemurs. Mistletoes are photophyllic (Bazzaz and Pickett, 1980) so that selective logging at RNP may have contributed to plant proliferation by opening up the understory. Typical of other tropical Loranthaceae (Richards, 1952; van Leeuwen, 1954), *Bakerella* grows on a broad range of hosts and at all forest heights, making it a widely distributed food source. *Bakerella* was found in small patches proportional to the needs of a small solitary forager. Lastly, unlike other epiphytes, the semi-parasitic nature of the Loranthaceae may decrease the sensitivity that epiphytes typically have to seasonal dry spells resulting in a more reliable food source. The ability of mouse lemurs to exploit small, widely distributed patches of fruit whose presence is enhanced by forest disturbance may contribute to their conservation.

Parasitic plants usually constitute just over 1% of flowering plants making their contribution to forest composition low (Nickrent, 2002). The Loranthaceae, the family to which *Bakerella* belongs, are usually rare in tropical forests because to ensure water and nutrient flow from the host, parasitic plants must transpire heavily in order to maintain lower water potential than their host (Nickrent, 2002). Therefore, large numbers of the parasitic Loranthaceae and Viscaceae are less likely to occur in the dense dark forests of the tropics, where high transpiration is not easily maintained (Nickrent, 2002). However, Talatakely, where this study took place at RNP, may have supported a high proportion of mistletoes, which are also known to favor younger trees (Kujt, 1969). That *Bakerella* appeared to be common in Talatakely may be a testimony to the area's history of human activity. Most parasitic plant species do not fare well in ecosystems disturbed by humans, but *Bakerella* may be an exception.

Mistletoes are significant in the feeding ecology of many New and Old World birds (Richards, 1952; van Leeuwen, 1954; Davidar, 1983; Godschalk, 1985; Reid, 1990; Stiles, 1993). Mistletoe fruits constitute high-energy food sources for birds (van Leeuwen, 1954; Davidar, 1983). In turn, the seeds of the mistletoe-rich families, the Loranthaceae and Viscaceae, are dispersed effectively through regurgitation or defecation and the fruits are considered to be consumed almost exclusively by birds (Kujt, 1969; Godschalk, 1985; Reid et al., 1995). Seed dispersal may be among the most important components of plant–animal interactions, and bird–mistletoe interactions can be highly specialized (Reid, 1990). Mammals such as tree shrews also engage in dispersing seeds of parasitic plants (Emmons et al., 1991), and some primates, particularly monkeys, are known seed dispersers (Gautier-Hion et al., 1985). Nevertheless, Smith and Ganzhorn (1996; citing Wilson et al., 1989) point to the rarity of mammal-dispersed fruits in tropical forests worldwide. The exception is areas where diversity of frugivorous birds is low. Madagascar is depauperate of frugivorous birds and of many kinds of mammals, including fruit bats, which could serve as fruit-seed dispersers (Fleming et al., 1987; Goodman et al., 1997; Wright, 1997; Hawkins and Goodman, 2003). Consequently, on the island, lemurs may be primary seed dispersers (and pollinators) (Smith and Ganzhorn, 1996; Dew and Wright, 1998). Indeed, just as I discovered through this study that brown mouse lemurs are good candidates for dispersal of mistletoe and other fruit seeds because these were almost always ingested and voided intact, similar observations have been made for various other species of cheirogaleid, including the grey mouse lemur and species of dwarf lemur (Lahann, 2007). However, little is understood of dispersal systems across the island, perhaps because of the high degree of endemism in the flora and fauna (Langrand, 1990; Schatz, 2001). The discovery of a close relationship between mistletoes and brown mouse lemurs is particularly exciting because mammals are rarely dispersers of mistletoes.

The relative frequency with which mouse lemurs consumed mistletoes compared with other frugivores at RNP was not examined, but elsewhere it has been documented that a single species in a community may be the primary consumer of mistletoes. For instance, at one site in South Africa, a single bird, the yellow-fronted barbet (*Pogoniulus chrysoconus*), was the most important disperser of several mistletoe species, consuming 94% of the fruits of one species (Godschalk, 1985). Rarer are the exclusive relationships between dispersers and plants. One such exclusive mutualistic relationship, between an endemic mistletoe in the family Loranthaceae and a small nocturnal arboreal marsupial, *Dromiciops australis*, was discovered in southern Argentina (Amico and Aizen, 2000). Amico and Aizen monitored all visitors to trees hosting mistletoes by placing automatic cameras to photograph potential dispersers. The research confirmed that only *D. australis* dispersed seeds of the plant. Germination experiments indicated that gut passage was necessary for seed development. This discovery may represent an example of a very primitive mutualism between two primitive species.

Whereas parallels can be drawn between these examples and that of brown mouse lemurs and *Bakerella*, an obligate relationship between the latter two has not been established. At RNP, three fruit bat species, nine primate species, and thirteen bird species are frequent or occasional consumers of fruit. Little is known of their dispersal potential (Goodman et al., 1997). Besides mouse lemurs, *Bakerella* is known to be consumed by at least one bird species (Razafindratsita, 1995) and by several large-bodied lemurs (*Eulemur fulvus rufus* and *Eulemur fulvus rubriventer*, Overdorff, 1993; *Propithecus diadema edwardsi*, Hemingway, 1995; Dew and Wright,

1998; *Varecia variegata*, White et al., 1995; *Cheirogaleus major*, personal observation). None of these species are confirmed seed dispersers of *Bakerella*. *Propithecus* is a seed predator (Hemingway, 1996; Dew and Wright, 1998) actively breaking down seeds before ingestion (Overdorff and Strait, 1998); according to RNP guides, this species feeds on *Bakerella* year-round. *E. f. rufus* damages seeds while eating fruit, and neither this species nor *E. f. rubriventer* would be good candidates for dispersing mistletoe because they spend too little time feeding on small fruits (Overdorff and Strait, 1998). In one study, *C. major* ate fruit in 86% of observations; none on epiphytic plants (Wright and Martin, 1995). I saw another nocturnal species *Avahi laniger*, spitting out the seeds of one fruit, suggesting that it too may not contribute to dispersal if gut passage is required.

In sum, although arboreal mammals are generally considered to be minor dispersers of mistletoe (Calder, 1983), at RNP the brown mouse lemur could very well be an important agent of mistletoe seed dispersal, especially since seeds were ingested and voided intact and sticky. Mistletoe berry structure may facilitate removal of the exocarp, an advantage if the skin is indigestible because the viscous material that surrounds the pericarp acts as a "slip zone" (Kuijt, 1969; Walsberg, 1975) that allows the skin to be peeled off. Once removed by the animal disperser, the sticky viscin layer acts to adhere the voided naked seeds to host surfaces, as has been demonstrated for mistletoes eaten by birds (Godschalk, 1983c; Martínez del Rio et al., 1996). On several occasions, we came across the characteristic sticky appearance of mouse lemur feces containing mistletoe seeds on various forest substrates, such as trunks of trees. Furthermore, by virtue of their wide-ranging movements at all forest heights, mouse lemurs are good candidates for disseminating seeds away from the parent plant. In other plants, the ranging behavior by animal dispersers has been found to reduce density-dependent mortality (Godschalk, 1983c).

Typically, color is an important feature attracting dispersers to fruit. Unripe fruits of *Bakerella* were green, a color often associated with mammalian dispersers (van der Pijl, 1982; Knight and Siegfried, 1983), including lemurs (Dew and Wright, 1998), a taxon that lacks trichromatic color vision (Jacobs and Deegan, 1993). Fruits of African mistletoes generally ripen while still green in color and later change to various colors (Godschalk, 1983a). At RNP, some varieties of *Bakerella* turned yellow when ripe. Mouse lemurs attracted to green mistletoe fruit may have been ingesting ripe fruit just as mistletoe-eating birds commonly do (Godschalk, 1983a). Indeed, mouse lemurs were observed feeding in *Bakerella* patches even when most of the available fruit was green. It was more difficult to determine from seeds in the feces the degree of ripeness of the fruit that had been eaten. However, I noted that seeds of what may have been unripe fruit were very soft and appeared in fecal samples as fragments, likely as a result of being inadvertently and easily chewed along with the fleshy part of the fruit. On the other hand, of the fruits eaten by brown mouse lemurs, I found the majority were red when ripe, a color preferred by diurnal birds and monkeys (Gautier-Hion et al., 1985) and to which the diurnal sifaka at RNP, *Propithecus diadema edwardsi*, was also attracted (Wright et al., 2005). Where attraction to vivid color might be expected for diurnal lemurs, especially because some species can distinguish color better than anticipated (e.g., Gosset and Roeder, 2000), how color figures into fruit selection for the nocturnal mouse lemur is not clear. In grey mouse lemurs, olfactory cues were sufficient to lure animals to fruit (Siemers et al., 2003). Clearly, more research is needed to clarify the cues by which mouse lemurs make their fruit choices.

Observations at RNP point to a potentially mutually beneficial relationship between mouse lemurs and mistletoes. However, many factors contribute to successful dispersal. Germination trials would show how well seeds fare following gut passage. Dew and Wright (1998) discovered that seeds passed by three diurnal lemurs sprouted significantly faster than unpassed ones, but Godschalk (1983a) observed that passage through an (avian) gut may not be mandatory for successful germination of mistletoe seeds. Furthermore, seeds must be deposited on the appropriate hosts, the branch's diameter must be of the right thin size, and the ectocarps must rupture to release the sticky viscin within (Reid, 1991; Larson, 1996). Finally, the more time a frugivore spends within host trees the higher the probability that defecated seeds will land on a suitable location to germinate (Larson, 1996). These and other studies highlight the complex relationships that characterize mistletoes and their host plants. These relationships can be complicated further by the possibility that mistletoes, being parasites, may harm the host by decreasing plant vigor, reducing fruiting, predisposing trees to attack by insects or fungi, and inducing premature mortality (Hawksworth, 1983; Martínez del Rio et al., 1996). For these reasons, birds are being studied not only as important dispersers but also as vectors of disease spread by disseminating mistletoe seeds. Often the problem is within plantations not in native forests (Hawksworth, 1983), and the mistletoe "infection" can be of only minor import (Wiegand et al., 1999). In other instances, the consequences of infection can be beneficial to the tree or to other animals. For instance, the Mexican spotted owl (*Strix occidentalis lucida*), a threatened species, was attracted to infected trees more than to noninfected ones because the former provided more suitable nest structures within mistletoe brooms (Seamans and Gutierrez, 1995). In another example, more than twice as many juniper tree seedlings sprouted in mistletoe-rich patches than in mistletoe-free ones because birds attracted to the mistletoe were involved in spreading tree seeds (van Ommeren and Whitham, 2002). These examples underline the dynamic relationship that exists between species, one that moves along a continuum, from mutualistic to antagonistic, depending on complex interactions within a changing environment (van Ommeren and Whitham, 2002). No doubt, mouse lemur dietary habits play an important role in the life cycle of mistletoes at RNP and may affect the host plant ecology. An investigation of this interaction may reveal important findings with respect to the long-term ecological dynamics of Ranomafana's rainforest.

MOUSE LEMURS AND BEETLES

Mouse lemurs at RNP ate beetles irrespective of habitat-wide insect availability. Although it is possible that beetle exoskeleton preserved better than that of other insects, the constant and high presence of beetles in the feces suggested that, like *Bakerella*, this insect order was a dietary staple and may have served as a keystone resource. Results indicated that other insects were added to the diet more opportunistically. The presence of chitin indicated that insects eaten were adult, but little is known about their habits. Brown mouse lemurs relied on several families of beetles that were largely phytophagous and nonterrestrial. Stark identified several families: Tenebrionidae (darkling beetles), Scarabaeidae (scarabs), Cerambycidae (longhorn beetles), and Curculionidae (weevils). A few fecal samples also contained Scarabaeinae, or dung beetles. Dung beetles are terrestrial with particularly high diversity in the tropics—over thirty species have been identified at RNP (Hanski, 2004). A few fecal samples contained members of the family Gryllidae (crickets), a family that has both arboreal and terrestrial representatives. Taken together, these observations hint that mouse lemurs can exploit ground-dwelling insects as food resources.

Commonly, most insects captured during our monthly insect collection sessions measured between 5 and 15 mm in length. Insects in this size class are important to vertebrates (Smythe, 1982), but the majority of beetles captured during insect sampling were smaller (<5 mm). Unfortunately, data on the size range of beetles and other insects actually eaten by brown mouse lemurs are not available, although we observed that brown mouse lemurs pursued prey of differing sizes including very large ones.

Beetles are a preferred dietary item not only of mouse lemurs but of other small mammals, particularly of bats for which fecal sampling is widely used to understand diet (Fenton et al., 1998; Bordignon, 2006). In one study, several species of bat consumed beetles preferentially over all other insects, although remnants of other insects were present in the feces (Fenton et al., 1998). As with brown mouse lemurs, one study discovered fragments of longhorn beetles and scarabs in fecal samples (Bordignon, 2006). Beetles may be preferred dietary items because they occupy an enormous variety of habitats and their nutritional value is high (McGavin, 2002). Generally, however, insects vary in the nutrients available to predators (Allen, 1989). Protein levels found in insects can be overestimated, and insect nutrients can be indigestible to insectivores (Allen, 1989). Flying insects, despite being excellent sources of potassium, nitrogen, and magnesium, were found to be low in calcium and iron resulting in nutrient deficiencies in insectivorous bats that ate them (e.g., Studier and Sevick, 1992; Studier et al., 1994a,b). Calcium is essential for skeletal development and the required levels of intake may be difficult to meet. Its availability is low not only in insects but in fruit and pollen as well (Barclay, 1995). Some primates, such as marmosets and tamarins, rely on gums to fulfill their calcium needs (Smith, 2000) and perhaps this is true for mouse lemurs as well. For brown mouse lemurs, it may be epiphytes that are a source of minerals, including calcium and phosphorus, because the plants trap, from the air, soil particles (Kricher, 1997), which are released from the rapid decomposition of dead organisms in the tropics. Additional data are required to investigate the vitamin and mineral composition of epiphytic fruits eaten by brown mouse lemurs and to see if they constitute sources of calcium that could offset a deficiency in this essential mineral.

COMPARING THE DIETS OF MOUSE LEMUR SPECIES

The relatively long palate and high sharp cusps on the cheek teeth of *M. rufus* compared with *M. murinus* suggest a species adapted to feeding on insects (Martin, 1995), whereas the low crowns of *M. murinus* point to greater intake of plant material (Martin, 1972b; Strait, 1993, using dental casts that I took of *M. rufus* at RNP). Given the high degree of frugivory of *M. rufus* at RNP, the morphological differences may support the hypothesis that dental morphology is more closely related to foods that represent a "biomechanical challenge" (Rosenberger, 1992), such as the tough exoskeleton of beetles, than to foods which are more frequently eaten.

Despite the differences in their habitats, there are many dietary similarities between *M. rufus*, a rainforest species, and *M. murinus*, a predominantly dry forest species. To begin with, the pattern in which fruit resources available during the latter part of the wet season fulfill specific needs of mouse lemurs, for that period of the annual life cycle, has also been documented for *M. murinus* (Hladik et al., 1980). As with brown mouse lemurs at RNP, *M. murinus* in Madena's littoral rainforest foraged extensively on fruits and flowers during the rainy season (Lahann, 2007). Moreover, in the latter part of the wet season, both *M. rufus* at RNP and *M. murinus* in certain west coast locations accumulate body fat prior to entering hibernation during the dry season (Chapter 4), and young mouse lemurs, the offspring of the most recent reproductive period, begin to feed independently (Chapters 4 and 6). Furthermore, specialization on local plant food, previously noted by Martin (1972b) for *M. murinus* was paralleled by the importance of *Bakerella* fruit in the diet of *M. rufus* at RNP. Martin identified several berries less than 1 cm in diameter in the diet of *M. murinus* although none were epiphytic. Fruits eaten by mouse lemurs at RNP were more diverse in size ranging from less than 0.5 cm to more than 2 cm. Both species consumed beetles and both sometimes pursued and consumed large insects (Martin, 1972b; Hladik et al., 1980; Radespiel et al., 2006). As with grey mouse lemurs (Martin, 1972b; Hladik et al., 1980), brown mouse lemurs exploited ephemeral insect food sources, a behavior made obvious by their attraction to the insects on the tree crowns of *Dombeya*. On the other hand, in *M. rufus* the quantity of insects consumed did not appear to increase during the wet season as reported for *M. murinus* (Hladik et al., 1980), even though at RNP, this was a time of high insect abundance.

Compared with *M. murinus*, mouse lemurs at RNP were rarely seen feeding on gums although this lack of detection may have been associated with the visibility challenges we faced. Nevertheless, resources in dry forests during the dry season are exceedingly sparse (Hladik et al., 1980), which may explain the high levels of gummivory there (Génin, 2001; Dammhahn and Kappeler, 2006; Radespiel et al., 2006) or the increased intake of insect secretions (Corbin and Schmid, 1995; Radespiel et al., 2006). These dietary items can function as alternative resources to other plant and animal foods such as insects and fruits. Gum, however, is not always considered a high quality food. It can be difficult to digest and may require fermentation by microorganisms in the gut to break it down (Power, 1996), which may be a challenge for mouse lemurs as they have an unspecialized gut (Ganzhorn, 1989b). Additionally, gum contains little protein, no fat, and no vitamins (Power, 1996) although it is a good source of calcium (Garber, 1984). Because gum is not a balanced food and probably requires fermentation to yield nutrients, Power (1996) describes it as a "problematic" food. As the digestive efficiency for gums may depend on special adaptations, such as a longer intestine (found in marmosets, Power, 1996), the nutritional value of this food source for mouse lemurs requires further assessment. At RNP, brown mouse lemurs appeared to have alternative food sources, such as high-energy fruits, to sustain themselves during the dry season.

In Ampijoroa, sympatric *M. murinus* and *M. ravelobensis* fed primarily on the secretions of homopteran larvae and on gums during the dry season; they also included fruits, insects, nectar, small spiders, and vertebrates in the diet (Reimann et al., 2003). The two species differed only in that *M. murinus* focused on a narrower range of plant items whereas *M. ravelobensis* fed on more diversified plant resources, a finding also confirmed in another study of sympatry. In this second study, which took place within the dry season when fruits were scarce, researchers discovered that insect secretions were the main food resource for *M. murinus* (Radespiel et al., 2006). *M. ravelobensis*, too, consumed insects to meet protein needs, specifically Coleoptera, Saltatoria (a division of Orthopteroids), Hymenoptera, and Arachnida (spiders). Overall, sympatric *M. ravelobensis* and *M. murinus* had similar diets, at least during the dry season, differing mostly in the degree of concentration on different plant foods (Radespiel et al., 2006). For *M. murinus*, three plants made up 65% of all food gum trees whereas four species accounted for 53% of food gum trees in *M. ravelobensis*, which distributed its time evenly among the remaining trees (Radespiel et al., 2006).

As with brown mouse lemurs at RNP, in Madena, Lahann (2007) discovered that grey mouse lemurs visited a diverse array of plants, for fruit (62 species) and flowers (8 species). Small fruits were preferred; berries and drupes were the most commonly consumed fruit types. The main forage plants belonged to the family Rubiaceae (10.4%), a family of plants commonly targeted by brown mouse lemurs at RNP as well (see Table 3–1). In this detailed dietary study, grey mouse lemurs were reported to consume *Bakerella*, making them potential candidates for dispersers of this epiphytic plant, as are brown mouse lemurs at RNP. Finally, although predominantly frugivorous, grey mouse lemurs in Madena also fed on a variety of arthropods, including maggots, spiders, stick insects, crickets, cockroaches, moths, and beetles. However, it may be that these mouse lemurs consumed less animal matter than mouse lemurs at RNP, since insect remains in fecal samples were rarely found.

By and large, the evidence indicates that mouse lemurs consume diverse diets that change seasonally, but perhaps not all mouse lemur species are as omnivorous as those just described. In this respect, interesting findings are emerging from an ongoing study at Kirindy, where researchers have discovered that sympatric mouse lemurs differ radically in their diets. While *M. murinus* does indeed enjoy a diverse diet that varies seasonally and includes plenty of fruits and gums, the tiny *M. berthae* appears to sustain itself predominantly on the sugary secretions produced by homopteran larvae, and on animal matter (Dammhahn and Kappeler, 2006). Feeding patterns of *M. berthae* in this study may be affected by its sympatric status with *M. murinus* and its small size. Differences in composition and seasonal variation in the diet of these two species may be a way to reduce interspecific competition (Dammhahn and Kappeler, 2006).

Another way to reduce competition between closely related sympatric cheirogaleid species is to feed at different forest heights. Lahann (2007) discovered that *M. murinus* and two species of *Cheirogaleus* fed on the same plant species and even in the same trees, but were separated in the vertical dimension; grey mouse lemurs fed in lower strata then did the dwarf lemurs. Additional long-term studies that include dietary choices througout the year will improve our understanding of mouse lemur feeding ecology, leading to additional insights on how closely related, sympatric lemurs diversify their diets and coexist within the same habitat.

WHAT CAN MOUSE LEMURS TELL US ABOUT PRIMATE ORIGINS

For students of primate evolution, shedding light on the relationship between fruiting trees and mammalian dispersers, especially the interaction between primates and rainforests, calls for special attention (e.g., Rasmussen, 1990; Sussman, 1991, 1995; Cartmill, 1992). In "How Primates Invented the Rainforest and Vice Versa," Sussman (1995) outlined a hypothesis for the initial evolution of this relationship. The main idea is that the appearance of modern primates in the fossil record paralleled the radiation of angiosperms (flowering plants). In particular, for the early small nocturnal and arboreal mammals of the Paleocene when angiosperms were reaching wide distribution, trees and other flowering plants may have held a store of diverse resources, buds, flowers, fruits, nectars, gums, in addition to insects, attracted to these potential foods. Eocene ancestors of modern primates, the first Euprimates, with their grasping hands and feet, were uniquely adapted to reaching the terminal branches of trees, which other mammals may have been unable to exploit as easily (Cartmill, 1990; Sussman, 1995). There, with their acute visual abilities, primates were, and are, able to take advantage of small food items, from fruits to insects (Rasmussen, 1990; Sussman, 1991; Cartmill, 1992). Finally, the relationship between flowering plants and primates evolved into what we see today, where primates constitute important dispersers of seeds in the tropics.

Despite some reservations that have been put forth regarding this evolutionary scenario (Soligo and Martin, 2006), it seems reasonable to state that there is a strong link between the diets of primates and the radiation of angiosperms. Today, this relationship can be illuminated through observations on mouse lemurs and other mammals. Observing mouse lemurs is akin to looking through an evolutionary time-window, for they incorporate both modern and early elements of the rainforest–primate relationship. Behaviors recorded while radiotracking Male 22, as well as other nocturnal observations, showcase how the terminal branches of tropical trees constitute a storehouse of plant and insect resources for mouse lemurs.

Additional field observations offer insights into how the early primates may have adapted to life in the trees. For instance, Rasmussen and Sussman (2007) have found many similarities, what they call *parallelisms*, between certain marsupial radiations and primates. In particular, observations on pygmy-possums of the genus *Cercartetus* draw strong parallels with primitive primates. These pygmy-possums are nocturnal and arboreal. They are characterized by hands capable of grasping, moderately convergent eyes, and diminutive sizes (6–70 g). As noted by Rasmussen and Sussman, many researchers have commented on the strong physical and behavioral resemblance of pygmy-possums to mouse lemurs. Pygmy-possums eat flowers, nectar, pollen, fruit, and arthropods while foraging alone. They can be found sleeping in groups, and they store fat in their tails and undergo seasonal periods of torpor-all mouse lemur behaviors. The authors (citing Atherton and Haffenden, 1983) note that one species, *Cercartetus nanus*, the eastern pygmy-possum, is known to specialize on flowers but captures insects opportunistically from the flowers by snatching them out of the air with its hands. This behavior, so strikingly similar to mouse lemurs as highlighted by my own observations on the feeding behavior of Male 22 in the crowns of *Dombeya*, is proposed to support the idea that it was the combined presence of insects along with fruits and flowers that set the stage for the development of primate-like adaptations. These observations reveal that there is much to be learned from ecological and behavioral comparisons of diverse taxa. Yet, although the high degree of similarity between primates and other taxa is often surprising, identifying their differences will be the true aid in distinguishing those traits that mark primates from other taxa leading to compelling insights into primate origins (Rasmussen and Sussman, 2007).

FECAL SAMPLING AS A WAY TO STUDY DIET

Long-term studies based on fecal analysis can be an effective way to decipher an animal's diet. Shorter-term studies cannot reveal the full complement of food items eaten, detect staple or keystone dietary items, or monitor seasonal dietary changes. Many studies on nonprimate mammals rely on fecal samples from live-trapped animals to monitor individual and population-level seasonal dietary patterns (e.g., Fenton et al., 1981). In primates, fecal analysis has been used to study diet in difficult-to-observe, small nocturnal species as well as in the large but elusive apes. One advantage in collecting samples from live-trapped animals is that the depositor's identity is known (Moreno-Black, 1978). In my study, sampling from a large number of known individuals helped us to avoid possible biases in dietary preferences.

Overall, fecal analysis is useful in compiling lists of fruits (when seeds are swallowed) and insects (when chitin is present) and constitutes an important method of determining seasonal dietary changes in species that are difficult to follow (Tutin and Fernandez, 1993). Fecal analysis is especially reliable in understanding the diet of insectivores because direct observations of insect feeding can be rare (Kunz and Whitaker, 1983; Dickman and Huang, 1988; Williamson et al., 1990).

The main disadvantage to fecal analysis is that it favors hard items such as seeds and chitin, and therefore results from fecal analysis may not reflect everything that is eaten (Harding, 1981). The soft parts of plants and soft-bodied insects such as flies, caterpillars, or larvae are underestimated (Whitaker, 1988; Williamson et al., 1990; Tutin and Fernandez, 1993). Even chitin can be so finely masticated that it becomes unidentifiable. Moreover, there is the problem of differential digestibility of different kinds of chitin, which makes certain hard-bodied insects more easily recognizable than others (Allen, 1989). Scanning electron microscopy (SEM) analysis has been used to identify small insect remains in bat fecal pellets, but this is costly, time-consuming, and impractical under most field conditions (Coutts et al., 1973).

Easily digestible carbohydrates, such as sap, can remain entirely undetected under macroanalysis, as can gums. Even with respect to fruit identification, fecal analysis has its shortcomings because although the underlying assumption is that fruit will be represented by seed presence, animals may avoid ingesting some seeds even while consuming the fruit. Moreover, identification requires practice and a reference library of whole fruit and insects found in the forest to which masticated bits of plant and animal matter found in the feces are compared. Hence, though fecal analysis is an efficient and widely used field method (Korschgen, 1969; Whitaker, 1988), not all seeds can be identified and seeds from species of the same genus cannot always be distinguished from one another (Tutin and Fernandez, 1993). In addition, even when soft plant parts such as pith and skins are found, they are frequently impossible to identify unless reference material has been previously prepared as a way of comparison.

Quantification, too, poses problems when attempting to compare quantities of different categories of food. In my study on mouse lemurs, the challenge was how to reasonably quantify and compare the relative consumption of insects and fruit. I followed the example set by researchers who studied ape diets and I avoided a direct comparison of quantities of different food categories. Instead, I presented the seasonal fluctuations that each category underwent as part of mouse lemur diet. Other methods can also be used. By applying a subjective volumetric score of 1–4, Harcourt and Nash (1986a) compared relative fruit and insect consumption in galagos by assuming that one volumetric unit of fruit was equivalent to one volumetric unit of insect. This assumption has no true justification, though the method provides a crude way of comparing the relative consumption of "apples" to "oranges". The comparison is more meaningful, but not necessarily more justifiable, if true volumes or mass of individual foods eaten are known so that they can be calculated as percentages of total food volume or mass (Korschgen, 1969; Whitaker, 1988). Ultimately, the relative importance of particular foods—such as fruit versus insects in the diet of brown mouse lemurs, or any other animal species—goes beyond the question of volume or mass ingested. It is a consequence of the interaction between nutrient content of food items (energy, protein, minerals, etc.), nutritional requirements of the individual, and the energy required to extract the contents of the food, that is, digestibility of the food. These factors can be assessed only by combining field and laboratory techniques and by monitoring both captive and wild populations (Harding, 1981; Sterling et al., 1994).

SUGGESTED DIRECTIONS FOR FUTURE STUDIES

This study highlights the importance of *M. rufus* as a possible seed disperser of the epiphytic plant *Bakerella,* suggesting that the ecological dynamic between mouse lemurs and epiphytic plants requires further and thorough investigation. Because epiphytes play an important role in forest ecology (Nadkarni, 1981, 1983, 1984), understanding the relationship between mistletoe prevalence and mouse lemur density can shed light on their influence on forest health. Studies on dispersal effectiveness, which measures the relationship between number of visits and seeds dispersed per visit, are also needed. Because little good comes to mistletoe seeds that fall to the forest floor as they must root on host branches, measuring the number of seeds dispersed per visit and the quality of the deposition would help establish germination patterns (Reid, 1989; Schupp, 1993). Effectiveness also includes the quality of seed treatment by the putative disperser. Trials to establish success of germination of seeds passed through the gut could answer questions regarding the quality of the brown mouse lemur as an effective seed disperser.

Generally, fatty acids play an important role in energy and water balance and in reproduction, among other functions, and high-lipid diets influence the duration and depth of hibernation in small mammals (Geiser and Kenagy, 1993; Florant, 1998). As hibernators (Chapter 4), brown mouse lemurs undoubtedly face pressures to reduce energy expenditures during the period of being lethargic, which may offer advantages when emerging from hibernation (Geiser and Kenagy, 1993). In brown mouse lemurs, males emerge earlier from hibernation than do females and the mating season begins shortly thereafter, within the dry season when resources are still relatively scarce. Because the uptake of an appropriate lipid diet may form part of the preparation for hibernation (Florant, 1998), male brown mouse lemurs, whose diet included beneficial components, may have more energy to spend in reproduction. Because there are intersexual and intrasexual differences in hibernating patterns, with some mouse lemurs remaining active, a comparison of the diets of hibernating mouse lemurs with those that do not hibernate may provide additional clues to our understanding of feeding ecology and the physiological consequences of diet.

SUMMARY

The diet of the brown mouse lemur was studied primarily through an investigation of 334 fecal samples from live-trapped individuals over the course of sixteen months. Mouse lemurs consumed a mixed diet of fruits and insects. Twenty-four different fruits were identified, whereas an additional 40–52 fruits remained unidentified. *Bakerella*, a high-lipid epiphytic semi-parasitic mistletoe was detected in 42% of fecal samples that contained fruit and was consumed year-round irrespective of habitat-wide fruit availability serving both as keystone and as staple resource. Other epiphytic plants were consumed as well. Fruit was less frequently absent from fecal samples than were insects. For the brown mouse lemur at RNP, fruit appears to be a primary source of energy. Fruit consumption increased in quantity and diversity during the latter part of the rainy season and early dry season, when fruit production in the forest was high. This pattern of fruit feeding was akin to that found for mouse lemurs in west coast dry forests and coincided with mouse lemur fattening in preparation for hibernation, and young individuals from the year's breeding season becoming independent. Coleoptera were present in 67% of samples examined and were consumed year-round. Insect consumption did not increase consistently during the rainy season when insect abundance was highest, possibly because mouse lemurs were consuming large quantities of fruit at this time or because the insects present were not favored. The most significant finding of this study was the reliance of mouse lemurs on mistletoes. The common assumption is that birds are dispersers of mistletoes, but at RNP we discovered the rare occurrence of a mammal acting as a significant seed disperser of several species of mistletoe plants.

4

Seasonal Changes in Body Mass and Activity Levels

HOW SMALL MAMMALS RESPOND TO CLIMATIC AND RESOURCE FLUCTUATIONS

Through homeothermy—the ability to maintain constant core body temperature (T_b) within a wide range of ambient temperatures (T_a)—mammals (and birds) maintain the high energy flow needed to digest efficiently, move fast, and occupy many different and extreme habitats (Malan, 1996). In turn, thermoregulatory heat production required for homeothermy demands a constant inflow of fuel. These energy demands can be particularly challenging for small-bodied mammals during seasonal food shortages and when animals experience temperature extremes that occur across diverse climates—from temperate to tropical (Bourlière, 1975). Energy needs can be significant for small mammals because their high surface area relative to their body volume results in increased heat loss. Consequently, the relatively high metabolic rates of small mammals require sustained intake of nutritious food (Lyman, 1982a,b; Schmidt-Nielsen, 1998). To conserve valuable energy, some mammals, usually those weighing less than 5 kg, enter periods of dormancy, during which body temperatures drop to near ambient levels and metabolic rates along with activity levels are drastically reduced (Vaughan et al., 2000; Blumstein et al., 2004; Perrin and Richardson, 2004).

Generally, hypothermic states may be daily (shallow) or seasonal (deep) (French, 1992; Vaughan et al., 2000). *Hibernation* is an ecological term defined as a prolonged period of time during which an animal stays inactive in a safe place (Michener, 2004). *Torpor* refers to the actual physiological changes that occur during dormancy, that is, the state of having cooler body temperature and slowing down of bodily functions (Michener, 2004). Although some authors use the term *torpor* to refer to either daily or seasonal hypothermia, when the distinction is possible I will usually refer to daily or occasional periods of lethargy as *torpor* and reserve the term *hibernation* for prolonged and deep periods of seasonal lethargy (following Altringham, 1996).

Dormancy is widespread among mammals, with hibernators using hypothermia to their advantage. Before becoming hypothermic and lethargic, most hibernators, such as woodchucks (*Marmota monax*), meadow jumping mice (*Zapus hudsonius*), woodland jumping mice (*Napaeozapus insignis*), and garden dormice (*Eliomys*), accumulate fat and then become dormant (Godin, 1977; Nowak, 1991). Accumulated fat stores serve as fuel reserves during the period of inactivity (Schmidt-Nielsen, 1998).

Entering a hypothermic state, once considered to be a primitive form of thermoregulation in marsupials (Lyman, 1963; Lyman et al., 1982), is now known to be an adaptation that occurs across a wide range of taxa in order to conserve valuable energy in environments that are physiologically stressful or where food supplies fluctuate daily or seasonally (Mrosovsky, 1977; Fleming, 1979; Lyman, 1982c). During seasonal periods of hypothermia, body temperature in temperate-zone hibernators can hover around 1°C or lower, although hibernators experience different temperature ranges depending on body size and environmental conditions (Barnes, 1989). For instance, marmots prefer to hibernate between 5°C and 10°C, whereas other rodents lower their body temperatures down to 1°C to 6°C. Although in daily or shallow torpor, body temperatures and metabolism do not drop as low as during seasonal or more profound periods of lethargy, in both shallow and deeper states of lethargy, metabolic rates are actively decreased to a fraction of basal metabolic rate (BMR) levels enabling animals to survive without the need for nutritional intake. As small mammals have relatively higher metabolic rates than larger ones (Heldmaier et al., 2004), they may enjoy greater energy savings compared with larger species because the amplitude of metabolic reduction during hibernation is greater (Heldmaier et al., 2004). Overall, keeping body temperatures low, on a daily or seasonal basis, can amount to important energy savings from the usually costly endeavor of maintaining homeothermy.

What are the triggers for entering a state of lethargy? The presence of an endogenous circannual rhythm, or exogenous factors such as temperature, resource availability, or photoperiod can set off hibernation. In many mammals, the effect of photoperiod—a predictable environmental cue—combined with the influence of seasonal fluctuations in resource availability and climate can prompt changes in activity levels (Petterborg, 1978;

Hoffmann, 1981). Specific physiological responses are manifested variably depending on the species (Rusak, 1981). Diminishing photoperiod associated with falling temperatures is a trigger for some species with annual cycles, such as the arctic ground squirrel (*Spermophilus parryii*) (Vaughan et al., 2000). The availability of food, water, and reproductive mates can also affect how animals enter a period of lethargy (Muchlinski, 1978; Nestler et al., 1996; Nomakwezi and Lovegrove, 2002). In deer mice (*Peromyscus*), torpor is triggered by lack of food (Nestler et al., 1996). In species such as pygmy mice (*Baiomys taylori*) (Hudson, 1965), European hedgehogs (*Erinaceus europaeus*), and South African hedgehogs (*Atelerix frontalis*) (Fowler, 1988; Gillies et al., 1991), seasonal reduction in activity can be modified by fluctuations in food availability and controlled by winter's low ambient temperatures. The same applies to North American heteromyid desert rodents (*Dipodomys microps, D. merriami,* and *Perognathus longimembris*) (Kenagy, 1973). Other species such as gray squirrels (*Sciurus carolinensis*) use only moderate heterothermy to conserve energy (Pereira et al., 2002). Cold winter temperatures are not a prerequisite for hibernation. In tropical species, shortage of food supply or water can trigger a hypothermic response (Ortmann et al., 1996, 1997; Schmid, 1996; Heldmaier et al., 2004). In one view, climatic conditions rather than body size may be the deciding factor influencing overall length of time spent in dormancy (French, 1988).

Deep hibernation in small mammals is interrupted by bursts of activity and rewarming (arousals), which do not occur in large-bodied hibernators that sleep less deeply (Heldmaier et al., 2004; Michener, 2004). The periods of inactivity are short at the start and end of the dormant period, but, in general, duration of inactivity, frequency of arousals, and time of emergence from hibernation are influenced by ambient temperatures and can change from year to year (Lyman et al., 1982). Because arousals are costly, more energy can be saved by remaining in deep hibernation. Arousals, although short in duration, emphasize that hibernating endotherms maintain control over homeostasis and point to the adaptiveness of high body temperatures (French, 1988). Kocsard-Varo (2000) hypothesizes that because hibernating animals exhibit a flat EEG (electron encephalogram; a recording of electrical signals from the brain), emerging periodically from the state of hypothermia is essential for these animals to reactivate their automation system in order to avoid death by freezing.

SEASONAL FLUCTUATIONS IN THE CHEIROGALEIDAE

Monotremes, some metatheria, and select members of the orders Insectivora, Chiroptera, Dermoptera, Carnivora, Rodentia and Primates have evolved the ability to use adaptive hypothermia. Torpor is also common in some bird groups such as the order Caprimulgiformes, which includes whip-poor-wills and nightjars (Fletcher et al., 2004). Among primates, the ability to enter periods of hypothermia is rare. Many primate species confront seasonal scarcity by adjusting their diets, subsisting on lower quality or more diverse foods (e.g., Olupot et al., 1997), by changing their grouping patterns to decrease competition (e.g., Symington, 1990; Moraes et al., 1998) or by reducing activity to conserve energy (Wright, 1999). Only certain members of the family Cheirogaleidae are known to experience marked seasonal behavioral cycles paralleling those described for small nonprimate mammals. Cyclicity in the annual life cycle is not restricted to small lemurs, because even large-bodied diurnal lemur species undergo photoperiod-driven seasonal changes such as those associated with pelage thickness and food intake (e.g., Morland, 1993; Pereira, 1993; Pereira et al., 1999). However, the seasonal cycles in cheirogaleids are much more dramatic. Observations on *Cheirogaleus* and *Microcebus* populations have revealed the presence of distinct, sometimes dramatic, cyclical changes in food intake (Petter-Rousseaux and Hladik, 1980), body mass (Petter, 1978; Hladik, 1979; Hladik et al., 1980; Atsalis, 1999a; Schmid, 1999), endocrine activity (Perret, 1972, 1985, 1995), and thermoregulation and activity levels, often culminating in torpor or hibernation (Petter, 1978; Hladik, 1979; Petter-Rousseaux, 1980; McCormick, 1981; Foerg and Hoffmann, 1982; Ortmann et al., 1996; Schmid, 1996; Atsalis, 1999a). Petter-Rousseaux's (1974, 1980) pioneering experimental work documented the influence of photoperiod on different behaviors in the grey mouse lemur and other cheirogaleids. By transferring animals to the northern hemisphere, thus reversing the photoperiodic cycles, Petter-Rousseaux was able to demonstrate that mouse lemurs adjusted their annual cyclical behaviors to the new photoperiod. For instance, whereas in Madagascar, as will be detailed shortly, mouse lemurs increase their body mass early in the austral winter in May–June when photoperiod is shortening, the transplanted subjects adjusted to their new annual photoperiodic schedule by increasing body mass in October, a response to decreasing photoperiod in the northern hemisphere.

Cheirogaleus species living in both dry and rain forest habitats exhibit the most-extreme behavioral cycles with substantial seasonal body mass gain followed by hibernation for up to eight months during the dry season (Petter, 1962; Hladik et al., 1980; Wright and Martin, 1995; Müller, 1999b; Dausmann et al., 2001, 2004). *C. medius* in the west coast begin hibernating in April after substantial body mass gain. Their body mass may be doubled, much of it stored in the tail (Petter et al., 1977; Fietz and Ganzhorn, 1999). Animals hibernate in tree holes, emerging in November to mate in December with the onset of the rainy season (Fietz, 1999a). Offspring hibernate the first year of their lives entering hibernation one month later than the adults (Müller, 1999c). Some dwarf lemurs did not require periodic arousals during hibernation, characteristic of other mammals;

while dwarf lemurs were huddled in their tree hole hibernacula, tempera-ture-sensitive radio tags indicated that their body temperatures fluctuated passively, between 15°C and 33°C, along with ambient temperatures (Dausmann et al., 2004). In short, these individuals remained in a hypometabolic state continuously for eight months. On the other hand, other dwarf lemurs exhibited regular but short arousal periods. Colder ambient temperatures made arousals more frequent, which was noted because dwarf lemurs tended not to arouse when ambient tempertures remained around 30°C (Harder, 2007-from an interview with Kathrin Dausmann, Phillips University). Periodic arousals may serve to dispose of metabolic substances, or to fight against muscle atrophy, which in non-hibernators is a significant danger during long bouts of inactivity (Harder, 2007-from an interview with Sandra Martin, University of Colorado).

Mouse lemurs experience daily and seasonal periods of lethargy. Sea-sonal hibernation differs from daily torpor, in that the former is part of a time-fixed seasonal regime, whereas daily torpor offers the flexibility required to maintain social and other activities (Heldmaier et al., 2004). In mouse lemurs, daily torpor is a flexible way to adjust to energy require-ments, but hibernation is essential for survival during unfavorable envi-ronmental conditions in the dry season. The grey mouse lemur increases body mass and tail volume (where fat is differentially stored) each winter during the nonbreeding period (approximately between March and May), prior to entering hibernation (Russell, 1975; Glatston, 1979; Hladik, 1979; Hladik et al., 1980; Petter-Rousseaux, 1980). Tail volume can increase from 5 to 20 cm^3; (Petter-Rousseaux, 1980). Body fat fluctuations are asso-ciated with changes in thyroid activity (Perret, 1972) and are under pho-toperiodic control (Perret, 1972; Petter-Rousseaux, 1974; Perret and Aujard, 2001), with increases induced by short day lengths (Perret and Aujard, 2001). Captive grey mouse lemurs experienced changes in body fat even when temperature, humidity, and nutrition were held constant (Bourlière and Petter-Rousseaux, 1966; Petter-Rousseaux, 1970, 1974; Russell, 1975), but longer bouts of hypothermia were induced through food restriction; mouse lemurs underwent daily bouts of torpor when food was in short supply even under high ambient temperatures, inde-pendent of photoperiod (Génin, 2000; Génin and Perret, 2003). Food-restricted animals experienced lowest body temperatures. In other words, given food freely, animals did not become torpid even during short photoperiod.

Studies of free-ranging individuals suggest that decreases in activity may occur for varying lengths of time during the dry season (Petter, 1978; Hladik, 1979; Petter-Rousseaux, 1980; Ortmann et al., 1996, 1997; Schmid, 1996). Daily torpor was studied from April through July in grey mouse lemurs and *Microcebus berthae* in the west coast dry forest of Kirindy (Ortmann et al., 1996, 1997; Schmid, 1996). Male and female mouse lemurs trapped in the forest were held in enclosures that permitted exposure to natural temperature and light conditions. Normal body temperatures during the active period hovered around 37.5°C in grey mouse lemurs and around 38°C in *M. berthae*. With food and water available, both species exhibited spontaneous torpor on cold days and warmer days. The longest torpor bout lasted eighteen hours with minimum T_b reaching 15.5°C, accompanied by metabolic depression of almost 90% (Ortmann et al., 1997). However, Schmid (1996) has reported body temperatures as low as 6.8°C. In both species, arousal from torpor was a two-step process. Body temperature,T_b, always rose passively initially, which occurred by following the rise in T_a. When T_b reached about 24°C to 25°C mouse lemurs initiated active body heat production in order to reach their normal body temperature. Schmid (1996) noted that the passive stage of the arousal helped mouse lemurs to conserve energy required for arousal to occur. With daily torpor, grey mouse lemurs can achieve energy savings of approximately 40% (Schmid, 1996, 2000; Ortmann et al., 1997). In one study, water loss conservation was also found to be an important benefit when entering torpor during the dry season (Schmid and Speakman, 2000).

In addition to daily torpor, mouse lemurs, like other small mammals, enhanced their energy savings seasonally by increasing body mass through fat storage before the dry season and entering hibernation for several months during the dry season, when temperatures, rainfall, and resources were reduced (Fietz, 1998; Schmid and Kappeler, 1998; Schmid, 1999). These changes were photoperiodically driven, triggered by short photoperiods. Whereas daily torpor characterizes all mouse lemurs studied thus far, seasonal changes seem to be species- and habitat-specific. *Microcebus ravelobensis* and *M. berthae*, both inhabitants of dry forests, were not observed hibernating seasonally (Ortmann et al., 1996, 1997; Schmid, 1996; Schmid et al., 2000; Randrianambinina et al., 2003a,b). Sympatric with *M. berthae*, grey mouse lemurs at Kirindy hibernated; however, at Ampijoroa in northwestern Madagascar, where they are sympatric with *M. ravelobensis*, they did not exhibit seasonal fattening and hibernation (Schmelting et al., 2000; Lutermann and Zimmermann, 2001). These observations suggest that both genetic variability and differences in local habitats may drive seasonal strategies. At the same time, both *M. murinus* and *M. ravelobensis* experience daily torpor, emphasizing the importance of energy savings at low ambient temperatures (Randrianambinina et al., 2003a,b).

In addition to interpopulational and interspecies differences in hibernating patterns, intrapopulational differences have also been discovered; some mouse lemur individuals remaine active year-round even within populations where seasonal inactivity was experienced (Martin, 1972b; Schmid and Kappeler, 1998; Atsalis, 1999a; Rasoazanabary, 1999; Schmid, 1999). This is unlike what happens in species of *Cheirogaleus* where no individuals are sighted in the forest in the dry season. In one study of grey mouse lemurs at Kirindy, nine of twenty males and same ratio of females entered states of hypothermia in the dry season, whereas others remained normothermic (Rasoazanabary, 1999). Male-biased trap sex ratios have been reported in both west and east coast populations of mouse lemur in studies that took place during the dry season (Harcourt, 1987; Fietz, 1998; Schmid and Kappeler, 1998; Atsalis, 1999a, 2000). Researchers proposed that behavioral differences between the sexes in seasonal patterns of hypothermia explain the presence of mouse lemurs in the forest in the dry season (Fietz, 1998; Schmid and Kappeler, 1998). Corroborating this proposal, in grey mouse lemurs, hibernation has been found to take place more commonly among females than among males (Schmid, 1999; Rasoazanabary, 2006). Moreover, results from one study that followed focal males throughout the dry season discovered that whereas both sexes hibernated, males were more likely to become active, and even females changed nests at least once during the period of dormancy (Rasoazanabary, 2006). On the other hand, even males that did not hibernate, occasionally became inactive during the dry season (Rasoazanabary, 1999, 2006).

INVESTIGATING SEASONAL FLUCTUATIONS
IN THE BROWN MOUSE LEMUR

The majority of studies on the Cheirogaleidae have targeted the species of the west coast, where climate and resource availability are markedly seasonal. In the dry deciduous forests of the west coast, observed seasonal behavioral cycles are associated with variations in food availability that are correlated with dramatic changes in precipitation. As seasonal fluctuations in availability of resources were presumably less pronounced in rainforests, it was suggested that east coast mouse lemurs were less likely to lay down fat stores (Martin, 1972b). However, at RNP certain months of the dry season are characterized by considerable scarcity of resources as well as decreased temperatures and less rainfall (Meyers and Wright, 1993; Overdorff, 1993; Hemingway, 1995; Atsalis, 1998). Therefore, it was probable that rainforest-dwelling mouse lemurs of the east coast would exhibit changes similar to cheirogaleids living in west coast dry forests. Because previous reports on body mass in brown mouse lemurs (Martin, 1972b; Harcourt, 1987; Wright and Martin, 1995) covered only short periods in the field, it was not possible to monitor seasonal changes. Therefore, with a long-term schedule of live-capture in place, I monitored body mass and activity levels, longitudinally and on a population level, to clarify patterns of seasonal changes.

The timing and frequency of capture of mouse lemurs was crucial to successfully interpreting longitudinal capture data. To answer questions regarding temporal changes in body fat and activity levels, I used data

The hut adjacent to the Talatakely research cabin where brown mouse lemurs were weighed and measured in RNP

from individuals that were trapped between February and September. The interval encompassed a period of relatively high resource availability (February–May), when mouse lemurs were expected to increase body fat, and that part of the dry season (June–August) when mouse lemurs were expected to undergo hibernation, emerging at the onset of the breeding season in August.

Given the information that mouse lemurs were seen active in the dry season, I hypothesized that some, but not all, brown mouse lemurs at RNP experienced seasonal changes in body mass, tail circumference, and activity levels (Atsalis, 1999b). I interpreted prolonged (a minimum of one month) and complete absence from traps during the dry season as seasonal inactivity a result of animals having entered hibernation. For individuals that became inactive during part of the dry season, I predicted that body mass and tail circumference taken the last time that they were captured just before their disappearance from the traps to enter hibernation (called "last capture" data) would differ significantly from values recorded at the time of their first capture following their disappearance from the traps (called "first recapture" data). Body mass and tail circumference were expected to be higher before hibernation and lower immediately after-wards. Because a 2–3 g difference in body mass between trappings can reflect chance fluctuations, which may be the result of food intake, a mini-mum criterion of 5 g in body mass difference between last capture and first recapture was set as a sign that hibernation had resulted in body mass loss. Simultaneous changes in body mass and tail circumference were con-sistent indicators of changes in fat storage, so I compared the correlation between these values.

To examine population-level differences between the sexes, male and female body mass and tail circumference averages were compared using all data points (1 and 2, Table 4–1). Additionally, to focus body mass comparisons on adults only, values from two periods were examined: June 1993–May 1994 (3 and 4, Table 4–1) and August 1993–May 1994 (5 and 6, Table 4–1). The rationale behind which months to include depends on how adulthood is determined or defined. Captive grey mouse lemurs and brown mouse lemurs (Petter-Rousseaux, 1964; Glatston, 1979; Perret, 1992) were weaned at seven weeks and they were able to breed by the first

Table 4–1 Mean Body Mass (g) and Tail Circumference (cm) of *Microcebus rufus* Males and Females Taken Over Different Sampling Periods in Talatakely, RNP

	Sample Population	Period	Mean Body Weight ± SD, n,[a] Range	Mean Tail Circumference ± SD, n, Range
1	All males	February 1993–May 1994	41 ± 6.6, 319, 30–88	2.7 ± 0.38, 2.2–5
2	All females	February 1993–May 1994	41 ± 9.3, 167, 20–76	2.7 ± 0.42, 2.2–4.4
3	Adult males	June 1993–May 1994	42 ± 5.3, 220, 31–68	2.7 ± 0.36, 2.2–5
4	Adult females	June 1993–May 1994	41 ± 8.2, 82, 27–72	2.7 ± 0.42, 2.3–4.4
5	Adult males	August 1993–May 1994	43.5 ± 4.4, 155, 34–56	2.7 ± 0.40, 2.2–5
6	Adult females	August 1993–May 1994	42 ± 7.6, 32, 27–61	2.7 ± 0.45, 2.3–4.4

Sample populations represent data for all mouse lemurs trapped, or for the subsamples that excluded young individuals. Young mouse lemurs have been reported to achieve adult body size within three months of birth (3 and 4) or by the first breeding season (5 and 6), so both periods were examined. See text for full explanation. Sample populations exclude data on pregnant and lactating females.

[a]Data points from all captures included.

Adapted from Table V in Atsalis, 1999b; used with permission from Springer Science and Business Media.

reproductive season after their birth, but it is unclear when young, independent mouse lemurs achieve full adult body size. Perret (1992) reported that captive grey mouse lemurs reached adult body size by three months following birth. At RNP individuals with low body mass, indicating that they were young, began making their appearance in the traps in February (Chapter 6), so that by June some young animals would be at least three months old and considered adult by Perret's criterion. In contrast to Perret, Glatston (1979) stated that mouse lemurs did not achieve adult body mass until the beginning of the breeding season. At RNP this would mean that young individuals reached adult body mass only by August or September. I compared body mass data for the period June 1993–May 1994 with data for August 1993–May 1994, to check for differences. I found no significant differences for females, but male differences were marginally significant (Student's t-test, $t = -2.0$, $p = .046$ for males; $t = -.71$, $p = .47$ for females). Consequently, I opted for a conservative approach and used data collected between August and May for the comparative analysis.

To test for seasonal differences between males and females at the population level, body mass and tail circumference averages for February–May were compared with the corresponding values for September–October. The first period represented the time when some mouse lemurs were found to increase body fat values, whereas the second followed seasonal hibernation when some individuals were expected to have reduced body fat values. Data on mouse lemurs that experienced more than one capture per month were averaged, minimizing the effect of chance fluctuations on recorded values for each individual. Averages for the first period were based on 1994 data because this removed young individuals trapped between February and June from the analysis as they may not have achieved full adult body mass. Young mouse lemurs were distinguished from older ones based on two criteria: lower than average body mass and not being captured in the previous year.

To identify periods of greatest magnitude in body fat changes, I calculated the percentage deviation of each monthly adult body mass and tail circumference average from overall averages (following Petter-Rousseaux, 1980). Data collected between August 1993 and May 1994 were used to determine monthly and overall averages.

To demonstrate graphically the proportional shifts in four population body mass classes, 20–30 g, 30–40 g, 40–50 g, and 50+ g, I used data based on monthly average body mass calculated for all trapped individuals. These four classes were chosen because they reflected the body masses of young individuals, those of the majority of mouse lemurs captured, and those reached by mouse lemurs during seasonal fattening. Monthly frequencies of each body mass class, as a percentage of all males or females trapped, were plotted as monthly histograms. Unless otherwise indicated, females that were lactating or pregnant were excluded from all analyses.

FATTENING AND HIBERNATION

A total of 102 males and 72 females were captured and marked, but only 6 males and 7 females were captured frequently enough to document seasonal changes during the required period (Table 4–2). For these individuals, last capture took place between March and June. The majority of males were recaptured for the first time in August. Females were recaptured in September or October. Males were absent from the traps an average of 14 weeks (SD, ±5; range, 6–19 weeks), whereas females averaged 21 weeks (SD, ±4; range, 15–25 weeks). Absence from traps was interpreted as seasonal inactivity. Of course, the data represent the number of weeks that the animals were absent from the traps, not the absolute time spent hibernating. The data are useful in that they reveal a seasonal pattern of absence and a significant difference between the sexes in the interval length (and presumably in the overall length of the period of hibernation) ($t = 2.2, p < .05$, degrees of freedom (DF) = 11).

Males in the analysis increased their body mass between 15% and 91% prior to their absence from traps to enter hibernation (see Table 4–2). When they were retrapped for the first time following hibernation, they had lost 16–44% of their body mass and tail circumference was decreased by 26–39% (Table 4–3). Male body mass decrease between last capture and first recapture in August ranged from 5 to 35 g and was even greater for recapture in September, ranging from 9 to 39 g (see M2 in Figure 4–1). Decrease in tail circumference between last capture and first recapture in August ranged from 0.4 to 0.8 cm, and for recapture in September it ranged from 0.9 to 1.6 cm. Body mass was positively correlated with tail circumference ($r_s = .762, p < .05, N = 31$) indicating that the former tracked changes in the latter. Last capture body mass and tail circumference were significantly different from first recapture values in September ($t = 3.8$ for body mass, $t = 4.7$ for tail circumference; $p < .05, N = 6$).

Female patterns mirrored those of males in body mass and tail circumference changes (see Table 4–2). For instance, F8 showed a dramatic 26% increase in body mass over a single month (see Figure 4–1). When females were retrapped for the first time following hibernation, they had lost 10–37% of their body mass and tail circumference had decreased by 9–32% (see Table 4–3). F32, F38, F42, and F49 were not trapped frequently enough to record the actual fattening process. Fattening in these females was inferred by the decrease in body mass from the last capture before hibernation to the first recapture following hibernation.

In females, body mass decrease between last capture and first recapture ranged from 5.5 to 23.0 g, whereas the decrease in tail circumference ranged from 0.5 to 1.2 cm (see Figure 4–1). Body mass and tail circumference were highly positively correlated ($r_s = .907, N = 37$). Last capture body mass and tail circumference values differed significantly from the

Table 4–2 Monthly Mean Body Mass (g) and Tail Circumference (cm) Fluctuations in Male and Female Brown Mouse Lemurs that Fattened and Hibernated in RNP

	February 1993	March 1993	April 1993	May 1993	June 1993	July 1993	August 1993	September 1993	October 1993	November 1993	December 1993	January 1994	February 1994	March 1994	April 1994	May 1994
M1	44			50.7 (53)			47.5	43.5								
	2.5			3.4 (3.8)			3.4	2.7								
M2	46.0		88				52 (53)	48.8								
	2.7		4.2				3.2 (3.4)	2.7 (3.1)								
M7	56.0	54.7					48.3 (45)	47.6 (46)	48.0	43.5						
	4.5	3.6 (3.7)					3.2	2.8 (2.7)	2.6	2.6						
M11		37.3	38.6	49.3	50 (50)		40.8 (40)	39.2 (38)	39.0	37.4	42.0		41.0	40.7	37.6	
		2.5	2.7	3.2	3.5 (3.5)		2.8	2.5 (2.6)	2.4	2.5	2.5		2.7	2.7	2.7	
M22			43.0	74				52 (48)								
			2.5	3.7				2.6								
M60				66	54			43.5 (42)	42.0							
				4.1	3.1			2.5	2.5							
F8	36.5	35	34	43				34	33	37			45			
	2.4	2.3	2.6	2.6					2.4	2.4			2.5	2.5		
F10	52	46.7	43	65					42.6	42.6		44.5	41	41		
	3.1	2.6	2.5	3.7					2.4	2.5		2.5	2.5	2.6		
F22		46.7	53.5					48	48	47		53		53	59	
		3.0	3.3					3	3	2.5		2.7		3.6	4	
F32			50					34 (36)						42		
			3.6					2.6						2.6		
F38			51					43								
			3.2					2.7						2.6		

F42	40		32	31.5
	3		2.5	2.4
F49	42		34	
	2.9		2.4	

For each subject, first series of numbers represents body mass; second row, tail circumferences. When values at the last time of capture in each month differed from the monthly averaged value, I included last capture data in parentheses. Before hibernation, body mass increased for males and females: M1 by 15%, M2 by 91%, M11 by 35%, M22 by 72%, F8 by 26%, F10 by 51%, and F22 by 15%.

Source: From Atsalis, 1999b; used with permission from Springer Science and Business Media.

Table 4–3 Mean Body Mass and Tail Circumference Values for Male and Female Brown Mouse Lemurs in RNP Before and After Hibernation

Sex	Last Capture Data—Before Hibernation[a]		First Capture Data—After Hibernation[b]		Second Capture Data—After Hibernation[c]	
	Body Mass (g) ± SD, N	Tail Circumference (cm) ± SD, N	Body Mass (g) ± SD, N	Tail Circumference (cm) ± SD, N	Body Mass (g) ± SD, N	Tail Circumference (cm) ± SD, N
Males	64 ± 14.7, 6	3.8 ± 0.27, 6	46.5 ± 5.4, 4	3.2 ± 0.29, 4	44 ± 4.1, 6	2.7 ± 0.21, 6
Females	50.8 ± 8.3, 7	3.3 ± 0.30, 7	38.6 ± 6.1, 7	2.6 ± 0.21, 7		

[a]Values recorded at the last time of capture just prior to disappearance from traps to enter hibernation.
[b]Values recorded at the first capture in August after hibernation.
[c]Values recorded when captured in September.

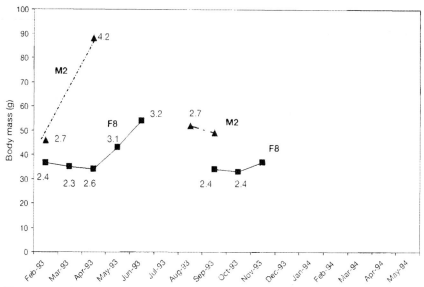

Figure 4–1 Seasonal fluctuations in body mass (g) and tail circumference (cm) in one brown mouse lemur male (M2), represented by closed squares, and one brown mouse lemur female (F8) represented by closed triangles. Floating numbers are tail circumferences corresponding to body mass values.

corresponding values at first recapture (t = 4.9 for body mass, t = 5.6 for tail circumference; p < .05, N = 6).

The average differences in male body mass and tail circumference between last capture and first recapture (18 g for body mass and 0.7 cm for tail circumference) and between last capture and second recapture (20 g for body mass and 1.1 cm for tail circumference) were higher than the average differences in the values for female body mass and tail circumference between last capture and first recapture (13 g for body mass and 0.6 cm for tail circumference). However, the differences were not statistically significant except when comparing tail circumference differences of females to second recapture tail circumference data for males (t = 1.2, p = .27 when test included male body mass data from first capture; t = 1.5, p = .17 when test included male body mass data from the second recapture; t = .8, p = .4 when test included male tail circumference data from first capture; and t = 2.9, p < .05 when test included male tail circumference data from second recapture; DF = 11).

For some individuals, only partial data existed to support that seasonal fattening took place (Table 4–4). The data indicated that several males that did not fatten in 1993 exhibited fattening tendencies or signs of fattening in 1994 (M16, M40, and M63). Several others too had increased values in 1994 (M9, M14, and M79). Some males were trapped with increased body mass and tail circumference values in August 1993 compared with

Table 4–4 Partial Data Available Demonstrating Seasonal Fluctuations in Monthly Mean Body Mass (g) and Tail Circumference (cm) Fluctuations in Male and Female Brown Mouse Lemurs in RNP

	February 1993	March 1993	April 1993	May 1993	June 1993	July 1993	August 1993	September 1993	October 1993	November 1993	December 1993	January 1994	February 1994	March 1994	April 1994	May 1994
M9	43.0		43.0				53.0	45.0	41.3	39.6			47			
	2.5		2.6				3.6	2.7	2.5	2.5			3			
M12		42.0	42.0				54.5	44.8	45.3							
		2.5	2.6				3.8	2.6	2.5							
M14		43.5						46.9	44.3	44.7				67.5 (72)		
		3.3						2.9	2.6	2.6				4.75 (4.9)		
M16		34.0	34.0	39.0	39.0	39.5	41.5	46.8	41.3	40.6				51		
		2.4	2.4	2.5	2.5	2.6	3.0	2.7	2.4	2.4				3.5		
M19		32.0				37.0		44.0	40.0							
		2.3				2.5		2.9	2.5							
M32			45.3				48.0	43.0								
			3.2				3.2	3.0								
M40			37.5	40.4	39.6	39.9	43.1	40.9	37.8	37.4	43.0	44.0	43.0	43.3	45.4	55 (56)
			2.3	2.6	2.9	3.0	2.9	2.6	2.4	2.4	2.4	2.5	2.7	2.6	3.0	4.2 (4.3)
M63					31.5	31.6	33.4	38.7	37.0	35.0	40.0			40.0	37.0	57
					2.4	2.4	2.4	2.5	2.3	2.4	2.4			2.7	2.5	3.3
M79								42.8	40.8	39.5		47.0			65 (65)	
								2.7	2.6	2.5		2.8			5 (5)	
F13		43.0	49.0											51		
		2.7	3.0											3.5		
F19		39	37	43												61
		2.5	2.4	2.7												4
F25		35.7		36.5	39.9	40.0	38.0	41.5	39.0	35.0	40.0					52.5 (54)
		2.4		2.3	2.6	2.7	2.6	2.6	2.6	2.3	2.4					3.4 (3.5)
F29		30	37	41	52											
		2.4	2.4	2.8	3.4											

For each subject, first series of numbers represents body mass, second row are tail circumferences. When values at the last time of capture in each month differed from the monthly averaged value, I included last capture data in parentheses.

Source: From Atsalis, 1999b; used with permission from Springer Science and Business Media.

April 1993 (M9, M12, M19, and M32). Possibly, these males increased their body mass after April, entered hibernation, and emerged from traps with body mass still high. Alternatively, it may be that these individuals never entered hibernation and, instead, used the dry season months to increase mass in preparation for the breeding season.

For some females, too, only partial data were available (see Table 4–4). In 1993, some females fattened (F13, F19, and F29). Their body mass and tail circumference increased between 10 and 73% and between 8 and 48%, respectively. These females ceased to be trapped by June implying that they went into hibernation, but recapture data between August and November were not available. Of the listed females, F13, F19, F22 (listed in Table 4–2), and F25 exhibited signs of fattening the following year as well. Although data from only a single trap session were available in some cases, recorded body mass was high: up to 20 g above average female body mass.

There were sufficient data to surmise that in 1993 some mouse lemurs did not fatten and did not enter hibernation, continuing to enter traps throughout the dry season (Table 4–5). Some of these individuals did fatten the following year. In this group, the body mass and tail circumference fluctuations that were observed in those individuals that hibernated are lacking. Nevertheless, monthly average body mass for the males varied significantly across months (repeated measures Anova, $F_{3,18} = 7.36, p < .5$), but not for females ($F_{4,14} = .64, p = .65$). These results may be associated more with differences in sample size than with actual biological variation. Body mass for each individual nonhibernating male, averaged from May to August (the time when hibernating males emerged), was below the population average of 43.5 g (SD, ±4.4), although the differences were not significant (M16: body mass = 39.8, Z-test $z = -.43$; M36: body mass = 40.3, $z = -.36$; M40: body mass = 40.8, $z = -.31$; M48, body mass = 40.3, $z = -.36$; M63: body mass = 32.2, $z = -1.52$; all at critical value of $\alpha/2 = 1.96$). Similarly, body mass for each individual nonhibernating female, averaged from May to September (when the hibernating females emerged), was below the population average of 42 g (SD, ±7.6), but values did not differ significantly (F20: body mass = 37.2, $z = -29$; F25: body mass = 39.7, $z = -.23$; F47: body mass = 37.6, $z = -.35$; all at critical value of $\alpha/2 = 1.96$).

POPULATION FLUCTUATIONS IN BODY MASS, TAIL CIRCUMFERENCE AND ACTIVITY LEVELS

Significant differences were not seen in body mass and tail circumferences between males and females when all capture data were included (1 and 2, Table 4–1) ($t = .19, p = .85$ for body mass; $t = .05, p = .96$ for tail circumference), nor when I included only values for adults (5 and 6 in Table 4–1)

Table 4–5 Male and Female Brown Mouse Lemurs that Did Not Experience Seasonal Fluctuations in Monthly Mean Body Mass (g) and Tail Circumference (cm) in the Dry Season in RNP[a]

	February 1993	March 1993	April 1993	May 1993	June 1993	July 1993	August 1993	September 1993	October 1993	November 1993	December 1993	January 1994	February 1994	March 1994	April 1994	May 1994
M16	34.0		34.0	39.0	39.0	39.5	41.5	46.8	41.3	40.6				51		
	2.4		2.5	2.5	2.5	2.6	3.0	2.7	2.4	2.4				3.5		
M36			40.0	41.5	40.0	37.1	42.6	42.8	41.3	41.0						
			2.5	2.6	2.9	2.7	2.6	2.6	2.5	2.5						
M40			37.5	40.4	39.6	39.9	43.1	40.9	37.8	37.4	43.0	44.0	43.0	43.3	45.4	55 (56)
			2.3	2.6	2.9	3.0	2.9	2.6	2.4	2.4	2.4	2.5	2.7	2.6	3.0	4.2 (4.3)
M48				41.0	39.0	39.9	41.4	40.7								
				2.5	2.7	2.5	2.5	2.4								
M63					31.5	31.6	33.4	38.7	37.0	35.0				40.0	37.0	57
					2.4	2.4	2.4	2.5	2.3	2.4				2.7	2.5	3.3
F20			33.0	32.5	42.0	41.8	34.0	36.0	32.0	33.5				45.5	46.0	
			2.3	2.3	2.5	2.5	2.3	2.5	2.3	2.4				2.5	2.5	
F25			35.7	36.5	39.9	40.0	38.0	41.5	39.0	35.0	40.0					52.5 (54)
			2.4	2.3	2.6	2.7	2.6	2.6	2.6	2.3	2.4					3.4 (3.5)
F47					37.0	39.0	35.5	40.0	36.5							
					2.6	2.8	2.7	2.5	2.6							

For each subject, first series of numbers represents body mass; second row, tail circumferences. When values at the last time of capture in each month differed from the monthly averaged value, I included last capture data in parentheses.

[a]Refers to 1993 values.

Source: From Atsalis, 1999b; used with permission from Springer Science and Business Media.

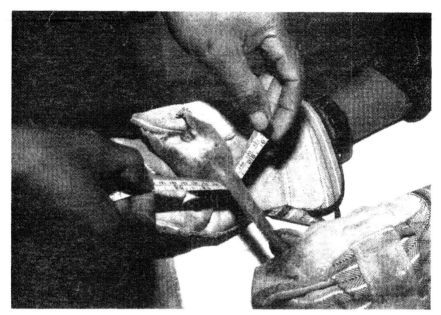

Measuring tail circumference of the brown mouse lemur in RNP. During periods of seasonal fattening, fat is stored in the tail.

($t = -.98, p = .33$), which suggests that brown mouse lemurs are not dimorphic in these traits. However, there were some minor differences between the sexes when looking at population-level data for body mass and tail circumference. Specifically, among females, average body mass decreased by 24% when comparing February–May with September–October (Table 4–6). There was a 14% decrease in tail circumference. Both differences were statistically significant ($t = -5.8, p < .0001$ for body mass; $t = -3.0, p < .005$ for tail circumference). In contrast, male body mass did not differ significantly between the two intervals ($t = -1.5, p = .128$) although the 13% difference in tail circumference was significant ($t = -3.2, p < .005$).

Table 4–6 Population-Level Body Mass and Tail Circumference Values for Male and Female Brown Mouse Lemurs for Two Seasonal Periods in RNP

	Mean Values for Females		Mean Values for Males	
Period	Body Mass (g) ± SD, N	Tail Circumference (cm) ± SD, N	Body Mass (g) ± SD, N	Tail Circumference (cm) ± SD, N
February–May[a]	48.3 ± 8.5, 22	2.9 ± 0.63, 22	45 ± 8.3, 26	3 ± 0.67, 26
September–October[b]	36.8 ± 5.3, 27	2.5 ± 0.19, 23	43 ± 4.2, 70	2.6 ± 0.18, 67

[a]Represents prehibernation period.
[b]Represents posthibernation period.

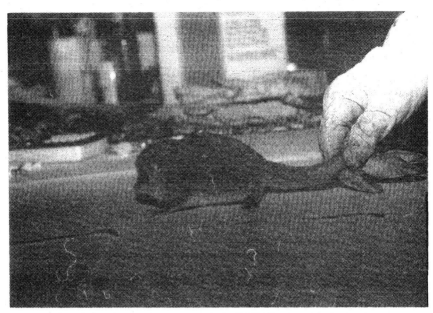

Fattened (88 g) brown mouse lemur male in RNP. Photo taken in April when some mouse lemurs fattened in preparation for seasonal torpor.

Population-level analyses generally mirrored the findings from longitudinal analysis. Monthly average body mass and tail circumferences in both sexes tended to deviate negatively from overall averages between August and November 1993 when animals emerged from hibernation and began breeding (Figures 4–2 and 4–3). Monthly averages tended to be at or above overall population averages at the onset of the new year, within the rainy season and at the onset of the dry season when seasonal fattening was observed. However, in December and January, when only a very small number of animals were trapped, the female pattern differed from the male pattern. Although the intention was to remove all pregnant and lactating females from these analyses, it is possible that the higher female body mass exhibited during this period, not tracked by corresponding increases in tail circumference, was the result of including data from recently parturient females.

Additionally, as would be expected, of the four body mass classes, the two middle-size classes constituted the highest percentage of individuals trapped throughout the annual cycle (Figures 4–4 and 4–5). Individuals in the lightest body mass class were trapped between February and May, most likely representing young newly weaned individuals. Young individuals could occur in the lower range of the 30–40 g size class as well. A single female represented the 20–30 g body mass class in July, August, and October 1993. Because she cycled during the breeding season, she

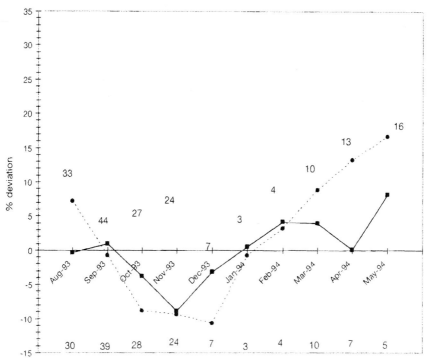

Figure 4-2 Percentage deviation of monthly average body mass (g) and tail circumference (cm) values from population averages (43.5 g and 2.7 cm respectively) in adult brown mouse lemur males in Talatakely, RNP. Floating numbers above x-axis denote monthly sample sizes for body mass. Numbers below x-axis denote monthly sample sizes for tail circumference. (From Atsalis, 1999b; used with permission from Springer Science and Business Media.)

would be considered an adult, but her body mass never exceeded 30 g. Individuals in the heaviest body mass class were present mostly between February and June, supporting results from the longitudinal analysis of a seasonal pattern in body mass increase. The two females trapped in December were both over 50 g, but neither was gestating or lactating at the time of capture. Two males trapped in August and September were heavy when trapped earlier in the season (M2 and M22 at 88 and 74 g respectively) and remained over 50 g (53 and 51 g) even after body mass loss during hibernation (see Table 4-2). In addition, M9 and M12 reached a mass of over 50 g values during the dry season (see Table 4-4). Three other males, over 50 g, had no trap history prior to August.

DIFFERENCES IN SEASONAL RESPONSE AT RNP

Mouse lemurs at RNP exhibited seasonal fluctuations in body mass, tail circumference, and activity levels. These findings are based on results from live-trapping, a method also used in studies on grey mouse lemurs to

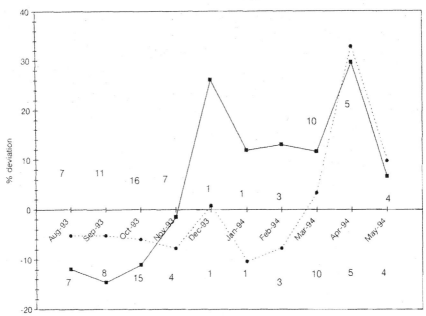

Figure 4–3 Percentage deviation of monthly average body mass (g) and tail circumference (cm) values from population averages (42 g and 2.7 cm respectively) in adult brown mouse lemur females in Talatakely, RNP. Floating numbers above x-axis denote monthly sample sizes for body mass. Numbers below x-axis denote monthly sample sizes for tail circumference. (From Atsalis, 1999b; used with permission from Springer Science and Business Media.)

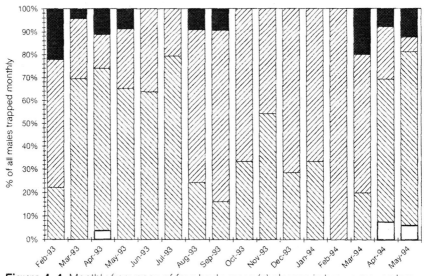

Figure 4–4 Monthly frequency of four body mass (g) classes in brown mouse lemur males as the percentage of all males trapped each month in Talatakely, RNP; 20–30 g, open bar; 30–40 g, thick-striped bar; 40-50 g, thin-striped bar; >50 g, black bar. (From Atsalis, 1999b; used with permission from Springer Science and Business Media.)

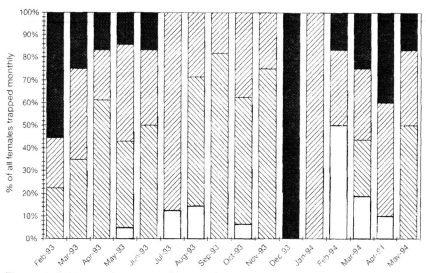

Figure 4–5 Monthly frequency of four body mass (g) classes in brown mouse lemur females as the percentage of all females trapped each month in Talatakely, RNP: 20–30 g, open bar; 30–40 g, thick-striped bar; 40–50 g, thin-striped bar; >50 g, black bar. (From Atsalis, 1999b; used with permission from Springer Science and Business Media.)

Comparison of fattened brown mouse lemur female (72 g) and a younger brown mouse lemur male (31 g) in RNP. Photo taken in April when some mouse lemurs fattened in preparation for seasonal torpor.

effectively document seasonal inactivity and body mass changes (Schmid, 1999; Rasoazanabary, 2006). At RNP direct observations agreed with the findings from our trap data. Fat and lethargic mouse lemurs were occasionally seen in the forest during the dry season, and they were not trapped. Our observations from nocturnal walks indicated that mouse lemurs were more conspicuous in the forest between February and May, a period when we were able to distinguish young mouse lemurs, as they made their appearance in the forest, from older ones. In August, a few fat as well as several very lethargic mouse lemurs were observed sometimes during our nocturnal walks, suggesting that individuals emerged periodically from torpor.

Risks are involved when allocating time and energy to deposit fat stores before hibernation, and there may be risks when emerging from torpor, daily or deep. When the RNP guides and I observed animals that had been trapped arousing from daily torpor, their reflexes were slow and the animals required time to regain normal active state. While in this state, mouse lemurs may not be able to react with readiness to the presence of predators. To illustrate, in May we radiocollared a female whose high body weight suggested that she was preparing for hibernation. One night, while we were following the radiosignal emitting from her nest, she emerged at the entrance and immediately froze upon seeing us—a typical response—but then she remained in a lethargic state for nearly three hours before moving away to seek cover. The female was so lethargic when she first emerged that she was unable to remain upright and instead slowly rotated, while holding firmly onto a vine with her hind feet, until she was suspended entirely upside down. In August, when mouse lemurs were emerging from lethargy, one individual was observed laying lengthwise holding onto a thin (9-cm circumference) branch, for over four hours, alternating between sleeping and lethargically rotating his head to follow the cloud of insects that flew around him. The behavior of lethargic animals, (and possibly even the heavier mass of those preparing to enter hibernation), may place them at increased risk of predation if mobility is compromised.

At the same time that some mouse lemurs were exhibiting these behaviors during the dry season, other mouse lemurs, predominantly male, continued to be energetically active (see Tables 4–4 and 4–5; see also Figure 5–5 for fluctuations in monthly trap sex ratio). Results from trapping indicated that some males even increased their body mass over this period. A few females, too, continued to be captured. The trap sex ratio for M. rufus was also male biased in the dry season in Mantadia National Park, another eastern rainforest (Randrianambinina et al., 2003a,b). Overall, then, the suggestion is that more females than males hibernate, and the implication is that males and females exhibit different seasonal adaptations.

In addition to sex-specific differences, at RNP, individual mouse lemurs exhibited different behaviors in different years during the dry season.

Some individuals fattened successively in both years of the study; others fattened only once. Several mouse lemurs had fattened in the first year of the study but did not show body fat increase by the time of their last capture in May 1994, when my study ended (M11, F8, F10, and F32) (see Table 4–2). One male weighed even less compared to the same time the previous year (M11). Other mouse lemurs displayed body fat increase in the second year, just as they had in the previous year (F13, F19, and F22) (see Tables 4–2 and 4–4). One female was recaptured in the second year of the study even heavier in body mass than she had been at approximately the same time in the first year (F13) (see Table 4–4).

In summary, I discovered that variation in seasonal behaviors may be reflected in the timing of the response, the extent of the response (e.g., degree of fat gain), or whether fattening and hibernation occur at all. Moreover, age may influence, although it may not determine, whether fattening and hibernation occur. Among mouse lemurs that fattened in the first year of study, some individuals could be classified as adult. Given that the breeding season activities peaked in November, these individuals were captured with body mass hovering around or above population-average values too close to the end of the breeding season to have been the offspring of that season (M1, M2, M7, M9, M12, M14, M22, F10, F13, F22, F32, F38, and possibly F19) (see Table 4–4). However, a small subsample of mouse lemurs that fattened in 1993 may have been newly weaned young, based on their body mass when they were first captured (M11, F8, and F29) (see Tables 4–2 and 4–4). Other mouse lemurs that may have been young did not fatten in the first year of study but did so in the second (M16, M40, M63, and F25) (see Table 4–4).

Social status may be another factor influencing seasonal changes in mouse lemurs. Researchers have suggested that different size classes among grey mouse lemur males reflected variable social and reproductive status (Martin, 1972b, 1973; Fietz, 1998). At RNP, the males that remained heavy, over 50 g, in August, may have held superior social status, especially with regard to males that continued to remain active throughout the dry season. I have proposed that the latter males may have been trying to establish themselves in the population, possibly seeking to find and maintain home ranges in anticipation of the mating season (Atsalis, 2000). Many of these males were new individuals, first-time captures, that may have been in the process of migration, migrating either into the population or through it. Therefore, these males may have been of lower social status than those that fattened and entered hibernation and that may have had established ranges. Overall, differences in seasonal behaviors among males may reflect differences in age, or social and "residency" status. Females showed variable patterns as well, but the highly-male-biased sex ratios during part of the dry season suggested the existence of more extreme patterns in males. Nevertheless, if males were active and dispersing, the same may be the case for the females that did not hibernate. This hypothesis was suggested for a related species, *Mirza coquereli* (Kappeler et al., 2002). Observed fluctuations in the sex ratio over the annual cycle will be more thoroughly discussed in Chapter 5, where patterns of social organization will be presented.

The male-biased sex ratios reported for grey mouse lemurs reflected differences in hibernation patterns, just as those found for the brown mouse lemur at RNP (Martin, 1972b; Fietz, 1998; Schmid and Kappeler, 1998; Schmid, 1999; Rasoazanabary, 2006). At Kirindy, the majority of adult females, but only a few adult males, became inactive for the duration of the dry season (Schmid and Kappeler, 1998; Schmid, 1999; Rasoazanabary, 2006), which is why grey mouse lemurs could be seen active in the forest year-round (Martin, 1972b). Mouse lemur variability in frequency of torpor is an indication that animals use foraging and inactivity tactics opportunistically and that they are not obligatory hibernators as are free-ranging species of *Cheirogaleus* (Schmid and Speakman, 2000; Génin and Perret, 2003). The differences in behavior between the sexes in mouse lemurs may relate to differing sexual adaptations while surviving under conditions of food scarcity (Schmid and Kappeler, 1998; Rasoazanabary, 1999).

Certain geographic regions of Madagascar are characterized by extreme climatic cycles (Pereira, 1993). Seasonal patterns of rainfall and temperature changes (Hladik et al., 1980; Petter-Rousseaux, 1980; Morland, 1993; Pereira, 1993) can explain cyclical variations in lemur behavior and, seasonal behaviors are present in a wide range of Malagasy climates (Richard and Dewar, 1991). This has long been known for nonprimate species in Madagascar such as the tenrecs (endemic insectivores), whose body mass and activity levels fluctuate in response to the dry season in a wide range of environments, including east coast rainforests (Eisenberg and Gould, 1970; Schmid and Stephenson, 2003). At RNP, brown mouse lemurs were faced with reduced resources and stressful climatic conditions during the austral winter. Rainfall and average temperatures decreased by 60% and 17% respectively between wet and dry seasons (see Chapter 2). These differences are comparable to those reported for the dry west coast forest of Kirindy, where mouse lemurs hibernated and where rainfall decreased by approximately 85% and mean temperature by 14% (Sörg and Rohner, 1996).

In Ampijoroa, the lack of seasonal response by *Microcebus ravelobensis* (Randrianambinina et al., 2003a,b) and by grey mouse lemurs (Schmelting et al., 2000; Lutermann and Zimmermann, 2001) was attributed to local ecological conditions: temperatures did not fall below 15°C (Randrianambinina et al., 2003a,b). If seasonally unfavorable environmental conditions, including low temperatures, instigate seasonal hibernation, minimal temperatures at other research sites should be lower than those in Ampijoroa. Reviewing some of the available evidence, researchers claimed that minimal temperatures at other locations where mouse lemurs have been studied were on average 5°C lower (Randrianambinina et al., 2003a,b). At RNP, I determined that temperatures could drop to 9°C in the dry season supporting the researchers' claim although temperatures averaged 12°C. There may be other factors, besides low temperatures, prompting the need to hibernate. Low resource availability associated with decreased rainfall, as was apparent at RNP (see Chapter 2), would be an obvious obstacle for mouse lemurs in meeting their energy demands. Captive data support this claim. In captive grey (Génin, 2000; Génin and Perret, 2003) and brown mouse lemurs (Wrogemann and Zimmermann, 2001; Wrogemann et al., 2001), unlimited food availability was key to remaining active even when animals were exposed to short photoperiod. Thus, even though short day length acts as the external trigger for prolonged seasonal hibernation in mouse lemurs, whether or not animals enter a hypothermic state depends on diverse factors including food availability, body mass achieved (see "Comparing Seasonal Responses of Mouse Lemur Species," this chapter), and ambient temperatures (Randrianambinina et al., 2003a,b).

Among small mammals, variation in seasonal response is not unusual. For instance, whereas in some species, such as dormice (*Glis glis*), circannual fluctuations in activity levels and body mass persisted for all individuals even under constant environmental conditions (Mrosovsky, 1977), in others, periodic inactivity was frequently used as necessity dictated (French, 1992) and was not always accompanied by fat storage (Godin, 1977; Fleming, 1979; Geiser, 1986; Geiser and Baudinette, 1987). In general, mammalian species that hibernate respond variably to diverse stimuli. As previously discussed, deprivation of food, water, reproductive mates, or changes in photoperiod can trigger torpor (Muchlinski, 1978; Nestler et al., 1996; Perrin and Richardson, 2004). Once triggered, the degree of seasonal response can be influenced by temperature and the availability of resources (Hudson, 1965; Kenagy, 1973; Gillies et al., 1991).

It is possible that at RNP, a larger segment of the population exhibited seasonal behaviors and that these were not made apparent because for so many mouse lemurs trap records were incomplete. Additionally, the fact that age, or at least life stage, of captured individuals could not be determined with certainty posed further challenges in deciding whether mouse lemurs that underwent fattening were older or recently matured young. Given the quick maturation period of mouse lemurs (about three months), it was possible that even newly weaned individuals entered hibernation, and certainly there were indications of this. Among some small mammals, such as woodchucks, even the young of a given year accumulate fat and disappear from above ground activity to hibernate (Snyder et al., 1961). On the other hand, mouse lemurs may resemble Belding ground squirrels (*Spermophilus beldingi*), whose propensity to enter seasonal torpor and reproduce the first year of their life is body-size dependent; in these squirrels, only animals that reached adult body mass became dormant

(French, 1988). This scenario was supported by one study on grey mouse lemurs that revealed that all the females captured in July, (i.e., they remained active in the heart of the dry season), were "juveniles," that is, newly matured individuals from the previous breeding season (Rasoazanabary, 2006). As will be discussed in "Comparing Seasonal Responses of Mouse Lemur Species," achieving a particular threshold body mass, rather than the particular age of the individual, may be the defining criterion for entering hibernation.

In addition to field observations, captive studies on grey mouse lemurs also offer evidence for the presence of diverse responses in mouse lemurs. Whereas in one captive study, no variation in the propensity toward fattening was discovered (Génin and Perret, 2000), in another, grey mouse lemurs decreased activity and food consumption during the winter but without ceasing either completely (Bourlière and Petter-Rousseaux, 1966). In some cases, age and sex-related differences in seasonal behaviors were reported. Adult male grey mouse lemurs remained lethargic and had lower body temperatures during the winter than did younger males that were never observed inactive at night (Russell, 1975). Storage of fat in the tail was most noticeable in older individuals, particularly in females (Glatston, 1979). Variability in seasonal response has been observed even in *Cheirogaleus medius*. Considered to be obligatory hibernators in the wild, in captivity, some individuals underwent seasonal body mass changes without always entering hibernation (Russell, 1975; Petter-Rousseaux, 1980; Foerg and Hoffmann, 1982).

Overall, findings from captive and field research point to the existence of facultative heterothermia in mouse lemurs at RNP. Comparable temporal responses, however, including the presence of flexible and multiple seasonal responses, occur in both dry and rainforest mouse lemur species. The observed variability may reflect multiple factors, including differences in age, social status, and other individual characteristics.

COMPARING SEASONAL RESPONSES OF MOUSE LEMUR SPECIES

Maximum body mass values reached by brown mouse lemurs at RNP were higher than values reached at Mantadia. At RNP, the maximum body mass achieved by a male was 88 g; at Mantadia, a male reached 70 g (Randrianambinina et al., 2003b). Correspondingly, a female at RNP reached 65 g, whereas 55 g was the record weight at Mantadia. At RNP, male mouse lemurs increased their body mass by 15–91% in the prehibernation period, whereas female body masses increased by 15–51%. In comparison, at Kirindy, female grey mouse lemurs had stored more fat than males before they became seasonally inactive (Schmid, 1999). One male increased body mass by 18%, whereas females increased their mass by 26% (Schmid, 1999). Even more dramatic body mass increases, more than

40%, have been reported for grey mouse lemurs at this site (Kappeler and Dill, 2000). Schmid (1999) speculated that females entered the seasonal period of inactivity once they had reached a critical mass that allowed them to remain in hibernation for several months. At Kirindy, the critical mass was approximately 60 g. Achieving a minimum target mass may be necessary for prolonged seasonal torpor. Randrianambinina and associates (2003b) found that lighter-mass brown mouse lemur males in Mantadia remained active, whereas heavier ones, which achieved a threshold of 50 g or more, entered seasonal torpor. Mouse lemurs that were low in body mass did not stop foraging to enter prolonged torpor. At RNP, too, with the exception of two females (F42 and F49), all other individuals, for whom there were indications of having entered hibernation, were at least 50 g (see Table 4–2). Even F42 and F49 may have fattened further although trap data were not available. Individuals that did not hibernate maintained body mass values below the population averages.

As stated, at RNP, body mass for males that remained active, but not for females, varied significantly over time. At Kirindy, both male and female grey mouse lemurs that remained active did not show significant changes in body mass and tail circumference (Schmid, 1999). Furthermore, in contrast to findings at RNP, body mass of inactive males at Kirindy did not change significantly during the period of inactivity; inactive female grey mouse lemurs experienced a body mass loss of 32% and a tail circumference decrease close to 28%, whereas male tail circumference decreased only by 12%. Schmid proposed that in contrast to females, males emerged from hibernation periodically to feed. This was confirmed in a more recent study, also at Kirindy, during which both hibernating males and females became active but it was the males that were more active throughout the dry season (Rasoazanabary, 2006). Males that remained active maintained their body mass between April and September, and focal animal follows indicated that inactive males became active and searched for food far and wide (Rasoazanabary, 1999, 2006). Energy savings for males may remain high with this tactic of periodic emergence from hibernation to feed, but more studies are needed to demonstrate if there are advantages to adopting one or the other behavioral pattern. At RNP, both inactive males and females lost mass and decreased tail circumference, with males showing greater loss in both mass and tail circumference than females (see "Fattening and Hibernation," this chapter). Why do mouse lemur species behave differently? Comparative studies could clarify and explain interspecies differences that occur in different environments.

EMERGING FROM HIBERNATION

The onset of the breeding season began in August, which is when male mouse lemurs first emerged from hibernation. Evidence from the longitudinal trap-capture data at RNP showed that females, assumed to be hibernating, were absent from the traps seven weeks longer than hibernating males. Male C. *medius* also emerged earlier than females from hibernation, having undergone drastic body mass loss (Müller, 1999b). In this monogamous species, early emergence may be a form of paternal investment as males take this time to secure a home range that will provide resources for the family that they will soon form (Müller, 1999b). In mouse lemurs, which are acknowledged to be promiscuous (Chapter 5), males may use the extra time to maximize mating opportunities by establishing territories and breeding hierarchy as was suggested for grey mouse lemurs, where a similar sexually biased pattern of inactivity was discovered (Schmid, 1999). In turn, by remaining dormant longer, females conserved body fat necessary toward breeding (Perret, 1992; Fietz, 1998). Early male activity may be a form of sexual competition that allows males to secure optimal territories, perhaps leading females to choose males with the best sites. Indeed, captive research has shown that females have the opportunity to choose their mates. Females preferred males with higher rank (Andrès et al., 2001), that were older in age, or that exhibited a higher frequency of mate calling (Craul et al., 2003).

Small nonprimate mammals that undergo torpor can provide additional insights into explaining early emergence of mouse lemur males from hibernation. In rodents, age and sex can determine when animals come out of dormancy. Most male hibernating rodents, such as woodchucks, Belding ground squirrels, and western jumping mice (*Zapus princeps*) emerge earlier than females (Snyder et al., 1961; Godin, 1977; French, 1988). Sex also determined the pattern of emergence: male jumping mice aroused more frequently as the dormancy period neared its end, but in the Belding ground squirrel, it was the females and small nonbreeding males that varied the time they spent aroused towards the end of dormancy, whereas large males spontaneously terminated hibernation (French, 1988). The timing of emergence may be associated with testicular development. In the Anatolian ground squirrel, males emerged from hibernation only one week earlier than females, with testes that were already spermatogenic, or would become so shortly afterwards (Gür and Gür, 2005). In contrast, the males of other ground squirrel species require euthermia to develop testes, emerging two to four weeks before females to complete spermatogenesis (Barnes 1996). Mouse lemur testes are regressed and nonspermatogenic during the nonbreeding season, increasing in growth as the photoperiod lengthens. In captivity, testicular growth was not complete until two months after the shortest day of the year (Glatston, 1979), suggesting that the early emergence of males provided the extra time to complete spermatogenesis. This hypothesis was supported by observations at RNP and elsewhere, where male testicular volume was shown to increase up to one month before most females were in estrus (Chapter 6).

As with grey mouse lemurs in the west coast (Fietz, 1998) and like other small mammals, such as male woodchucks and Anatolian ground squirrels

(Gür and Gür, 2005), male brown mouse lemurs continued to lose body mass immediately after emerging from hibernation, even as testicular volume increased. Indeed, results from both longitudinal and population-level data indicated that during this brief interval, body mass was low for both sexes. At least for males, results from captive studies on brown and grey mouse lemurs concur with these findings (Perret and Predine, 1984; Wrogemann et al., 2001). Researchers have attributed the decrease in body mass to metabolic changes, a result of increased hormonal activity during mating (Perret and Predine, 1984; Wrogemann et al., 2001).

SLEEPING NESTS

Although occasionally seen sleeping on open branches, brown mouse lemurs, like other mouse lemur species, occupied either spherical leaf nests or tree hollows, which they shared when sleeping in the daytime and when in seasonal hibernation (Martin, 1972a; Atsalis, 1998; Weidt et al., 2004). Like the behavior of huddling in larger lemurs, communal sleeping in nests has been proposed to be a social thermoregulatory behavior that conveys energetic advantages to a solitary forager by significantly reducing metabolic costs (Perret, 1998; Schmid, 1998). Behavioral thermoregulation (curling up when sleeping to reduce exposed body surface area), social thermoregulation, and nest building in protected areas are critical to reducing seasonal stress in small mammals (Vaughan et al., 2000). Ambient temperature in nests of mouse lemurs increases with the number of sleeping partners, probably providing survival benefits to a solitary primate through the warmth of the nest's microclimate (Charlot and Perret, 2000). Thermoregulatory benefits of social sleeping may be particularly essential when mouse lemurs sleep on branches and in leaf nests that are less insulated than tree holes (Weidt et al., 2004). Finally, during hibernation, sleeping together may offer other benefits besides those associated with thermoregulation. Social hibernation increases the opportunity for social bonding and allows males to associate with females, even monopolize them, before reproduction (Arnold, 1990; Armitage, 1998; Blumstein et al., 2004).

The building of spherical leaf nests has been proposed to be an ancestral strepsirrhine trait (Martin, 1972a). At RNP, leaf nests were ball-shaped structures of tightly woven leaves, suspended from trees. The leaf composition of the nests varied. They consisted of fifty to more than one hundred leaves from several different plants, although one nest was composed exclusively of 240 guava leaves. The small entrance (averaging 4-cm wide) and the tightly woven leaves ensured that the interior, a hollow sphere averaging about 20 cm in diameter, remained warm and dry. The nests were not always hidden within heavy vegetation. Suspended from the corner of a tree crown, the open location of some nests may have been a way to avoid predators like the mongoose-like carnivore *Galidia elegans*. Larger-sized predators may have had a difficult time reaching the terminal location of a suspended nest, or it may be that the nests themselves served as sufficient camouflage. The leaf nest structures were remarkably durable; we monitored the life of one unoccupied nest and observed that it successfully weathered two cyclones, all the while remaining suspended from the tree.

Occasionally, mouse lemurs at RNP bedded down in the hollows of dead trees for sleeping or entering torpor, rather than constructing a freestanding nest. Villagers in the area sometimes reported finding mouse lemurs sleeping deeply in the hollow of a tree chopped down for firewood. Occasionally, we too observed mouse lemurs using tree hollows. In October 1993, F22 slept deeply in the hollow of a dead standing tree and had not emerged by 12 midnight when we departed. Another dead tree was felled months later, after M40 was seen entering one of four entrances. The entrance to the tree hole was 30-cm long and 14-cm wide and was located approximately 6.25 m high in an 8-m tall. The entrance led to a 70-cm-long dry tunnel where the animal had nestled. The tunnel located 30–60 cm away from the entrance probably provided sufficient protection from predators.

In western Madagascar, tree holes have been found to be important dry season refuges (Ortmann et al., 1997 citing Fietz's thesis, 1995; Radespiel, Ehresmann et al., 2003; Rasoazanabary, 2006). One study at Kirindy indicated that animals preferred the tree holes of dead trees to living trees perhaps because of the greater number of holes and their larger size, in one case accommodating sixteen sleeping members (Rasoazanabary, 2006)! In Ampijoroa, 86% of sleeping sites for the grey mouse lemur and 46% for the sympatric *M. ravelobensis* were tree holes. The remaining sites consisted of branches, and of hollows under dead leaves on the ground. A constructed nest was discovered only once (Radespiel, Ehresmann et al., 2003), possibly because of the lack of leaves during the dry season. Indeed, sometimes mouse lemurs retreated to nests found at the base of tree hollows because the trees themselves were bare. As a result, the hollows offered greater protection than leaf nests (Ortmann et al., 1997 citing Fietz's thesis, 1995). Tree hollows are ideal in that they allow mouse lemurs to use the warmth of the day as it progresses to passively arouse themselves from torpor with minimal energy expenditure (before beginning the active arousal phase of torpor) (Ortmann et al., 1997).

At RNP, we searched extensively for the location of hibernating animals, scanning trees for hollows and gently poking sticks into tree holes. But we never discovered seasonally torporing animals in this manner. However, while radiotracking F19 in the austral spring of 1994, we found that her body mass jumped to 61 g suggesting impending seasonal hibernation. Indeed, while in the leaf nests that she occupied, she slept deeply but did not remain in the same location; over the course of approximately one month, she switched between four different nests located at a distance of 14–120 m from each other. These observations suggested that mouse lemurs at RNP used a combination of tree holes and leaf nests during seasonal torpor, moving between them during periodic arousals.

THE EFFECTS OF TRAPPING

Trapping was an exceptionally useful method for gathering data at RNP on brown mouse lemur diet, body mass, activity levels, social organization, and reproduction. However, stress and duration within the trap without food may influence the body mass of small mammals (Kaufman and Kaufman, 1994). The extent of loss is dependent on age, sex, reproductive condition, season, precipitation, and temperature. Beach mice (*Peromyscus polionotus phasma* and *P. p. niveiventris*) trapped for three consecutive days lost an average of 4% of their initial body mass on the second day and 8% on day three (Suazo et al., 2005). At RNP, similar trends in body mass reduction among the animals in the sample population were not noted perhaps because mouse lemurs are larger and have the advantage of daily torpor, a factor that may minimize the influence of trap capture. Moreover, at RNP, body mass and tail circumference data for mouse lemurs that experienced repeat monthly captures were averaged to minimize the effect of chance fluctuations in the values measured for each individual.

Researchers at other study sites have used precalibrated, temperature-sensitive transmitters to serve as permanent identifiers of trapped mouse lemurs (Ortmann et al., 1996; Schmid, 1996; Heldmaier et al., 2004). The use of this technique requires special training because the transmitter must be implanted into the abdominal cavity while mouse lemurs are under deep anesthesia. The transmitters replace the need for ear notches, which are nevertheless very small. However, notches, with time, heal over making identification difficult. Transmitters have another advantage, in that they provide easy long-term recording of body temperatures, which I found could not be taken reliably using an ordinary rectal thermometer.

SUGGESTED DIRECTIONS FOR FUTURE STUDIES

Small mammals use torpor in anticipation of seasonal stresses. But, why do some individuals become torpid and others do not? The factors that influence different annual behaviors require further study through longitudinal monitoring of targeted individuals. Seasonal hibernation offers advantages during periods of resource dearth, but at the same time, there are risks that come from suspending activity. For instance, torpid mammals are less conscious of predatory risks, nor are they able to defend territories (French, 1992; Heldmaier et al., 2004). At the same time, the consequences of seasonal torpor on the dynamics of social relationships and the establishment of social organization remain unknown.

The striking seasonal changes in food intake of mammalian hibernators are associated with dramatic physical responses that remain to be explored. How do hibernators avoid the tissue damage that normally would result from lack of blood flow as a consequence of lowered heart rate and decreased blood pressure? In addition, fasting, decreased metabolism, and reduced body temperature lead to changes in the gastrointestinal tract, including notable decreases in intestinal mass and protein content, reduced intestinal cell proliferation, and decreased pancreatic exocrine function (Carey, 2005). The reduction in gastrointestinal tissue during hibernation benefits the hibernator because the mammalian intestine is an expensive organ to maintain energetically, but fasting also eliminates protective molecules such as antioxidants that are taken in through food putting the animal at risk for oxidative stress. Following hibernation, considerable energy is expended to restore gut mass, energy that could be directed toward reproduction, territorial defense, and so on. Feeding during periodic arousals would maintain the intestine closer to normal size, requiring less energy expenditure to return to normothermic levels. But for those individuals that arouse from hibernation periodically, little is known about their behavior. Do they, like echidnas, inspect the environment to determine the remaining length of the hibernation period (Nicol and Anderson, 2002)? Do they increase the number of arousals as the breeding season approaches? How does their behavior affect physical changes while they are hibernating? Why do they change hibernating sites during arousal? Do they engage in social interactions?

These and so many other complex and intriguing questions, including the study of the hormonal mechanisms and the genetic basis behind the physiology of hibernation, offer prospects for exciting and innovative research on mouse lemurs and other cheirogaleid species that hibernate.

SUMMARY

The data presented here document seasonal changes in body fat and activity levels in a rainforest species of mouse lemur through a long-term field study. Longitudinal data offered a rare look at temporal changes in specific individual mouse lemurs. Small-bodied mammals inhabiting a variety of environments, including tropical ones, undergo cyclical changes in thermoregulatory and metabolic behaviors that are related to maintaining energy balance during periods of seasonal climatic and resource stress. Among primates, only some members of the Cheirogaleidae enter periods of substantial seasonal fat increase followed by inactivity. In several species of mouse lemur, both daily torpor and photoperiodically driven seasonal rhythms in activity, metabolic rates, body temperatures, and body mass have been documented. Important energy savings are achieved through both daily torpor and seasonal hibernation, and these are valuable adaptations for survival under adverse conditions such as those presented during the dry season in varied Malagasy habitats. At RNP, body mass and tail circumference of mouse lemurs were seasonally influenced, but the effect depended on the individual's phase in the annual life cycle. At RNP, mouse lemurs faced environmental challenges during the dry season that spurred some individuals of both sexes to increase body mass by 15–91%, disappear during part of the dry season presumably to hibernate, and to reappear having lost 10–44% of body mass. Other mouse lemurs, predominantly male, continued to be trapped throughout the dry season. Many of these males were first-time captures and may have been migrating. Among mouse lemurs that underwent fattening in the first year of the study, some individuals were most likely adult. Some young individuals, the offspring of the most-recent breeding season, appeared to have hibernated the first year of their life, whereas others waited until the following year. The data also supported the presence of interannual variation in the behavior of the same adult individuals in response to seasonal environmental changes. Taken together, the observations suggest the occurrence of multiple seasonal behaviors or strategies for both males and females—a facultative heterothermy that is reflected through differences in age, social status, and individual reaction to resource and climatic conditions—indicating that mouse lemurs are not obligate hibernators. Male *M. rufus* emerged earlier from hibernation, and weighing more, than females that emerged on average seven weeks later. Males may need the additional active time for regressed testes to develop and to establish social hierarchy before the breeding season. Results from the study suggest that there are comparable temporal responses between dry and rain forest mouse lemur species. Nevertheless, there appears to be a great deal of flexibility in the expression of seasonal response among mouse lemur species, among populations of the same species when they experience different environments, between the sexes, and even within the same individual from year to year.

5

The Social Life of the Brown Mouse Lemur

SOCIALITY IN NOCTURNAL STREPSIRRHINES

At first glance, nocturnal strepsirrhines appear to lead solitary existences because they commonly forage alone and often shun group life. Primates, however, are social animals—even those species in which direct social encounters are relatively rare. Although many nocturnal primates are not found within cohesive social groups while active at night, their social life can be deciphered through an understanding of its social structure and social organization. *Social structure* has been defined as the composition of a group or population and the way that animals within the group distribute themselves in space, whereas *social organization* constitutes the sum total of social relations and interactions (van Schaik and van Hooff, 1983; Richard, 1985). The ways that animals meet their basic needs—including feeding, avoiding predators, and mating—are influenced by species-specific patterns of spatial distribution and social relationships (van Schaik and van Hooff, 1983). To understand these patterns is to understand the nuts and bolts of social life.

The social patterns of diurnal gregarious primate species have been extensively analyzed (e.g., Crook and Gartlan, 1966; Eisenberg et al., 1972; Clutton-Brock and Harvey, 1977a; Wrangham, 1980, 1987; Sussman and Kinzey, 1984; Terborgh and Janson, 1986; Dunbar, 1988). However, until recently, sociality in nocturnal nongregarious species has been only incompletely researched, in part because social interactions are frequently temporally and spatially displaced, with animals commonly communicating through scent-marking and vocalizations (Sterling and Richard, 1995). Dispersed social networks, typical of nongregarious primates, combined with nocturnal conditions and solitary foraging habits, make observation of interactions between individuals a challenge (Eisenberg et al., 1972; Bearder, 1987; Martin, 1995). Despite these constraints, in recent years there has been a veritable explosion in research on nocturnal strepsirrhines. Evidence now shows that despite their outwardly isolationist habits, nocturnal primates often engage in rich social associations. Through the significant efforts that have been made toward clarifying their complex social patterns, we now have an improved understanding of the social relationships between the sexes as well as more accurate descriptions of the spatial distribution and composition of populations.

Research into nocturnal social life has been carried out with varied methodologies, including radiotracking, trail censusing, trapping, genetic analyses, and investigation of daytime sleeping groups. Patterns of spatial distribution and social relations have been studied by investigating the way that home ranges among and between the sexes are shared, the frequency that individuals are seen in proximity to others, the number and sex of individuals sharing daytime sleeping nests, and dispersal patterns, in the tarsier (*Tarsius*—MacKinnon and MacKinnon, 1980; Nietsch and Niemitz, 1992; Gursky, 1995), bushbabies (*Galago*—e.g., Charles-Dominique, 1972, 1978; Bearder and Doyle, 1974; Doyle, 1974; Clark, 1978, 1985; Harcourt and Nash, 1986b; Nash and Harcourt, 1986), the aye-aye (*Daubentonia madagascariensis*—Sterling, 1993a,b; Sterling and Richard, 1995), the sportive lemur (*Lepilemur*--Warren, 1994), the fork-marked lemur (*Phaner*—Schülke, 2005), Coquerel's dwarf lemur (*Mirza coquereli*—Pagès, 1980; Kappeler, 1997a), the fat-tailed dwarf lemur (*Cheirogaleus medius*—Müller, 1998, 1999a; Fietz, 1999a,b), and mouse lemurs (*Microcebus*—e.g., Martin, 1972b, 1973; Barre et al., 1988; Pagès-Feuillade, 1988; Radespiel et al., 1998; Fietz, 1999c; Atsalis, 2000; Radespiel, 2000; Schwab, 2000; Wimmer et al., 2002; Weidt et al., 2004; Dammhahn and Kappeler, 2005).

The wealth of information now available on the social life of nocturnal primates has made abundantly clear that each nocturnal species studied is remarkable and different in its own way. Nocturnal primates are neither uniform in their social behavior, nor are they always particularly solitary. Among nocturnal species, the spectral tarsier, *T. spectrum*, exhibits substantial gregariousness relative to other nocturnal primates including other tarsier species. Studied extensively on the island of Sulawesi, spectral tarsiers were found to spend over a quarter of the night in close proximity to other individuals (Gursky, 2002b). Vocalizations drew the family group to the nest at the end of the night (Nietsch and Niemitz, 1992; Gursky, 1997). Food distribution figured importantly in the high degree of sociality exhibited by this species; tarsiers tended to be more gregarious

Author walks along steep trails surrounded by dense vegetation in RNP

when insects were plentiful (Gursky, 2002b). They were also more social when young infants needed protection from the infanticidal tendencies of other tarsiers (Gursky, 2002b). And, lastly, social contact increased when predators were near (Gursky, 2002b). In short, this nocturnal primate was gregarious for the same reasons that have been put forth to explain sociality in diurnal primate species.

Malaysian slow lorises, *Nycticebus coucang coucang*, were found to live as adult pairs with their young, maintaining dispersed distribution and found within 20 m from each other in only 8% of observations (Wiens and Zitzmann, 2003). The Asian Mysore slender loris, *Loris lydekkerianus lydekkerianus*, engaged in gregarious social behavior interacting frequently with the opposite sex, as well as with young during the night (Nekaris, 2001). Spending 10–20% of its time with other animals (Nekaris, 2000), this species extended its social period by frequently forming daytime "sleeping ball congregations" (Nekaris, 2003).

In mainland Africa, the large males of the bushbaby, *Galago moholi*, were dominant, territorial, and responsible for the majority of copulations (Martin and Bearder, 1979; Pullen et al., 2000). Males increased their ranges to find more mates, yet they did not have exclusive access to females (Martine and Bearder, 1979; Pullen et al., 2000). In another African nocturnal primate, *Perodicticus potto*, more social interactions than expected were maintained through a high degree of home-range overlap (Pimley et al., 2002), with conspecifics spending 22% of observations within 20 m from each other (Pimley et al., 2005). Pottos associated in male–female pairs, engaging in many social interactions of nonsexual nature and occasionally sleeping together (Pimley et al., 2005).

Among the nocturnal lemurs of Madagascar, the social organization of the aye-aye was found to be more complex than originally thought because the occurrence of animals feeding together was higher than expected for a solitary animal (Sterling and Richard, 1995; Sterling, 2003). Males participated in many more affiliative and aggressive interactions than did females (Sterling and Richard, 1995), and their home ranges overlapped greatly, more so than those of females (Sterling, 1993b).

Within the family Cheirogaleidae, dwarf lemurs, despite their long absence from active life when hibernating, are able to maintain social ties. At least one species studied, *C. medius*, maintained family groups consisting of a bonded pair accompanied by the offspring of several breeding seasons (Müller, 1998, 1999a,b,c; Fietz, 1999a,b; Fietz et al., 2000). Dwarf lemurs are among the few primates that live as monogamous pairs (Müller and Thalmann, 2000), which are thought to be permanently bonded (Fietz, 2003a). Pairs actively defended the boundaries of their territories, with males and females taking turns protecting infants that remained in nest holes for the first two weeks of their life (Müller, 1998; Fietz, 1999b; Fietz, 2003a). Pair-bonded males, however, engaged in extra-copulatory activities; genetic analyses revealed an unusually high percentage of young sired by neighboring male members of other pair bonds (Fietz, 2003a). Females typically raised their offspring together, and offspring left the family in the second year of their life (Fietz, 2003a). Surplus males, called floaters, which were reproductively suppressed, were not able to find mates but instead roamed within large ranges that overlapped those of other floaters as well as the territories of family groups (Fietz, 2003a). Because active social life is interrupted annually by prolonged hibernation, there remains the question of how family cohesion is maintained. *C. medius* used the same nest for more than one season, with members of family groups commonly sleeping together (Müller, 1999b). It may be that through their daytime sleeping associations, family groups maintain close social cohesion, thus reestablishing active social contact following emergence from hibernation.

The fork-marked lemur, another cheirogaleid, also lives in pair bonds. These lemurs were found to spend the majority of the night alone, but they maintained contact with their pair-bonded mate through vocalizations, and they engaged in conflicts with other pairs over access to the exudate trees that served as their main dietary resource (Schülke, 2003, 2005). Sportive lemurs, too, are solitary foragers, but the few species studied appeared to live in monogamous pairs (Ganzhorn and Kappeler, 1996; Thalmann, 2001; Thalmann and Ganzhorn, 2003). *Mirza coquereli*, a close relative of the mouse lemur, lives in matrilinear clusters maintained through female philopatry. Members of clusters actively defended territorial borders (Kappeler, 1997a, 2003; Kappeler et al., 2001, 2002).

Most of the currently recognized species of mouse lemur have not been studied. Research has shed light on the social patterns of *Microcebus ravelobensis* and *M. berthae*, but it is the grey mouse lemur that has been the focus of most studies. This species has been studied at several different locations where it naturally resides. Along with captive studies, an impressively informed picture of the social organization of this small nocturnal primate has unfolded. Grey mouse lemurs are said to be promiscuous (Fietz, 1999c; Radespiel, 2000; Schmelting et al., 2000), living in multimale–multifemale communities with considerable home-range overlap between the sexes and with males competing fiercely for fertile females (Barre et al., 1988; Pagès-Feuillade, 1988; Radespiel, 2000; Andrès et al., 2001; Radespiel, Ehresmann, et al., 2001). Captive research revealed that high-ranking males enjoyed significantly more success in siring litters (Andrès et al., 2001), and because female grey mouse lemurs were dominant over males (Radespiel and Zimmermann, 2001a), female aggression was probably associated with mate choice (Andrès et al., 2001). In the wild, females formed stable matrilinear social cores within which home ranges overlapped extensively (Radespiel, 2000; Radespiel, Sarikaya, et al., 2001). Grey mouse lemurs were found sleeping in tree holes, females choosing ones with better insulation than those selected by males (Radespiel et al., 1998; Lutermann and Zimmermann, 2001). Whereas males frequently snoozed alone, related females slept communally and raised their young ones together making sleeping group an essential unit of social life (Radespiel et al., 1998; Fietz, 1999c; Radespiel, 2000; Eberle and Kappeler, 2003, 2007).

Microcebus ravelobensis, too, was discovered to be promiscuous exhibiting high inter- and intrasexual home-range overlap, but in contrast to *M. murinus* and *M. berthae*, males did not increase their home ranges during the mating season (Weidt et al., 2004). As with grey mouse lemurs, sleeping associations were stable suggesting that individuals may be related (Weidt et al., 2004). Members even moved together to new sites

(Weidt et al., 2004). Females are philopatric, with female offspring settling close to their mothers (Radespiel, Ehresmann, et al., 2003). In nests, this species was found in large groups of variable sex composition, sleeping together (Weidt et al., 2004). In contrast to *M. murinus*, in which males mostly slept alone and females slept with conspecifics, in *M. ravelobensis*, there was no significant difference between genders in sleeping habits; both sexes slept in groups, often in mixed company (Radespiel, Ehresmann, et al., 2003). Overall, *M. ravelobensis* was found to sleep in groups more frequently than did *M. murinus* (Radespiel, Ehresmann, et al., 2003). Animals even waited for each other outside the nest and filed in together (Weidt et al., 2004). Differences in sleeping arrangements may support the coexistence of sympatric *M. murinus* and *M. ravelobensis* at Ampijoroa (Rendigs et al., 2003).

In *M. berthae*, during the mating season, large home ranges of males compared with those occupied by females suggested that males were competing for access to mates (Schwab, 2000; Schwab and Ganzhorn, 2004; Dammhahn and Kappeler, 2005). Male ranges overlapped those of several females but also those of several males, whereas female ranges did not overlap each other as much (Dammhahn and Kappeler, 2003). Though the animals sometimes slept together, more commonly they slept alone. Overall, this species is considered to be less social than other mouse lemurs because sleeping associations did not usually consist of genetically related individuals, established matrilines were not found, and the frequency of social contact at night was rare (Schwab, 2000; Dammhahn and Kappeler, 2005).

In short, considerable strides have been made in understanding the social organization of mouse lemurs. Mouse lemur species exhibit variety in their social life and the newly discovered taxonomic diversity among them highlights the need for detailed comparative studies. Perceived differences in past reports on behavior between different mouse lemur populations may now reflect actual interspecies differences and variability (Martin, 2002). Taken together, behavioral studies on mouse lemurs reveal some intriguing interspecific differences and generate many questions that remain to be investigated. Equally exciting is the prospect of new discoveries on social behavior from the large number of mouse lemur species that have not been studied. New discoveries on these species in conjunction with additional studies on other nocturnal primate taxa, promise to continue transforming the way we understand nocturnal primate social life.

Whereas there is a great deal of variability in the manifestation of social indicators among nocturnal primates, a review of available data suggested that dispersed multimale–multifemale social networks or dispersed family groups (associated with monogamy) were the prevailing social systems among nocturnal strepsirrhines (Müller and Thalmann, 2000). Because the former pattern is common among cheirogaleids and other nocturnal strepsirrhines (taxa sometimes considered to be the most primitive of primates), the multimale–multifemale social pattern based on promiscuous mating was proposed as the ancestral one for primate social organization (Müller and Thalmann, 2000). Thus, the study of nocturnal strepsirrhine social life can lead to important insights in our understanding of the evolution of primate social life.

INVESTIGATING SOCIAL ORGANIZATION IN THE BROWN MOUSE LEMUR

In this chapter, I discuss social structure and organization in the brown mouse lemur by presenting information on spatial distribution of individuals and their degree of solitary behavior. Moreover, with data covering more than one year, it was possible to monitor seasonal changes in population composition.

To investigate the occurrence of social interactions in the brown mouse lemur, we examined data from observations during nocturnal walks, radiotracking, and daytime sleeping associations. The frequency that mouse lemurs were seen within 10 m from other mouse lemurs during the total number of hours that were spent in trail censusing during nocturnal walks was calculated. Visibility beyond 10 m was often compromised by rain, fog, and density of vegetation. We followed radiocollared individuals, recording their activities and the frequency of social interactions. Sleeping associations were investigated by searching for leaf nests in the daytime (for description of nests, see Chapter 4), and counting the number of animals that appeared at or exited from the nest entrance at dusk.

Data gleaned from the year-round mark–recapture schedule of trapping were used to infer patterns of intra- and intersexual spatial distribution, patterns of monopolization of females by males, and seasonal changes in population composition. The main hypothesis with respect to trapping was that if multiple individuals were captured in the same trap location, their ranges probably overlapped.

For information on intra- and intersexual spatial overlap and spatial monopolization of females by males, the number of mouse lemurs captured at each trap site and the number of different males and females captured at each trap site (individual trap sex ratio) were determined. The number of different trap sites in which individual mouse lemurs were captured, the frequency of capture for each individual, and the frequency of capture for males and females in total were also determined and compared.

Spatial overlap between the sexes, which influences the degree that males can monopolize females, was also checked by establishing the number of males that were captured in traps where females also had been captured. An association index between sexes was calculated using the formula: $AI = a/[a + 0.5(b + c)]$, where a is the number of traps with males and females, b is the number of traps with males only, and c is the number

RNP guides, Raliva Pierre, Jean-Marie, Rakotoniaina Le Jean, Ratalata François (from left to right) waiting for the rain to cease before venturing into the forest to search for mouse lemurs and to set live-traps

of traps with females only (adopted from Radespiel, Ehresmann, et al., 2001, as per Dice, 1945). The index ranges from 0 (sexes never associated) to 1 (sexes always associated). If males were monopolizing females, we expected the index to be low indicating that sexes rarely associated. A high index would indicate that sexes associated frequently.

To compare how spatial distribution of males and females changed as a result of life-history events associated with mating, trap data were analyzed based on totals over the study period and then by comparing male to female individuals trapped within three periods: July–August, September–October, and November–December. To examine access of males to potential mates, I determined the number of females accessible to each male in each period. July–August covered the period before the onset of the mating season when some individuals of both sexes were hibernating and then when some of the inactive males became active. September–October covered the period marked by the onset of the mating season. Because the majority of females captured in November were already gestating, the third period included gestation and birth events. Mouse lemurs were counted once per period. Newly independent young began appearing in the traps in January. Because they were considered adult by three months and were able to mate in the first year of their life, animals captured between July and December were considered reproductively active adults.

Among mammals, males tend to disperse whereas females are usually philopatric (Greenwood, 1980), an observation that is generally true for primates (Pusey and Packer, 1987; Johnson, 1988) and for strepsirrhines specifically (Waser and Jones, 1983). Information from live-trapping has been used to infer migration activity in small, nocturnal, solitary mammals (Gaines and McClenaghan, 1980), including some nocturnal strepsirrhines (e.g., Clark, 1978; Harcourt and Nash, 1986b; Nash and Harcourt, 1986; Bearder, 1987). In bushbabies, dispersal was inferred by comparing the patterns of change in male and female membership in the population (Harcourt and Nash, 1986b; Nash and Harcourt, 1986). In his pioneering work, Martin (1972a, 1973) suggested that grey mouse lemurs migrated in and out of the population. Biased sex ratios, said to be associated with male dispersal patterns, have been documented for M. *murinus* (Martin, 1972b; Fietz, 1998; Schmid and Kappeler, 1998; Radespiel, 2000; Wimmer et al., 2002), M. *berthae,* (Dammhahn and Kappeler, 2003), and M. *rufus* (Harcourt, 1987; Wright and Martin, 1995; Atsalis, 1999b, 2000). In small nonprimate mammals, dispersal is dependent on season, density, and life-history events (Lidicker, 1985; Gaines and Johnson, 1987). Given these observations, I hypothesized that the continued activity reported for males in the heart of the dry season was the result of male migration (Harcourt, 1987).

To investigate the possibility that male brown mouse lemurs may be migrating in or out of the population and to evaluate the degree of continuity in the composition of this population of brown mouse lemurs, trap data were divided into four periods to compare changes in population composition. The periods corresponded to natural phases in the annual mouse lemur life cycle (February–May 1993, June–August 1993, September 1993–January 1994, and February–May 1994). In the first and fourth, young mouse lemurs from the year's breeding season, distinguishable from older ones because of their lower body weight, made their appearance in the traps, whereas other males and females underwent seasonal fattening in preparation for hibernation (see Chapter 4). In the second period, some individuals hibernated (June–August), whereas others, predominantly male, continued to be active. Some of the males emerged from hibernation in August. The third period included the mating season when females were in estrus, gestating or lactating, and males exhibited testicular enlargement (Chapter 6).

To check for patterns of change in male and female membership in the population, monthly trap sex ratios of all captured males and females as well as monthly trap sex ratios of new, previously uncaptured males and females were compared. Given the generally philopatric nature of female mammals, it was hypothesized that, at RNP, female brown mouse lemurs would exhibit greater stability in the population than would males. If males were the dispersing sex, then fewer of the males marked and captured in the first period of the study would be expected to be recaptured in the last period. To check for patterns of change in male and female membership in the trap population, the number of individual males to individual females (e.g., not the total number of captures that were male but the number of different male individuals) captured in all traps (Sex Ratio 1), and the number of new, previously uncaptured males to previously uncaptured females (Sex Ratio 2) were compared across the four periods. Each individual was counted once per period.

To examine continuity in the composition of the trap population, I compared the percentage of individual males and individual females that remained the same between the first and the fourth periods because these periods were identical in terms of annual life cycle. To compare the data, differences in monthly trap effort were accounted for by calculating the average number of individual males (ANM) and the average number of individual females (ANF) captured nightly in each period. Differences in capture rate of male and female individuals between the first and the fourth periods were investigated by comparing the ANM and ANF captured nightly in all traps.

In June, August, and September a number of newly captured individuals remained unmarked, and therefore they could not be identified when they were recaptured. Based on the location of capture, unmarked individuals were estimated to be three to fourteen males and one to four females, one to five males, and one to three males, respectively for each month. These estimates were not included in analyses or figures. They are noted here to indicate that for June, August, and September, the number of captured individuals included in analyses and figures was underestimated. Conversely, some of these individuals may appear as unknown ones later, overestimating results in later months.

SOCIAL INTERACTIONS OF THE BROWN MOUSE LEMUR

Nocturnal walks, which were described in Chapter 2, lasted between forty minutes and five hours. During 75 walks, totaling 230 hours, we encountered mouse lemurs on 342 occasions. The vast majority of sightings were of lone individuals, that is, no other mouse lemur was seen simultaneous to the first sighting. Two or more mouse lemurs were seen within 10 m from each other only thirty-three times. On four occasions, mouse lemurs were seen in close affiliative contact, either allogrooming or sitting adjacent to each other. On two other occasions, pairs consisting of an adult and a young mouse lemur were observed. Both occasions occurred in April, when one would expect to see newly independent young; in one case, the two were foraging together with another individual nearby. During nocturnal walks, only once were mouse lemurs observed together for more than a few minutes. That occasion, which occurred in May, when young would be present, consisted of a long episode of proximity, lasting over fifty minutes, during which mouse lemurs remained within 24 cm from each other. One mouse lemur was clearly adult, but I could not see the other well enough to classify it. During this time, the two mouse lemurs moved together searching for insects in tangles of dry lianas, moving about in the trees, and once taking time to groom each other. At intervals, a third mouse lemur was seen within 10 m from these two.

On four occasions, peaceful triads were observed, but on a different occasion, a fight ensued between a third mouse lemur and a pair. Following the bout of aggression, the initial pair remained together. As with pairs, triads were observed in months when young mouse lemurs would be expected to be present. An aggressive interaction, during which an adult displaced a young individual through loud vocalizations and physical contact, occurred in April of one year. Because of that interaction, the younger individual finally fell off the branch.

Radiocollared individuals were tracked for 116 hours, during which time they were seen 478 times. For most of the time that mouse lemurs were tracked, only the radio signal could be heard. The subject was rarely seen. The majority of sightings, 405 in total, were on one of the radiotracked individuals, Male 22. While following three of the four other individuals, mouse lemurs were noted in proximity of less than 10 m to a conspecific in only two instances. One of these individuals was a mother of two. Although her offspring were seen playing and traveling together, she was never seen interacting with them in the seven hours that she was radiotracked.

Male 22, was radiotracked for a total of thirty-nine hours over the course of seven nights. Between the fourth and seventh night he remained within or in the vicinity of two flowering trees of *Dombeya hilsenbergii* and was located 0–10 m of other mouse lemurs for sixteen hours. While in the trees, mouse lemurs darted back and forth to feed on insects and plant foods (see Chapter 3 "Observations of Mouse Lemurs Feeding" for additional details of these nightly observations). Twenty-two interactions were observed between Male 22 and other mouse lemurs that visited the tree to feed, twenty-one of which were aggressive in nature, involving chases, vocalizations, and physical contact (two cases). Two bouts of vocalization were prolonged, lasting thirteen and seventeen minutes respectively. Not included in these data are several aggressive bouts with dwarf lemur individuals that also visited the two trees.

To describe nest associations, we located fifty-six nests, of which thirty-two were occupied at some point during our periodic checks. In 47% of occupied nests only one occupant was counted, 22% had two occupants, 16% had three, 9% had four, and 6% had five. Both nests with five occupants contained young mouse lemurs; in one nest we caught a glimpse of one youngster, whereas in the other we saw two. At least one adult was detected in each of these nests. Of the nests that contained four individuals, two were occupied by one adult with three young. All five nests with three occupants contained one adult and two young. Nests containing between three and five occupants were located during the months when young were expected to be present, between mid-January and mid-March. In double-occupant nests, individuals were identified as being adults in all cases with the exception of one. Male individuals were identified in two cases in the single occupant nests. In the remainder of cases, the sex and age of occupants could not be determined.

THE SOLITARY MOUSE LEMUR

Evidence from observations during nocturnal walks, radiotracking, and investigation of nest associations suggested that the brown mouse lemur displayed strong solitary tendencies. During this study, observations of social contact among mouse lemurs were rare. When mouse lemurs crossed paths in the forest, we observed that they did not react to each other, acting as though they were indifferent to each other's presence. How much of this tolerance was associated with the possible relatedness of individuals involved remains unknown. In general, it would seem that despite overlapping home ranges, the small size of mouse lemurs and their ability to use all heights of the forest allowed them to space themselves within the heterogeneous forest environment so that they could forage solitarily and cryptically.

Most interactions that my guides and I noted were aggressive in nature, with mouse lemurs becoming especially rowdy when competing for resources. Aggressive interactions involved boisterous behavior and loud vocalizations, which of course drew our attention to these kinds of behaviors as opposed to other social interactions that were potentially quieter and thus may have gone unnoticed. The most boisterous displays of aggressive behaviors occurred while radiotracking Male 22 (see Chapter 3). These observations took place between September 27 and October 6, within the mating season, a period when agonistic interactions associated with mating would be expected (Perret, 1992; Radespiel et al., 2002; Weidt et al., 2004). For instance, in M. ravelobensis only 16.8% of encounters were agonistic—chasing and fleeing—but they all occurred slightly before or during the mating season (Weidt et al., 2004). At RNP, although the sex of Male 22's competitors remained unknown, and even though the animals were clearly competing for food resources, the possibility of breeding-related competition can not be excluded. Competitive interactions may have been instigated by the presence of females, or as part of increased aggression because of mating-related hormonal changes (Andrès et al., 2001), or as a result of males increasing home-range size during the mating season (Radespiel, 2000).

While conducting nocturnal walks at RNP, brown mouse lemurs were seen within close proximity of another only fourteen times in 100 hours of walking, accounting for only 10% of sightings. That brown mouse lemurs at RNP were strongly solitary accords with other reports on this species. Kappeler (1997c, citing results from trail censusing conducted by Ganzhorn), reported that brown mouse lemurs were seen within 10 m from each other in only 6.2% of encounters. In another study, all but one of the encounters were of single animals, but at a second location about one-quarter of animals were seen in pairs (Duckworth et al., 1995). In Schwab's (2000) study at Kirindy, *M. berthae* individuals were seen in close proximity to another only 3.2 times per 100 hours. In another study, 7–8% of observations on this species were social (Dammhahn and Kappeler, 2005). *M. ravelobensis*, too, foraged mostly alone (Weidt et al., 2004). In one study on feeding behavior, focal females of *M. ravelobensis* were never seen sharing feeding plants. *C. medius*, known to live in pairs with young, was seen in proximity to others 11 times per 100 hours (Schwab, 2000), but *Phaner*, another pair-living cheirogaleid, spent 75% of nightly active time alone (Schülke, 2005).

Grey mouse lemurs may be among the most social of mouse lemurs studied. They were seen in close proximity to other conspecifics 96 times per 100 hours (Schwab, 2000), and female grey mouse lemurs were found frequently in close proximity at night (Radespiel, Ehresmann, et al., 2001). That grey mouse lemurs exhibited a relatively high degree of sociality compared to other mouse lemur species concurs with results from other sources of information regarding their social life. Compiled research, including genetic analyses based on microsatellite markers, confirmed what is often hypothesized for other nocturnal strepsirrhines: the presence of matrilinear groups found in dispersed spatial organizations (Radespiel, Sarikaya, et al., 2001). Given this information, it is not surprising that female grey mouse lemurs exhibited greater nest fidelity than males and slept communally in stable groups of related females, whereas males generally slept alone (Radespiel et al., 1998; Lutermann and Zimmermann, 2001).

What are the forces that favor the nongregarious nature characteristic of most nocturnal primates that live in dispersed networks, and the particularly solitary nature of *M. rufus*, *M. ravelobensis*, and *M. berthae*? Traditionally, it was thought that an insectivorous diet promoted solitary behavior (Crook and Gartlan, 1966; Eisenberg et al., 1972), but this is not always the case, as the aggregated abundance of some insects can influence the expression of sociality in a positive way. In the spectral tarsier, gregariousness increased when insects were abundant (Gursky, 2002b), and in the Mysore slender loris, the availability of superabundant ants, the dietary staple of this species, decreased competitive interactions (Nekaris, 2003; Nekaris and Rasmussen, 2003). The strong competition exhibited by Male 22 while feeding on plant and insect matter within flowering tree crowns suggested that brown mouse lemurs were not likely to share resources willingly, perhaps because adequate concentrations of their favorite foods were not common. Brown mouse lemurs fed selectively on high-quality foods, favoring fatty epiphytes and beetles. Overall, these foods were found in small, scattered patches more conducive to solitary than to gregarious feeding arrangements. For instance, we never saw more than one individual feeding in *Bakerella* patches.

Whereas mouse lemurs can be solitary when active at night, especially while foraging, they often sleep together in the daytime. Several reasons have been proposed to explain the gregarious nature of sleeping arrangements in mouse lemurs, including thermoregulatory benefits, ease of male access to fertile females, maintaining association with family, and antipredator advantages derived from concealment and superior predator detection (Martin, 1972a; Perret, 1998; Fietz, 1999c; Radespiel, 2000; Weidt et al., 2004). Sleeping associations are an essential component to maintaining mouse lemur social life. In one study, the temporal stability of sleeping associations, the associated vocalizations that called group members to the nest, and the behavior of meeting outside of the nest to file in together, suggested that mouse lemurs knew each other individually (Weidt et al., 2004). The need for warmth and social contact, both offered through communal sleeping, are not mutually exclusive and certainly energy-saving benefits can be derived while sleeping with potential partners or family members.

Social thermoregulation has been proposed to explain the evolution of sociality in some mammalian groups because it enhances social associations or acts as a reproductive strategy, where males associate with females with whom they plan to mate following hibernation (Arnold, 1993; Blumstein et al., 2004). The benefits of social thermoregulation—in association with hypothermia—have been put forth to explain successful long-distance migrations, such as the scenario that rafting on drifting vegetation from Africa was responsible for transporting the first primates to Madagascar (Martin, 1972a; Kappeler, 2000).

Large assemblages of sleeping mouse lemurs have been found at other sites (e.g., sixteen in one tree hole, Rasoazanabary, 2006). In comparison, at RNP, the groups we discovered were small. Given the frequent presence of young individuals in nests at RNP, it is likely that many sleeping groups represented mother–offspring associations. As a result of their small body size, mouse lemurs do not carry their young, which often include two or more in a litter, and they require nests to secure their young while they are foraging (Martin, 1972a). With mouse lemurs sexually maturing within the first year of their life, and with females entering hibernation during the dry season within a few months of weaning the young, the time spent together in the nest most likely figures importantly in parent–offspring social interactions.

Nocturnal strepsirrhines are generally thought to be cryptic in their habits. Because their small size makes them frequent targets of predators, they should behave inconspicuously in order to avoid predation (van Schaik and van Hooff, 1983). Indeed, mouse lemurs are at high risk of predation. Through studies based on bones recovered from owl pellets collected in areas across Madagascar, Goodman et al. (1993) estimated that up to 25% of a population may be eaten in a year by the barn owl (*Tyro alba*), and the long-eared owl (*Asio madagascariensis*)—a rate higher than that reported for other primates (Cheney and Wrangham, 1987). Given their vulnerability, the expectation is that mouse lemurs should behave cryptically to remain undetected not only by owls but by the other raptors, viverrids, and snakes that eat them (see Chapter 2). In support of this hypothesis, mouse lemurs at RNP were more frequently trapped in areas of dense plant growth such as in tangles of the invasive guava plant (Musto et al., 2005), and experimental set-ups at RNP have shown that brown mouse lemurs are wary of snakes, responding with flight or other fear reaction to a moving rubber snake (Deppe, 2005, 2006). However, as Kappeler (1997c) observed, mouse lemurs often eschew their secretive ways by vocalizing loudly—perhaps to maintain territorial boundaries or contact with other conspecifics. In addition, despite the risk of predation, at RNP, we observed individuals behaving in risky ways that would attract attention rather than avert it: animals sleeping in open leafy areas, lounging about while in a lethargic state, oblivious to commotion, vocalizing extensively while competing for resources, and emerging from nests at dusk when it was still light outside.

Undoubtedly, a constellation of causes, ecological and behavioral, influence the ways that social and solitary behaviors are expressed. Factors such as the distribution of food and shelter, local climate, the risk of predation, seasonal life-history events, activity patterns, social structure and organization, and finally the phylogenetic constraints imposed by small body size and nocturnality, all influence social expression. Comparative studies that include mouse lemurs, other cheirogaleids, and nonprimate nocturnal mammals, to probe further into behavioral differences can clarify specific causal relationships.

UNDERSTANDING SPATIAL DISTRIBUTION THROUGH TRAP DATA

Trap capture data and statistical tests are summarized in Table 5–1. To begin with, multiple mouse lemurs were captured in the vast majority of traps; with the exception of three traps that did not capture mouse lemurs and two in which only one individual was captured in each, in all others at least two different mouse lemurs were captured. On average, eight mouse lemurs were captured in each trap in the main trap area (MTA), but as many as 19 were captured in one of the traps (column 1, Table 5–1; Figure 5–1).

Traps differed in the number of males and females that they captured. In approximately 11% of traps only males were captured, whereas in approximately 4% (3.6%) of traps only females were captured. More males than

Table 5–1 Summary of Trap Results for *Microcebus rufus* in Ranomafana National Park

	Mean Number of Individual Mouse Lemurs Captured Per Trap	Mean Number of Traps Entered/ Individual	Mean Frequency of Trap Capture/ Individual
Males	5.5 (±3.4, 0–14, 57)	3.6 (± 2.9, 1–16, 87)	9.8 (±13., 1–81, 102)
Females	2.5 (±1.6, 0–7, 57)	2.4 (±1.9, 1–10, 57)	5.7 (±8.5, 1–54, 72)
Males and females	8 (± 4.5, 0–19, 57)	3.1 (±2.6, 1–16, 144)	na
Statistical tests comparing males to females	$t = 6.2, p < .05, DF = 81$	$t = 3.0, p < .05, DF = 142$	$t = 2.4, p < .05, DF = 170$

t— Student *t*-test; *p*—probability; DF—degrees of freedom; the values in the parentheses denote the standard deviation, range, and *N* respectively.

females were captured at approximately 85% of traps: on average 5.5 males to 2.5 females (column 1, Table 5–1). Though this difference was significant (column 1, Table 5–1), each trap was equally likely to capture males as females: that is, the probability of capturing a male or a female did not vary depending on trap location (chi-square test $\chi^2 = 43.7, p = .816, DF = 53$).

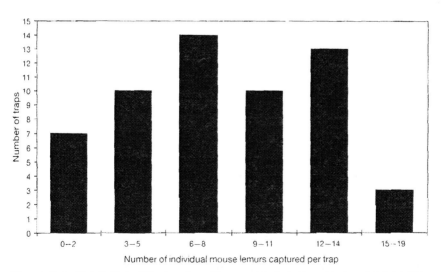

Figure 5–1 Distribution of the number of brown mouse lemurs captured at trap sites from February 1993 to May 1994, in Talatakely, RNP; for example, up to two mouse lemurs were captured in seven of the traps. (From Atsalis, 2000; reprinted with permission of Wiley-Liss, Inc., a subsidiary of John Wiley & Sons, Inc.)

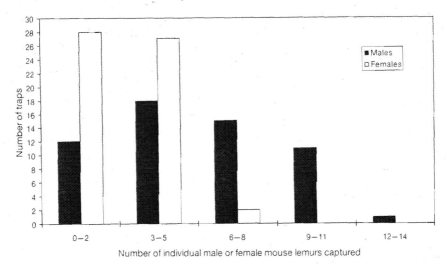

Figure 5-2 Distribution of the number of male and female brown mouse lemurs captured at trap sites from February 1993 to May 1994 in Talatakely, RNP; for example, up to two males were captured in 12 of the traps and up to two females were captured in 28 of the traps. (From Atsalis, 2000; reprinted with permission of Wiley-Liss, Inc., a subsidiary of John Wiley & Sons, Inc.)

Most traps captured three to five males. However, up to fourteen males were captured in one of the traps (Figure 5-2). No more than seven females were captured in any trap (column 1, Table 5-1; see also Figure 5-2).

The association index was 0.94 indicating a high degree of association between males and females (only traps where at least one mouse lemur was captured were included; $N = 55$). All but one of the males were captured in one or more traps where females were captured. Only one male was captured in a trap where no females had been captured.

Many mouse lemur individuals were captured in more than one trap (Figure 5-3). An individual mouse lemur in the MTA entered an average of 3.1 different traps (column 2, Table 5-1). Males were captured on average in 3.6 traps and females in 2.4 traps, a difference that was statistically significant (column 2, Table 5-1). Lastly, individual males entered traps more frequently than did females (Figure 5-4). An individual male mouse lemur entered a trap on average 9.8 times, whereas each female averaged 5.7 captures: a difference that was significant (column 3, Table 5-1).

CHANGES IN POPULATION COMPOSITION

Overall, more males were captured than females: 102 versus 72 (87 versus 57 in the MTA). The proportion of males captured over the course of the study period varied significantly ($\chi^2 = 72.39$, $p < .05$, DF $= 15$) (Figure 5-5). The number of males to females captured (Sex Ratio 1,

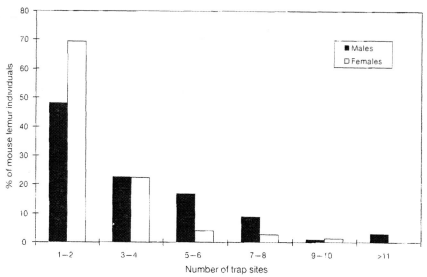

Figure 5–3 Percentage of male and female brown mouse lemurs captured and the number of different traps that they entered from February 1993 to May 1994 in Talatakely, RNP; for example, approximately 48% of males and 69% of females entered 1–2 traps. (From Atsalis, 2000; reprinted with permission of Wiley-Liss, Inc., a subsidiary of John Wiley & Sons, Inc.)

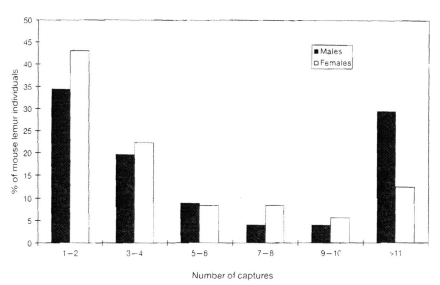

Figure 5–4 Percentage of male and female brown mouse lemurs captured and the number of times they entered traps from February 1993 to May 1994 in Talatakely, RNP; for example, approximately 34% of males and 43% of females entered traps only 1–2 times. (From Atsalis, 2000; reprinted with permission of Wiley-Liss, Inc., a subsidiary of John Wiley & Sons, Inc.)

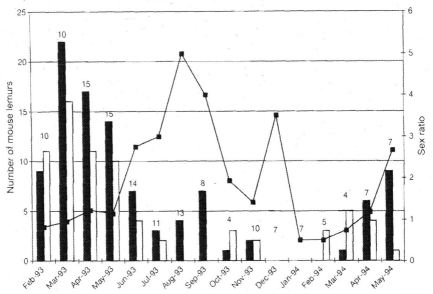

Figure 5–5 Trap results for brown mouse lemurs captured between February 1993 and May 1994 in Talatakely, RNP. Left y-axis (males shown by closed bars, females shown by open bars) is the monthly number of previously uncaptured males and previously uncaptured females. Right y-axis (line diagram) is the monthly sex ratio (total number of males captured to the total number of females captured). Previously uncaptured mouse lemurs were not trapped in December and January. Trap effort across months not equal; floating numbers above x-axis denote monthly number of trap nights. (From Atsalis, 2000; reprinted with permission of Wiley-Liss, Inc., a subsidiary of John Wiley & Sons, Inc.)

Figure 5–6) across the four designated periods also differed significantly ($\chi^2 = 12.75$, $p < .05$, DF $= 3$). The male bias in the sex ratio was highest in the second period. The increase was due, in part at least, to the greater number of previously uncaptured males than previously uncaptured females (see Figure 5–5; Sex Ratio 2, Figure 5–6) that entered the trap population although this proportion did not differ significantly across the four periods ($\chi^2 = 1.84$, $p = .05$, DF $= 3$). Within the second period, a minimum of fourteen previously uncaptured males compared with a minimum of six previously uncaptured females entered the trap population (in the MTA, the ratio was 11:3) (see Figure 5–5). Only the minimum number was determined because, as explained, a subset of newly captured individuals, were not included in the analyses because they had gone unmarked.

Within the fourth period, only 9.7% (6 of 62) of all male individuals captured originally in the first period were recaptured (11.3%, 6 of 53, in MTA). In comparison, 27%, or 13 of 48, of the original females were recaptured (28.9%, 11 of 38, in MTA). The capture rates of males and of females between the first and fourth periods did not differ because the ANM and ANF, captured nightly in the two periods, were not significantly different

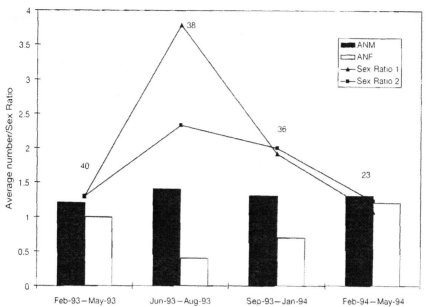

Figure 5–6 Average number of individual brown mouse lemur males (ANM) and average number of individual brown mouse lemur females (ANF) captured per night in each of four periods from February 1993 to May 1994 in Talatakely, RNP (see text for full explanation). Males shown by closed bars; females, by open bars. Closed-triangle line diagram represents the ratio of individual males to individual females captured (Sex Ratio 1). Closed-square line diagram represents the ratio of previously uncaptured males to previously uncaptured females (Sex Ratio 2). Trap effort across months not equal; floating numbers above x-axis denote monthly number of trap nights. (From Atsalis, 2000; reprinted with permission of Wiley-Liss, Inc., a subsidiary of John Wiley & Sons, Inc.)

(Student's t-Test $t = -.07, p = .9, \mathrm{DF} = 6$ for males; $t = -.6, p = .6, \mathrm{DF} = 6$ for females). These results suggest that over the course of the year, the female population was more stable than the male population, implying that females contributed more strongly to the continuity of the local population.

The continued presence of certain males and females in the trap area may indicate that these were "resident" members within the area. As an informal experiment, from August 1993 to the end of the study, two additional traps were placed at select trap site locations. I found that even within a single night, both traps could contain mouse lemurs, corroborating other trap results already described regarding overlap of ranges. The results from the experiment also hinted that new individuals attempted to establish themselves spatially among those already resident in the population; whereas some mouse lemurs were consistently captured, there were frequent changes in the identity of others trapped at the same location. At one site, a male that was captured throughout the duration of the study was trapped, on separate nights, with one of four other males and two females. By the end of the study, he continued to be trapped at this location with only one of the other males and one of the two females. These observations suggested that some individuals, at least, were able to establish themselves in areas where permanent residents already resided. Perhaps, as in *C. medius* (Fietz, 2003a), surplus individuals roamed the ranges of residents, attempting to establish their presence.

SEASONAL FLUCTUATIONS IN TRAP SEX RATIO

Although the evidence suggests that brown mouse lemurs have strong solitary tendencies, mating activities call for social interactions, which may result in changes in the spatial distribution between the sexes. At RNP, all but one of the males were captured in one or more traps where females were also captured, suggesting the occurrence of spatial overlap between male and female ranges. Moreover, with multiple males captured in the majority of trap sites, it would appear that male spatial use overlapped as well. Concurrently, multiple females were captured at the majority of trap sites, also reflecting shared spatial use, although the number of females captured at each trap was smaller than the number of males. Given the existence of intra- and intersexual spatial overlap, it seems unlikely that brown mouse lemurs at RNP were territorial or that males had exclusive access to females. Additionally, males were captured on average in more traps than were females suggesting that they were more active or had larger ranges within which to discover and enter more traps. Perhaps they roamed widely for access to females as in *M. murinus* and *M. berthae*, in which home ranges of both sexes overlapped extensively and males increased the size of their home ranges during the mating season, so that their ranges became larger than those of females (Barre et al., 1988; Pagès-Feuillade, 1988; Fietz, 1999c; Radespiel, 2000; Schwab, 2000; Eberle and Kappler, 2002).

Overall, judging by the number of multiple individuals captured at a majority of trap sites, there can be considerable spatial overlap in the distribution of brown mouse lemurs; approximately 70% of traps captured more than five individuals. By focusing on the interval from July to December, it became apparent that much of this overlap was seasonally biased (Figure 5–7). Between July and October, the number of females trapped doubled. The increase may have been the result of females that were becoming active following seasonal hibernation. The smaller increase in male captures could mean that more males than females remained active during the dry season and, therefore, had been trapped already. Thus, the trap sex ratio decreased in this interval, but not because of a smaller number of males present but rather because of more females being trapped. With the number of males also increasing, it was unlikely that males already present in the population were able to exclude the newcoming males.

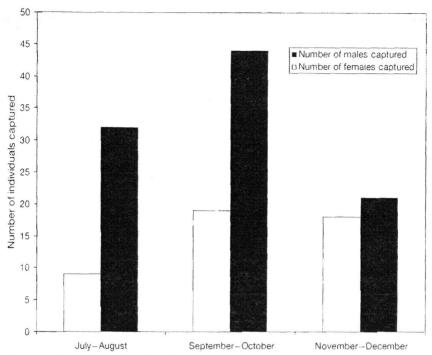

Figure 5–7 Number of individual brown mouse lemur male and female trap captures before the onset (July and August) and during the main part (September through December) of the breeding season in Talatakely, RNP. The majority of females captured in November were already gestating. December was a month of low trappability (seven males and two females captured).

The extremely seasonally biased male trap sex ratio was a significant finding at RNP. Previous short-term studies had reported a male bias occurring in Ranomafana; while trapping in June and July, Harcourt (1987) captured twenty-three males and five females, whereas Wright and Martin (1995) reported eighteen males and two females while trapping in September. These studies at RNP and others conducted elsewhere on the grey mouse lemur (Martin, 1972b; Harcourt, 1987; Fietz, 1998; Schmid and Kappeler, 1998; Radespiel, 2000) and on *M. berthae* (Dammhahn and Kappeler, 2003), where male bias has been observed too, took place almost entirely within the dry season (with the exception of the study by Schmid and Kappeler, 1998), and in the period either before, or within, the breeding season, that is, between June and December. Grey mouse lemurs exhibited a male-biased sex ratio in August but not in September and October, when more females were captured, leveling the inequality (Fietz, 1998). At RNP, more males than females were captured in the majority of traps and a high male bias was discovered between June and August, in the heart of the dry season. The bias continued into the mating and birthing season from September to December. Then, between February and May, the trap sex ratio changed dramatically again, with approximately equal numbers of both sexes trapped.

Biased birth sex ratios are known to occur in primates (Paul and Thommen, 1984; MacFarland Symington, 1987; Johnson, 1988), including captive *M. murinus* (Perret, 1990). In wild grey mouse lemurs, litters are often male-biased but the adult sex ratio is even (Eberle, personal communication, 2007). Similarly, at RNP, trap data reflected post-weaning sex ratio and not birth sex ratio. Furthermore, newly weaned young individuals appeared earlier than the June–September period when the highly biased sex ratio was noted.

Seasonal fluctuations in spatial use, even in the degree of exclusive use of home ranges, are common in small nonprimate nocturnal mammals such as voles, which have been studied extensively through mark–recapture (Ostfeld, 1990). Differential use of space by the sexes, as a result of seasonally differing life-history strategies, was displayed by mouse lemurs as well (see Chapter 4). In grey mouse lemurs, most adult males remained active while females hibernated between June and September (Schmid and Kappeler, 1998; Schmid, 1999; Rasoazanabary, 2006). In the brown mouse lemur, both males and females underwent seasonal fattening and entered hibernation, but the difference in the trap sex ratio between February–May and June–September indicated that more males than females remained active. I proposed that this difference was the result of male migration (see "Migration Patterns and Population Continuity," this chapter) (Atsalis, 2000). The biased sex ratio between August and October coincided with the onset of the breeding season when male mouse lemurs, like the males of other small mammals (e.g., jumping mice and woodchucks: *Zapus* and *Marmota*, respectively, Snyder et al., 1961; Godin, 1977), emerged from torpor earlier than females (see Chapter 4). Like grey mouse lemur males, in whom this also occurs (Perret, 1992; Fietz, 1998), brown mouse lemur males may be establishing breeding hierarchies before the emergence of females. The male bias in October and November, the main part of the breeding season, may be the result of highly active males in search of females in estrus.

The reasons behind the decline in male presence from December to February are unclear (see Figure 5–5). A similar situation was documented for *M. ravelobensis* in Ampijoroa in northwestern Madagascar during the rainy season, between November and April (Schmelting et al., 2000; Randrianambinina et al., 2003a,b); in this location, no animals were trapped in January and February but they continued to be sighted in the forest. Sympatric grey mouse lemurs also exhibited reduced trappability from January through March, although less dramatic than than what was noted in *M. ravelobensis* (Schmelting et al., 2000). In the spectral tarsier, which typically "parks" its offspring through the entire night by caching them in a tree, Gursky (2002a) discovered that mothers remained near their young during the early weeks of life. Although this is a plausible explanation for the reduced trappability of female brown mouse lemurs in December and January, which is the period when they would be giving birth and nursing their young, why male mouse lemurs would also avoid traps at this time remains to be discovered. There are no data to support that male mouse lemurs participate in infant care, and an alternative explanation whereby increased rainfall at RNP negatively affected trappability was not consistent with observations in March 1993 and March 1994, when both rainfall and number of individuals trapped were high.

MIGRATION PATTERNS AND POPULATION CONTINUITY

Ideally, the population captured through trapping represents the natural population at large, but in actuality, it represents only the trappable fraction. Capture in live-traps may create a male-biased sex ratio if males are more active than are females and/or have larger home ranges. In general, biased trap success may result in erroneous information concerning the age structure, sex ratio, and size of the population. Consequently, trap data are useful tools for investigating patterns of population change throughout the year rather than for describing exact population structure (O'Farrell et al., 1994). Moreover, with trapping, loss of individuals from

RNP guide Le Jean preparing to return a trapped brown mouse lemur at site of capture.

the trap population due to emigration is indistinguishable from the loss because of simple avoidance of traps (Branch et al., 1993). Furthermore, loss due to death and predation cannot be distinguished from emigration and trap shyness. Yet, patterns in the trap data, such as trends in the disappearance of a particular group from a population, can suggest a specific activity, such as emigration (Branch et al., 1993). In *Galago garnettii* (Nash and Harcourt, 1986) and *G. zanzibaricus* (Harcourt and Nash, 1986b), migration was inferred by the pattern of frequent change in the male population. Similarly, in brown mouse lemurs at RNP, the patterns in the appearance and disappearance of individuals differed between males and females. A subset of individuals of both sexes captured in the beginning of the study was not recaptured in the second year. The percentage of recaptured females was triple that of males, even though ANM and ANF remained at similar levels in these two periods. If new individuals were leaving the population but the rate of capture remained approximately the same, then the implication is that males and females replenished their numbers. Some of the new individuals entered the trap population between February and June of the second year, and their lighter body weight compared to average adult body weight signaled that they were the young from the year's breeding season (Chapters 4 and 6). Indeed, there was a natural break in the trap record between the time when new individuals (never trapped) ceased to be trapped in November 1993 and when new individuals began to be trapped once again in February 1994.

Between June and August, another pattern became clear: a difference in the number of previously uncaptured males compared with previously uncaptured females. Previously marked males were also active throughout this period, but the appearance of previously uncaptured individuals and the disappearance of known ones may be indicative of migration in and out of the population. Some of these second-period males were trapped only once, whereas others remained in the area into 1994. In particular, three of eleven male mouse lemurs captured new between June and August in 1993 continued to be present in the trap population in the last period of the study in 1994, perhaps establishing themselves as local residents.

Higher predation rates in males, because of their continued activity during the dry season, no doubt accounts for some of the loss in the male population. Predation on mouse lemurs is extremely high (Goodman et al., 1993). Indeed, research at Kirindy using a 9-year database on marked animals revealed that mean annual rate of mortality in adult females was 34%, climbing to 49% in adult males (Eberle and Kraus, personal communication, 2007). Predation episodes on mouse lemurs have been documented at RNP (Deppe et al., in prep), and given the Kirindy data, loss to predation assuredly is behind the lack of recapture of many of the subject animals in my study.

Predation notwithstanding, as with other small mammals (e.g., Fairbairn, 1977), the pattern of disappearance of male brown mouse lemurs from the particular study area at RNP, compared with that for females, may also be attributed to migration activity. Without excluding the possibility that some females migrated, the phenomenon of migration seems to be male biased. Female brown mouse lemurs contributed more strongly to population continuity than did males, and a larger percentage of females than of males appeared to be "resident." Yet, between June and September, more than twice the number of males than females was captured at the majority of trap sites. Given these observations, it appears that seasonally migrating males were partly responsible for the high degree of spatial overlap seen at RNP. Consequently, migration was a seasonal event that played an important role in influencing the composition and spatial distribution of the local population. Among male individuals that were trapped in the first period of the study in 1993 but were not retrapped in 1994, there were those whose trap history was very short and ended early in the study. Others continued to be trapped into the second period, but their trap history terminated in September, October, or November. Most females whose trap history did not continue into 1994 disappeared from the trap population early in 1993, but the fact that some males stayed in the area during part of the breeding season may reflect their attempts to compete for breeding rights.

The findings at RNP are comparable to those of other mouse lemur populations. Male dispersal has been proposed for *M. berthae* (Dammhahn and Kappeler, 2005) and documented for the grey mouse lemur (Radespiel, Sarikaya, et al., 2001; Wimmer et al., 2002). In *M. ravelobensis,* approximately twice as many known females as males were recaptured in the last year of the study (Weidt et al., 2004), suggesting that males had migrated out of the population. Martin (1972b), too, noted that female grey mouse lemurs marked in the first year of his study were still occupying the same area two years later. Genetic analyses revealed high diversity in Kirindy's grey mouse lemurs—especially in males—which was attributed to a high degree of population turnover due to male dispersal, predation, and a promiscuous mating system that sometimes resulted in litters of mixed paternity (Wimmer et al., 2002). Results from additional genetic analyses revealed that population turnover in the grey mouse lemur in Mahajanga, another west coast location, was also high; less than a third of the population was recaptured in one year, and less than half in another (Radespiel, Lutermann, et al., 2003). In this population, not all males dispersed, but only 11.5% of male offspring were present in their first mating season, as opposed to 58% of daughters.

As with other locations, including RNP, potential immigrants came into the population mostly before the mating season, giving them enough time to establish home ranges, assess resource availability, and search for mating opportunities. Genetic analyses confirmed that males sometimes migrated more than once in the six years of one study, occasionally returning to the vicinity of their natal area (Wimmer et al., 2002; Radespiel, Lutermann, et al., 2003). Therefore, male migration may constitute a significant source of gene flow in mouse lemur populations (Wimmer et al., 2002; Radespiel, Lutermann, et al., 2003).

Female dispersal is also possible. In one population of grey mouse lemurs, female dispersal was detected in 14% of cases (Radespiel, Lutermann, et al., 2003). Female dispersal from the natal region has been suggested for other cheirogaleids, *C. medius* (Müller, 1999b) and *M. coquereli* (Kappeler et al., 2002), in which male dispersal has been documented. In *M. coquereli*, the proportion of females recaptured after three years was three times higher than for males, yet both unmarked males and females continued to be captured for several years into the study, suggesting that emigration characterized both sexes (Kappeler et al., 2002). In addition to female dispersal, studies on mouse lemurs provided evidence that some males were sedentary, (whereas others moved over large distances), and that not all males dispersed upon reaching adulthood (Radespiel, Sarikaya, et al., 2001; Radespiel, Lutermann, et al., 2003). Wimmer et al., 2002). In fact, philopatry and dispersal could be facultative options for males (Kappeler et al., 2002). Mouse lemurs are able to reproduce within the first year of their life. So if dispersal occurs as a way to avoid the costs of inbreeding as has been suggested (Pusey and Packer, 1987), then we may expect frequent changes in the male mouse lemur population in order for males to avoid reproducing with their own daughters. Yet, even for those males that remain in the natal group, high predation rates and the presumably promiscuous mating system operate against inbreeding (Wimmer et al., 2002; Radespiel, Lutermann, et al., 2003).

In one important study on the genetic relationships of grey mouse lemurs at Kirindy, nineteen females were followed over three breeding seasons (Eberle and Kappeler, 2007; Eberle, personal communication, 2007). The females formed eight different clusters, with mother-daughter pairs and sisters forming the majority of clusters. Female offspring stayed with the mother, while males dispersed, doing so before reaching maturity. Having dispersed, males often remained in their new location for years. Taken together the various lines of evidence strongly support the proposal that females form the stable core of populations in several species of mouse lemur. As the philopatric sex, females contribute to population continuity despite occasionally dispersing themselves, and female philopatry is at the core of matriline formation.

Many years ago, Martin (1972a, 1973) proposed that grey mouse lemurs lived in concentrations of female-biased resident populations (population nuclei) with central males encompassing the ranges of several females and where excess males settled in the periphery (Martin, 1972a, 1973). Applying genetic analyses has clarified the intrapopulational relationships of mouse lemurs, confirming the presence of concentrations of closely related females in the grey mouse lemur (Wimmer et al., 2002), which has been suggested by other studies as well (Radespiel 2000; Radespiel, Ehresmann, et al., 2001; Eberle and Kappeler, 2007). Indirect support for this claim comes from Radespiel (2000), who discovered that female grey mouse lemurs associated in temporally stable sleeping groups, and Wimmer et al. (2002) pointed out that the presence of closely related female clusters, or matrilines, was typical of other mammals that exhibited female philopatry. Yet, results from some studies on mouse lemur populations has revealed a high degree of intersexual spatial overlap, which seemed to preclude the presence of spatial clustering of one or the other sex (Harcourt, 1987; Barre et al., 1988; Pagès-Feuillade, 1988; Radespiel, 2000). At RNP, trap data also did not reflect a spatial configuration consistent with the presence of clusters of females and clusters of males. One explanation for the varied findings may rest in the different methodologies applied. For instance, only studies using advanced technologies, such as genetic analyses, are sufficiently refined to determine relatedness among clusters of trapped individuals. Additionally, populations may vary in how they are spatially organized depending on local ecologies.

While there may be a tendency to apply findings from one species of mouse lemur to all mouse lemurs, only additional studies using similar methods will reveal the true commonalities among species and populations. At RNP, the bulk of available data on the brown mouse lemur support conclusions regarding the social organization and structure found for other mouse lemur populations, pointing to a solitary species that lives in a dispersed multimale–multifemale system in which most females are philopatric and males migrate.

POPULATION RESIDENTS

Trap data at RNP were not analyzed to determine home-range sizes. Nevertheless, graphical representation of spatial relationships among mouse lemurs can illuminate how individuals share space. By way of example, I show the spatial distribution of select, resident mouse lemurs based on their location of trap capture (Figure 5–8). In this graphical depiction, male ranges overlap each other more than the ranges of females. Generally, the ranges of males appear larger although they vary widely in size: M9, M11, and M16 were trapped within much larger areas than M26, M40, and M69. Likely, this result was not associated with frequency of capture because with the exception of M69, an individual that was captured only five times, the other males were trapped between twenty-one and fifty-five times over the course of the study period, yet their ranges never increased. Generally, females were trapped in a narrower range than were males. As with males, these results were not associated with frequency of capture.

The ranges of the majority of selected males overlapped, to some degree, with at least one other male. M16, whose range was large and relatively

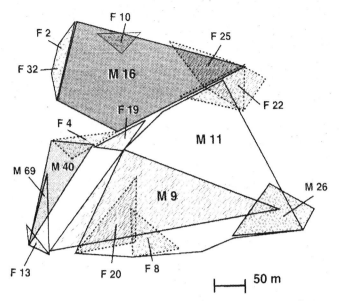

Figure 5–8 Spatial distribution of resident brown mouse lemur males (M16 etc) and resident brown mouse lemur females (F10 etc) based on locations of trap capture in Talatakely, RNP Female trap ranges shown dotted, male ranges are solid. The map was originally hand-drawn and scale is approximate.

exclusive of other males, was the only exception. With the exception of some females, such as F10 and F13, the ranges of other females overlapped each other to some degree despite their small size. Lastly, the ranges of males and females overlapped. Each male, with the exception of M26, was in contact with at least two females. The range of M16 overlapped that of six females, and for three of these females, F2, F10 and F32, he was the only resident male captured in their area. His large, relatively exclusive range and association with many females may indicate a male of high status.

SCRAMBLE AND CONTEST COMPETITION

Of late, considerable attention has focused on the nature of male–female relationships among mouse lemurs and on addressing the question of how males gain access to females. Understanding how the sexes distribute themselves spatially, particularly during the mating season, provides clues to how they interact socially. It is commonly held that males and females should distribute themselves in space according to the location of resources, and with the intention of avoiding predators (Clutton-Brock and Harvey, 1977a, 1978). The accepted reasoning is that fertile females constitute a "resource" to which males must gain access in order to reproduce successfully (Trivers, 1972; Emlen and Oring, 1977). For males, females are a "limited" resource because having conceived, females are for a period of time no longer available for breeding. As a consequence, males will compete for females, distributing themselves in space according to female location (Trivers, 1972). When competition among males commonly occurs through physical contact, called *contest* competition, sexually dimorphic traits, such as large body size and canines, will evolve (van Hooff and van Schaik, 1992). Through "contest," males attempt to monopolize as many females as they can, a strategy which may result in the formation of the polygynous mating system often observed in diurnal primate species (Clutton-Brock, 1989). An alternative strategy, called *scramble* competition, usually occurs when females are spatially dispersed, challenging male ability to monopolize them (Clutton-Brock, 1989). Under these circumstances, a multimale–multifemale promiscuous mating system may evolve in which males are not dimorphic. Male competition is manifested through superior skills in locating females and through sperm competition by which large testes produce copious amounts of sperm (Harcourt et al., 1981). As more than one male can mate with the same female, the increased volume of sperm enhances chances at fertilization.

To demonstrate strong contest competition, dominance and reproductive success in mouse lemurs should be correlated with rank: high-ranking males would be expected to sire more offspring than subordinate ones. Results from one captive study on grey mouse lemurs, however, indicated that there was no correlation between dominance and number of offspring produced, supporting that contest competition is not what drives male reproductive success (Radespiel et al., 2002). In contrast, other captive studies have revealed that intense sexual competition can arise between males for priority of access to females in estrus (Andrès et al., 2001), with males establishing dominance hierarchies before mating (Perret, 1992) and older males exerting dominance over younger ones (Radespiel et al., 2002). Spurred on by the presence of females, males in one study exhibited a great deal of aggression (Andrès et al., 2001). High-ranking males exhibited greater frequency of marking and chemosensory investigation of females (Andrès et al., 2001), whereas components in their urine inhibited sexual development of subdominant males (Perret and Schilling, 1995). Notably, a robust relationship was found between male rank and reproductive success (thirty-three of thirty-five offspring produced were sired by the highest-ranked males; Andrès et al., 2001). Female choice also played a role in mating (Andrès et al., 2001). Not surprisingly, because mouse lemur females are dominant over males (Kappeler, 1996a), highest-ranking males were attacked less frequently by females during sexual solicitations, and older females exerted the most control over choice of sexual partners (Andrès et al., 2001). Females strongly preferred males that showed a high frequency of trill mating advertisement calls (Craul et al., 2003).

In the wild, heavier males were found closer to females during the mating season, supporting the claim that contest competition occurs in mouse lemurs (Fietz, 1998). However, in the wild, males have not been found to monopolize females as would be the case through contest competition. Moreover, mouse lemurs have larger testes than expected based on body size, with the smallest living primate, M. *berthae*, exhibiting the largest relative testicular size of all primates (Harcourt et al., 1981; Kappeler, 1997b; Fietz, 1999c; Schwab, 2000). Additional evidence, including data from RNP, points to males that engage in scramble competition: the presence of new males migrating into the population and a high degree of male home-range overlap (Atsalis, 2000), as well as the increase of male home-range size during the mating season suggesting an active search for females (Radespiel, 2000; Schmelting et al., 2000). The occasional presence of sperm plugs, coagulated sperm that remains in the female vagina after copulation preventing another male's sperm from vaginal entry, further supports the claim that mouse lemurs are a promiscuous species that engages in scramble competition (Schmid and Kappeler, 1998; Schwab, 2000).

Food distribution and density, predation risks, and space requirements influence daily survival strategies leading to particular types of social groupings, mating strategies, social composition, migration patterns, and patterns in social behavior, including competitive interactions. Generally, when resources are distributed in patches, animals may be able to secure access by excluding others through direct competition (van Hooff and van Schaik, 1992). Therefore, although animals feeding on cryptic insects, which are sporadically and patchily distributed, will scramble for them, when feeding on fruits, which usually occur in patches, they will engage in contest competition leading to exclusive access to resources (van Hooff and van Schaik, 1992). In grey mouse lemurs, distribution of fruits (Martin, 1972b; Pagès-Feuillade, 1988) and insect secretions (Corbin and Schmid, 1995) were found to influence spatial distribution of individuals but exclusive use of resources was not documented. At RNP, contest over food resources was evident, but no single individual could exclude others from feeding in the same tree for insects and plant resources when they were plentiful. Male mouse lemurs may not be able to monopolize spatial use and females, but they do exhibit fierce contact aggression over patches of vital resources. Therefore, to summarize, evidence suggests that mouse lemurs engage in a mix of both scramble and contest competition, depending on specific social and ecological circumstances (van Hooff and van Schaik, 1992).

SUGGESTED DIRECTIONS FOR FUTURE STUDIES

Ecological and climatic factors may influence trapping results. In cotton rats and prairie voles, physiological stresses from temperature extremes and the need to avoid predators affected nighttime activity, with warmer temperatures on winter nights driving up the rates of capture (Stokes et al., 2001). Also, trapping results of small mammals, including prosimians, can be affected by the intensity of moonlight, which is associated with both increased (Nash, 1986; Gursky, 2003) and decreased activity (O'Farrell et al., 1994). Lunarphobia acts to decrease the activity of many small nocturnal mammals that are fearful of predation, including primates (Nash, 1986; Wolfe and Summerlin, 1989; O'Farrell et al., 1994; Bearder et al., 2002). But whereas some small mammals make themselves less conspicuous when the moon is bright, Gursky (2002b; 2003) discovered that the spectral tarsier increased activity in the full moon possibly to capture more insects (tarsiers captured approximately 3.2 insects per full moon night versus 1.2 insects per new moon night). At RNP, the trap schedule was not adjusted based on moonlight levels. My casual observations, however, hinted that mouse lemurs at RNP were less active during new and full moons, although on many occasions, mouse lemurs could be seen active at dusk under relatively high light conditions. A future study might check for fluctuations in activity and foraging patterns by monitoring trap and census results based on moon phase.

Social and ecological factors, including differences in male social status, the high incidence of predation, seasonal torpor, migration, and changes that occur in the mating season (Martin, 1972a; Goodman et al., 1993; Atsalis, 2000; Radespiel, 2000; Schwab, 2000), have been proposed to influence mouse lemur spatial distribution. How these and other factors interact to determine social organization in mouse lemur species merit further research. In light of the highly seasonal character of mouse lemur behavior, analyses should always consider the effect of seasonal life-history events. Dispersal, a significant component of the demography of small mammals, including cheirogaleids (Gaines and McClenaghan, 1980), requires further exploration. Dispersal generally occurs when population density is highest, such as shortly after the addition of newly independent young into the population, but how far and where animals go and what threats they face along the way are questions that remain open for study in mouse lemurs. Information from trapping, radiotracking, and genetic analyses can shed light on demographic, behavioral, and genetic traits of dispersers (Radespiel, Lutermann, et al., 2003).

Results from nocturnal studies strongly underscore that even remarkably similar-looking species can show varied social behavior (Bearder, 1999). One area that offers great promise in this domaine, is the study of nocturnal primate olfactory and auditory communication—poorly understood modes of social interaction. Mouse lemurs are quite vocal, and exciting strides toward clarifying how these vocalizations are learned and used have already been made. Captive research has shown that during the breeding season, male grey mouse lemurs are attracted to the breeding calls of females (Buesching et al., 1998). In free-ranging populations eleven different vocalizations were discovered for M. *murinus* and M. *rufus* (Zimmermann, 1995a,b). A gathering call was detected in M. *ravelobensis* (Braune et al., 2003; Braune et al., 2005). Sympatric species of mouse lemur have strikingly divergent advertisement calls (Braune et al., 2001), and genetically related populations of mouse lemurs living adjacent to each other have their own dialects of advertisement trill calls (Zimmermann, 1995a; Hafen et al., 1998). These calls, most often emitted by males, attracted both sexes (Zimmermann, 1995b). Females could exercise mate choice by recognizing individual trill calls (Zimmermann, 1995a; Hafen et al., 1998). It has also been suggested that by adopting local calls, new, perhaps young, males may be accepted more easily into the population, thus gaining access to females (Zimmermann, 1995a; Hafen et al., 1998). Because migration is as an important life-history event for males, possibly even for females, exciting new arenas are open for research into the mechanisms by which migrating individuals select and attempt to establish themselves into new locations.

SUMMARY

Overall, results from nocturnal walks, radiotracking, investigation of nest associations, and analyses based on a continuous mark–recapture trap study suggested that the brown mouse lemur has strong solitary tendencies. Evidence for social interaction was found in adult (presumably mother)–offspring sleeping associations, and during agonistic encounters over food. Male and female home ranges overlapped. All males, with one exception, were captured in traps where females had been trapped, and multiple males were captured at each trap site. Altogether, the evidence suggested that most males did not have exclusive home ranges and likely could not monopolize females. However, there were hints that a few males, perhaps high status resident individuals, maintained relatively large ranges with access to several females. A substantial bias was noted in the trap sex ratio during the dry season in the months preceding and immediately following the onset of the mating period. During the period of seasonal hibernation in the dry season, more males than females remained active. Some of these males were identified as new to the population. The percentage of recaptured females at the end of the study was approximately triple that of males when comparing the first period with the last period of the study. Taken with the pattern of frequent changes in the male population, results suggested that females were philopatric forming the basis of population continuity, whereas some males at least dispersed seasonally, with new males migrating into the study population. Lastly, research at RNP and elsewhere indicated that mouse lemurs compete in various ways, depending on the resources under contention.

Existing evidence hints that the brown mouse lemur is similar to other species of *Microcebus*, proposed to be nongregarious and promiscuous and to live in multimale–multifemale social organization characterized by dispersed spatial distribution. Further, various lines of evidence from other locations support that female mouse lemurs studied were generally philopatric and that, in many cases, they formed spatially clustered matrilines whereas the males dispersed. Much work remains to understand social patterns and processes involved in the evolution of particular expressions of primate social organization. With so much current effort being devoted to the study of nocturnal primates, we are gaining dramatic insights into the diverse ways that nocturnal species exhibit sociality. Additional research at RNP, using improved radiotracking techniques, additional analyses of trap data, and genetic studies can shed more light on the social organization of the brown mouse lemur.

6

Reproduction in the Brown Mouse Lemur

REPRODUCTIVE PATTERNS OF MOUSE LEMURS

With habitat loss constituting a major threat to the survival of lemurs throughout Madagascar, an understanding of behavior is essential to the conservation of these primates. Improving our understanding of reproductive behavior, reproductive potential, and how reproductive patterns are associated with local ecological conditions is important in establishing conservation directives (Schmelting et al., 2000). Until recently, little was known about reproduction in mouse lemur species, especially in wild populations. Martin (1972b, 1973), in his landmark field study, was among the first to research reproductive behavior in free-ranging mouse lemurs. Along with Petter-Rousseaux's (1970, 1981) and Glatston's (1979) studies on captive animals, Martin's research provided essential information on reproductive activity and offspring development. As with other aspects of mouse lemur behavior, in the past, the majority of studies on reproduction were on *M. murinus*, but of late considerable efforts have been made to understand reproductive dynamics of several other mouse lemur species. Table 6–1 summarizes some of the available information.

Many primates are characterized by reproductive seasonality, with mating activity and births concentrated in certain months of the year. The degree of reproductive seasonality is strongly influenced by the supply of food resources (e.g., Koenig et al., 1997; Wright, 1999), which in Madagascar is highly seasonal (Wright, 1999). As a result, mating activity is seasonally restricted in many lemur species (e.g., van Horn and Eaton, 1979;

Table 6–1 Summary of Results from Studies on Reproductive and Mating Patterns of Various Mouse Lemur Species

Species	Region	Population	Methods of Research	Male Patterns. Testicular Volume (TV)	Female Patterns	Mating System
Microcebus berthae (the pygmy mouse lemur)	Western dry forest[a,b]	Kirindy, Madagascar[a,b]	Mark–recapture, radiotracking, sleeping associations;[a] Mark–recapture, radiotracking, sleeping associations, DNA analysis[b]	Testes well-developed in October, peak TV in November at 625.7, 17.4%, above expected value—the largest relative testicular size of all primates;[a] TV increased September–November[b]	Sexual swelling began in November, last gestating female in April, reproductive period from November to June;[a] Swelling in November, with all females in estrus within 10 days[b]	Promiscuous with sperm competition, long mating season compared to grey mouse lemurs[b]
Microcebus murinus (the grey mouse lemur)	Western dry forest;[a,b,c,f] Littoral rainforest;[n] Captive study[c,d,h]	Kirindy, Madagascar;[a,b,f] Germany;[c,d,h] Ampijoroa in Ankarafantsika National Park, Madagascar;[e] Mandena in Fort Dauphin, Madagascar;[n]	Mark–recapture radiotracking;[a,b,e,n] Observations on mating, microsatellite DNA analysis;[d] Filming in nests, DNA analysis;[f] Basic reproductive measurements[c,h]	TV average highest in October: 898.4 ± 255.5 mm,[a] 55% above expected value;[a] TV average highest in August 1300mm;[c,e] Dominant, subdominant males, year old, older males sire offspring comparably;[d] Testicular activity for 7 months, highest volume~2400 mm³[h]	Sealed vulvas, anestrous until end of October;[b] High degree of estrous synchrony at onset of breeding season, weakening from second to third estrus;[c] Mating season began in September with first litters in Nov/Dec, and second litters in Feb/Mar;[c] Captured females gestating in October and lactating in November with first infants appearing in December and January. Captured females gestating in January and lactating in February with infants appearing again in February. Likely a third litter was born in April and May;[n] In estrus for 8 months[h]	Promiscuous with sperm competition;[d] Multiple paternity of litters;[d] Male home range size and overlap increases in September;[a] Cooperative breeding, allogrooming and allonursing of young among related females in sleeping groups[f]

Species	Habitat	Location	Methods	TV / reproductive measurements	Mating season / estrus	Mating system
Microcebus ravelobensis (the golden brown mouse lemur)	Western dry forest[e,g]	Ampijoroa, in Ankarafantsika National Park, Madagascar[e,f,g]	Mark–recapture, radiotracking,[e,f] Mark–recapture, radiotracking, sleeping associations[g]	TV average highest in August~1300 mm[3,e] TV increased~1500–2000 mm[3] from September to October, highest in October, resident males increased testicular volume earlier[f]	Mating season began in September, females in April with recent signs of lactation;[e] Estrous females trapped August–November, most in September, gestating females from September, with offspring in November[f]	High degree of intra and intersexual home range overlap before and during mating season-suggesting promiscuous mating system with sperm competition[s]
Microcebus rufus (the brown mouse lemur)	Eastern rain-forest,[f,k,o] Captive study[h,m]	Mantadia National Park, Madagascar;[f] Germany;[h,m] Ranomafana National Park, Madagascar[k,o]	Mark–recapture, radiotracking;[f] Mark–recapature, radiotracking, sleeping associations;[k] Basic reproductive data,[h] Basic reproductive measurements;[m] Mark–recapture and GPS vaginal smears.[o]	TV increased and remained~1200–2500 mm[3] in September–November but highest in October,[f] High TV for 6 months, highest volume~2500 mm[3,h] TV increased and remained high only in September and October, highest in September 2159 mm[3][k]	In estrus in November, first detected gestating in December;[f] In estrus for 6 months, and gestation shortest reported for any primate;[h] Polyestrous seasonal breeder;[h,k,m] Possible postpartum estrus;[h,k] Females can breed 2X/season;[m] In estrus beginning in August, majority of gestating females captured in November, last gestating female in February and lactating females Jan–April;[k] In estrus, mid-October to mid-November; Gestating and lactating females in December; lactating females in January too; Indications of estrous synchrony.[o]	Proposed promiscuous mating system.[h]

[a]Fietz, 1999b.
[b]Fietz, 1998.
[c]Radespiel and Zimmermann, 2001.
[d]Radespiel et al., 2002.
[e]Schmelting et al., 2000.
[f]Randrianambinina et al., 2003.
[g]Weidt et al., 2004.
[h]Wrogeman et al., 2001.
[i]Schwab, 2000.
[j]Dammhahn and Kappeler, 2005
[k]This study
[l]Eberle and Kappeler, 2003
[m]Wrogemann and Zimmermann, 2001
[n]Lahann et al., 2006
[o]Blanco, 2007

Rasmussen, 1985; Wright, 1999; Lewis and Kappeler, 2005), including mouse lemurs (e.g., Atsalis, 1998; Fietz, 1999c; Radespiel, 2000). As with seasonal changes in body mass and activity levels (see Chapter 4), reproductive activity in mouse lemurs and other lemurs is triggered by changes in photoperiod (Petter-Rousseaux, 1970, 1974, 1980). Sexually quiescent during the short days of the austral winter or dry season when resources are scarce, mouse lemurs are long-day breeders, with seasonal onset of sexual activity associated with dramatic changes in the genital appearance of both sexes. In Madagascar, increased photoperiod begins toward the end of the dry season, approximately from August to October (Petter-Rousseaux, 1970, 1974, 1980; Atsalis, 1998; Perret and Aujard, 2001). With the onset of the breeding season, the vulval area of females, which at other times is sealed by a membrane, begins to redden and swell. Then the vagina opens, signaling the start of estrus (Martin, 1972c; Glatston, 1979; van Horn and Eaton, 1979; Perret, 1990). In males, the testes undergo considerable enlargement from their usually reduced size (Martin 1972b; Andriantsiferana et al., 1974; Schmid and Kappeler, 1998; Schwab, 2000; Randrianambinina et al., 2003a,b; Dammhahn and Kappeler, 2005). In captivity, the reproductive period in female brown mouse lemurs was shorter than that for grey ones, and male testicular activity spanned fewer months (Glatston, 1979; Wrogemann et al., 2001). Relative testis size in mouse lemurs can range up to 6% of body mass (compare this with 0.27% in chimpanzees and 0.06–0.1% in humans, Harvey and Harcourt, 1984; Aslam et al., 2002), comparable only to *Mirza coquereli*, another cheirogaleid (Kappeler, 1997a). Some argue (Kappeler, 1991) that the presence of large testes, indicating that copious sperm is produced, suggests that males engage in sperm competition, an indirect way to vie for females.

In captive grey mouse lemurs, mating behavior was observed typically on the first or second day of vaginal perforation, only one night per estrous cycle (Glatston, 1979; Radespiel and Zimmermann, 2001b). Vaginal opening lasted between five and eleven days (Wrogemann et al., 2001), and the average cycle length was fifty to fifty-eight days (Glatston, 1979; Radespiel and Zimmermann, 2001b; Wrogemann et al., 2001). But there was a degree of intrapopulational variability with respect to estrous cycling. For instance, in one study, female grey mouse lemurs exhibited differences in the duration of cycling length, which varied from forty-eight to sixty-nine days (Buesching et al., 1998). Researchers have suggested that cycling variability—noticed under captive conditions—was an adaptation that allowed females to respond to varying environmental cues (Wrogemann and Zimmermann, 2001).

Mouse lemurs are characterized by high reproductive potential. Like other cheirogaleids (Foerg, 1982; Stanger et al., 1995), early studies discovered that mouse lemurs were sexually active in the first year of their life, typically producing litters of two to three offspring (ranging from one to

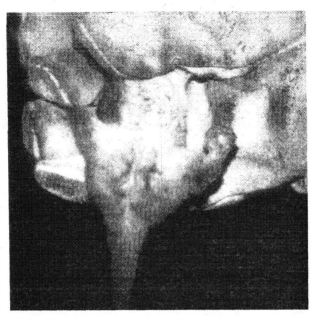

View of female brown mouse lemur vaginal opening during the breeding season in RNP

four) (Martin, 1972c, 1973; Andriantsiferana et al., 1974; Glatston, 1979), and females were polyestrous, undergoing two to four consecutive estrous cycles (Andriantsiferana et al., 1974; Perret, 1990). Traditionally, infants are born precocial, eyes are open within a few days of birth, and they are weaned within forty days (Glatston, 1979; Colas, 1999).

New field studies have added to these observations (e.g. Schmelting et al., 2000; Wrogemann and Zimmermann, 2001; Wrogemann et al., 2001; Lahann et al., 2006). At Kirindy, young remained in the maternal nest for four weeks, and afterwards were parked in vegetation when females were foraging, until finally they were weaned at six to nine weeks (Eberle and Kappeler, 2007; Eberle, personal communication, 2007). Studies have also revealed intriguing information on mouse lemur breeding patterns, including cases of multiple paternity in the grey mouse lemur-a rare occurrence in mammals (Radespiel et al., 2002; Andrès et al., 2003). Moreover, through genetic analyses and with the skillful use of infrared equipment to film inside sleeping nests, researchers discovered that related female grey mouse lemurs raised their young cooperatively, a behavior supported through the seasonal breeding pattern (Eberle and Kappeler, 2002, 2003, 2007).

Not all lemurs are seasonal breeders. Other nocturnal species— *Daubentonia madagascariensis* (Sterling, 1992), a rainforest lemur, and *Mirza coquereli*, a dry forest species (Stanger et al., 1995)—breed year-round.

These observations raised the possibility that the brown mouse lemur, a rainforest dweller, could be less seasonally restricted in the wild with respect to reproduction (Martin, 1990). Another intriguing possibility was that female mouse lemurs could produce two litters within a breeding season, the result of postpartum estrus. Admittedly a rare phenomenon, two litters have been produced by captive and free-ranging grey mouse lemurs (Andriantsiferana et al., 1974; Schmelting et al., 2000) as well as by captive female brown mouse lemurs, the latter occurring over the course of a six-month reproductive period (Wrogemann and Zimmermann, 2001).

At the same time as brown mouse lemurs continue to face pressures in their natural environment, for poorly understood reasons they also suffer from low breeding success in captivity (Wrogemann and Zimmermann, 2001). For these reasons, data from wild populations are needed to help in clarifying the parameters required to improve reproduction in captivity, thus helping to safeguard the survival of the species. In this chapter, I outline basic information that I discovered about brown mouse lemur reproduction at RNP. Another study by Blanco (2007, in press), which focused specifically on establishing mouse lemur reproductive schedules, has also added to our knowledge of reproductive patterns of brown mouse lemurs at RNP.

ASSESSING REPRODUCTIVE CONDITION IN THE BROWN MOUSE LEMUR

In this study, I assessed the reproductive condition of mouse lemurs whenever they were captured. The study overlapped two reproductive seasons, the latter part of the 1992–1993 reproductive season (January–April 1993) and the entire 1993–1994 season (August 1993–April 1994). The 1993–1994 season included the first sexual activity of young females born the previous year. Through regular trapping throughout the study period, reproductive activity of individual females and testicular enlargement in males were monitored. Observations on infant mouse lemurs became available through *ad libitum* examination of nests.

Captured individuals were designated as young or mature. Young females were those judged to be the offspring of that year's breeding season. Given that reproductively active females and males were captured predominantly in September through November 1993, young individuals were expected to be captured after January 1994. Similarly, in the first year of this study, which began in January 1993, young individuals captured would have been born in the previous year's breeding season. Criteria for distinguishing between young and mature mouse lemurs were somewhat subjective. Immature status was judged on overall appearance and body mass. Young females were lighter in body mass, ranging from 20 to 34 g (SD, ±4.2; $N = 11$), compared to the average mass of 42 g (SD, ±7.6) of adult females (see Table 4–1). The average body mass of young females and young males was based on values recorded when they were captured for the first time. Young males were distinguished from mature ones because older individuals sometimes exhibited loss of fur and signs of past injury. Younger males were characterized by lower body mass that averaged 35 g, ranging from 30 to 39 g (SD, ±2.6; $N = 15$), compared to the average body mass of 43.5 g (SD, ±4.4) of adult males (see Table 4–1).

Reproductive activity in females was described as quiescent, in estrus, or lactating, depending on the appearance of the nipples and the genital area. Gestation was detected through abdominal palpation. The vulval area was reported as imperforate, red and swollen, or open. When the vulval area was imperforate, and neither red nor swollen, the female was quiescent, considered anestrous. In the days before vaginal opening, the vulval area became red and swollen. Thus, a female was reproductively active when the vulval area was red, swollen, or in any stage of perforation. Based on captive observations, females with wide vaginal openings surrounded by swollen skin were at the peak of receptivity and fertility (Glatston, 1979; Wrogemann and Zimmermann, 2001).

Nipples were described as undeveloped, developed but currently not in use, prominent, or lactating. Lactation was indicated when fur around the nipples was conspicuously absent, and there was milk leakage. Prominent nipples, with fur missing but no milk leakage, indicated current or very recent lactating activity. Sometimes, nipples were developed but fur was not missing, suggesting past but not recent lactation.

The monthly number of females in estrus was tabulated based on individuals that showed signs of estrus at any time during the month. A female would be characterized with postpartum estrus if the presence of milk in the nipples coincided with vulval activity (Andriantsiferana et al., 1974).

Females exhibited atypical estrus if vaginal perforation was not associated with prior vulval swelling noted during previous captures or if the vulval area was characterized by superficial opening of the skin not followed by full perforation (Glatston, 1979; Buesching et al., 1998).

Average body mass calculated for gestating females was based on mass when pregnancy was first detected. For evidence of more than one pregnancy per season, I checked the reproductive records of frequently captured females, to detect individuals with signs of successive pregnancies in one season.

In species that are subject to marked seasonal variation in the size of testes, the testes of adult males are small in the nonbreeding season and are close to the inguinal canal. At RNP, in early August, the testes began to enlarge and remained large until November. Changes in testicular size were based on measurement of length of each testicle (and then averaging the two) and the width across both testicles (total width) using vernier calipers. Testicular volume was determined using the formula: volume = [3.14 × total width × (mean length)²]/6, following Bercovitch (1989), commonly used among mouse lemur researchers to document changes in testes size. Data for each male were averaged monthly in the case of multiple captures, and data were averaged across all males captured monthly. Data for testicular volume are shown for August–December; for all other months only width data were recorded because the testes were too small to obtain a useful measurement.

TESTICULAR ENLARGEMENT, ESTROUS CYCLES, GESTATION, AND BIRTHS

Forty-eight females were captured between January and May 1993, the first five months of the field study. I judged twenty-four to be adult females and twenty-two to be young, new additions to the population from the previous year's mating season. The level of maturity of the remaining two remained undetermined. In the mature sample, I discerned signs of current or recent pregnancy in fifteen females. Of the forty-eight females, fourteen (five of the young and nine of adult females) were recaptured frequently enough in the subsequent breeding season (which began in August/September 1993) to establish reproductive status; all of them, with the exception of one of the young females, experienced gestation.

The onset of the 1993–1994 breeding season was signaled by one female that was captured with a perforated vulva on July 19. That was the first sign of female reproductive activity of the season, but most female reproductive activity occurred between August and November (Figure 6–1). Female vaginal areas reddened, became rough, and started to swell. Red skin turned white, remained swollen, and finally split open. By taking vaginal smears, Glatston (1979) discovered that peak receptivity occurred on the second or third day of vaginal opening of the white swollen skin. Indeed, at RNP, pregnancy was observed in the majority of females after the appearance of white swollen skin. The synchronous nature of reproductive activity in females was most evident in November, when four females captured were already gestating and all but one of the remaining females displayed wide vaginal orifices with white swollen skin. Four of these females were gestating later that same month.

In males, testicular enlargement began in August (Figure 6–2). All males captured during the mating season, including those that had hibernated, had enlarged testes. Male testicular volume peaked in September but began to decrease by the following month. By December, testicular width was at prebreeding levels.

Some females were trapped frequently enough to monitor reproductive activity fairly closely, but regular trapping of the same female was not guaranteed. Therefore, because of the vagaries that characterize trapping,

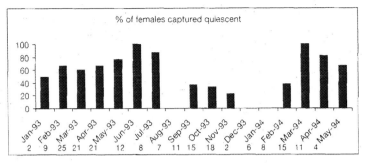

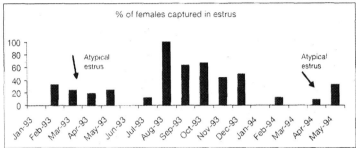

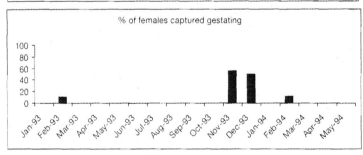

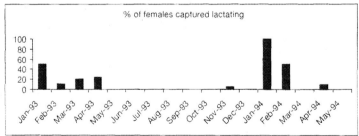

Figure 6–1 The reproductive pattern of *Microcebus rufus* females in Talatakely, RNP Shown are the monthly percentages of females captured in specific reproductive phases. Floating numbers below the x-axis in the first figure represent the total number of individual females captured each month. March 1993, April 1993, and April 1994 each include one female with atypical estrus. All estrous cycles in May 1993 and May 1994 are atypical. March 1993 and February 1994 include one female each that is both lactating and cycling. In April 1993 two females included as both lactating and cycling. In November 1993 four females are included as both cycling and gestating.

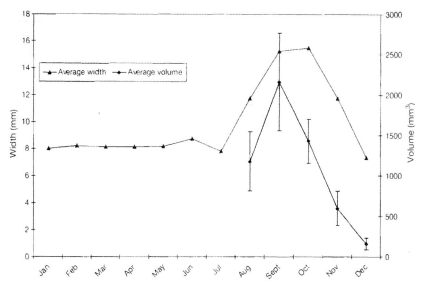

Figure 6–2 Fluctuations in male brown mouse lemur monthly average testicular width (mm) (left y-axis) and average testicular volume (mm³) (right y-axis) shown with standard deviations. Data are shown from males captured from January 1993 to May 1994 in Talatakely, RNP. January–June data are averaged over two years.

the length of the estrous cycle and the number of estrous cycles typical for a female could not be determined. There were hints that females experienced two consecutive estrous cycles. For instance, the female that was in estrus in July appeared to have cyc'ed twice before conceiving.

Seventy-one percent of gestating females were trapped in mid- to late November (see Figure 6–1). Based on a 58-day gestation observed in captive brown mouse lemurs (Glatston, 1979) and on an eleven-day minimum period between vaginal perforation and my ability to detect pregnancy (Table 6–2), I estimated that females captured in November were approximately a quarter to half way through their pregnancies. For four females captured between November and February, pregnancy was not detected even though each had undergone at least one estrous cycle. Two females were not captured frequently enough to detect pregnancy if it had occurred, but one may have conceived based on changes in the appearance of her nipples between two capture dates. Only in one female was it clear that gestation had not taken place.

Thirteen pregnancies were detected in thirteen different females. Five of these females carried two young, four females carried three young, and another four females appeared to carry singletons. Several trapped females illustrate the sequence of changes in the vulva, detection of gestation, and the number of fetuses they carried (see Table 6–2). Only through repeat capture could I confirm the number of offspring that a female was

Table 6–2 Sequence of Reproductive Events Detected and Changes in Body Mass of Select Brown Mouse Lemur Females During the Breeding Season in RNP

F25	11/2/1993 perforated vagina (38 g)	11/10/1993 sealed vagina (38g), no fetus detected	11/16/1993 fetus detected (40 g)	11/18/1993 fetus detected (41 g)	11/22/1993 two fetuses detected (44 g)
			→ 14 days		
					→ 20 days
F28	11/2/1993 perforated vagina (44 g)				11/22/1993 three fetuses detected (54 g)
					→ 20 days
F32		11/11/1993 perforated vagina (42 g)			11/22/1993 three fetuses detected (41 g)
					→ 11 days

carrying, and in the case of the four females bearing one offspring, only one was confirmed gestating a singleton.

The body masses of females before gestation compared with those following detection of gestation are shown in Table 6–3. For females captured a second time after first detection of gestation, body mass values were not significantly different from body mass values recorded when captured before gestation. These second capture data were available only for females carrying two fetuses ($t = -2.6$, $p = .076$, $N = 4$). Overall, these observations and the data in Table 6–3 indicate that there was some variability among females in body mass changes when gestating and that body mass increase was moderate even when there was more than one fetus, which may indicate that females were losing body fat during this seasonally resource restricted period. On the other hand, Blanco (2007, in press) discovered that gestating females at RNP experienced a 54 to 73% body mass gain, when gain was measured as maximum mass during pregnancy minus body mass at time of estrus. In my study I could not confirm that the data corresponded to maximum masses during pregnancy, and perhaps this also contributed to the more moderate increases that I noted, only up to 39% increase (for F37) based on available data (see Table 6–3). In addition, females presumed to carry only one offspring may have actually been carrying more than one, which could explain the high body mass found for some of these females (F17; see Table 6–3), none of which were recaptured to confirm their exact number of offspring.

Given the timing of gestations and gestation length, births would be expected to occur in mid- to late December or early January, and the capture of lactating females would also begin at this time. The data confirmed

Table 6–3 Changes in Body Mass of Gestating Brown Mouse Lemur Females During the Breeding Season in RNP

	Date	Body Mass (g) Before Detection of Gestation	Date	Body Mass (g) at First Detection of Gestation	Date	Body Mass (g) at Second Capture Following Detection of Gestation
Females with one fetus						
F42	10/25/1993	32	11/22/1993	37		
F37	11/10/1993	39	12/29/1993	51		
F20	11/11/1993	38	11/18/1993	40		
F17			2/21/1994	65		
Mean ± SD		36 ± 3.8		48 ± 12.7 (42.7 ± 7.4[a])		
Females with two fetuses						
F6			2/16/1993	73		
F14	10/25/1993	43	11/16/1993	48[b]	11/23/1993	47[d]
F56	11/10/1993	43	11/16/1993	42[b]	11/18/1993	44[d]
F25	11/11/1993	38	11/16/1993	40[b]	11/22/1993	44[d]
F10	11/11/1993	38	11/16/1993	43[b]	11/22/1993	43[d]
Mean ± SD		40.5 ± 2.9		49 ± 13.6 (43.3 ± 3.4[c])		44.5 ± 1.7
Females with three fetuses						
F22	10/18/1993		11/18/1993	44		
F28	11/11/1993	47	11/22/1993	54[e]		
F32	11/11/1993	42	11/22/1993	41[e]		
F59			11/24/1993	50[e]		
Mean ± SD		44.5 ± 3.5		47 ± 5.9		

[a]Excluding F17—see text;
[b]Only one fetus detected;
[c]Excluding F6's high body mass;
[d]Two fetuses detected;
[e]Three fetuses detected.

these expectations. In fact, only two females were captured in December. One was gestating. The other, which had been trapped exhibiting vulval activity in November, had not conceived. With the exception of one female captured lactating in November, all other lactating females were trapped between January and April (see Figure 6–1). All six females captured in January 1994 were lactating but only two females were captured in that same month in 1993, with only one exhibiting signs of lactating. The other exhibited signs of having gestated but was not lactating at the time of capture. Only one of nine and one of eight females captured in Februray 1993 and February 1994 respctively were gestating. After February, additional gestating females were not captured.

My estimate of the timing of most births was confirmed by Blanco's (2007, in press) study at RNP, in which, in addition to visual examination of female vaginal areas, vaginal smears of live-trapped females were inspected. In Blanco's study, females with vaginal openings were trapped from mid-October through mid-November. Pregnant and lactating females were captured in December. Lactating females continued to be trapped until the study ended, in early January. Taken together the data collected by Blanco indicated that births occurred in the second and third week of December, as I had also estimated. Since the research period of Blanco's study was shorter than my own, it was not possible to confirm a breeding season protracted by the reproductive activities of some females as was seen in my study.

In my study, a number of females displayed individual peculiarities in their reproductive patterns in both breeding seasons. F10 had signs of estrus at approximately the same time each year, and she was also among the last females captured lactating in both years of the study (April 1993 and February 1994) (see Figure 6–1). Similarly, another female experienced reproductive activity late in the season in both years, exhibiting normal vulval activity in February 1993 and lactating at the same time the following year. Lastly, two females were among a group of individuals to exhibit atypical reproductive activity in the same months of both years (April and May respectively).

REPRODUCTIVE SEASONALITY

To reduce sensitivity to seasonal food scarcity and adverse climatic conditions, some mouse lemurs use tactics widespread among mammals such as seasonal fattening followed by hibernation, and seasonal breeding (see Chapter 4). In many mammals, photoperiod is an important cue for timing reproductive events within the annual cycle, with additional environmental cues contributing to drive seasonal reproduction (Goldman, 1999; Perret and Aujard, 2001). Seasonality characterizes many lemur species inhabiting a variety of climatic conditions including east coast rain forests (Richard and Dewar, 1991). In mouse lemurs, mating was found to be seasonal in *M. murinus* (Martin, 1972b; Hladik et al., 1980; Fietz, 1999c; Radespiel, 2000), *M. ravelobensis* (Schmelting et al., 2000; Randrianambinina et al., 2003a,b; Weidt et al., 2004), and *M. berthae* (Schwab, 2000). Whereas these species live, for the most part, in dry forests, seasonal control and synchronization of reproduction also occur in brown mouse lemurs, a rainforest species (Randrianambinina et al., 2003a,b; this study). Indeed, it is commonly accepted that both temperate and tropical mammalian species time their reproductive activities so that births and lactation occur during the season that is the most energetically favorable for raising young (Goldman, 1999).

Under some conditions, however, it seems that seasonal control can be relaxed. The reproductive season of *M. berthae*, a species that was not shown to hibernate, was protracted, extending to June (Schwab, 2000) (see Table 6–1). Grey mouse lemurs in Ampijoroa, where this species did not hibernate (see Chapter 4), also experienced an extended reproductive season, commonly producing second litters in February and March (see Table 6–1). Females of *M. ravelobensis*, another species that did not hibernate in Ampijoroa (see Chapter 4), displayed recent signs of lactation in April (see Table 6–1). In grey mouse lemurs, local seasonality has been linked to reproductive potential, with the number of litters per year increasing as the severity of seasonal fluctuations decreased (Lahann et al., 2006). Specifically, in the highly seasonal region of Kirindy, characterized by the low annual rainfall of 800 mm, grey mouse lemurs were found to have 1 litter per year, whereas in Ampijoroa, with 1200 mm of rainfall, the number of litters increased to 2 per year. Furthermore, there were hints that in the litoral rainforest of Madena, characterized by 1600 mm of annual precipitation, grey mouse lemurs may have had the time to produce 3 litters per year (Lahann et al., 2006). Taken alone the data indicate that there may be an association between an extended reproductive season and the lack of seasonal response to the dry season, which may occur not only on a species level, dependent on the local habitat (as the shown by the above examples) but also on an individual level in species where hibernation is experienced variably.

Although it has emerged that a few lemur species, diurnal as well as nocturnal, breed throughout the year (Sterling, 1992; Stanger et al., 1995; Mutschler and Tan, 2003), most lemurs, even those that do not hibernate, follow a seasonal pattern of breeding that is similar throughout Madagascar, perhaps as a way to avoid reproducing when resources are scarce. Therefore, mating and gestation typically occur in the dry season, and lactation and weaning in the wet season, which is the time of greatest resource abundance (Martin, 1972a; Rasmussen, 1985). For mouse lemurs in general, and especially for those that hibernate, it remains important to time reproductive events according to optimal seasonality. The timing should allow the mothers the ability to prepare for seasonal torpor by increasing their body fat.

In captive studies, changes in female reproductive activity can be closely monitored through vaginal smears performed at particular stages of vulval morphological change (Wrogemann and Zimmermann, 2001). In the field, there is rarely the opportunity to monitor reproductive physiology so directly and so closely, even when vaginal smears are performed. On the other hand, with mouse lemurs, the usual constraint of limited sample size is tempered by the relative ease with which individuals are trapped. Thus, through trapping, reproductive information on the brown mouse lemur was gathered within the ecological context of its natural environment and as part of its annual life cycle. In this manner, we discovered that, as with other lemur species (Pereira, 1993; Wright, 1999), brown mouse lemur births were timed so that lactation and maturation of the young coincided with maximum food availability. Available food resources for brown mouse lemurs declined during most of the dry season (see Chapter 2), so mouse lemurs would need to take advantage of the period of abundance (see Chapter 3); in February through May, brown mouse lemurs consumed more fruit than during the rest of the year and some accumulated body fat in preparation for hibernation. In that period, young mouse lemurs attained independence from their mothers. Consequently, the seasonal regime of mating activity, parturition, weaning of the young, fattening and hibernation, centered around the period when food resources were at their most abundant: the second half of the rainy season and the very beginning of the dry season.

At RNP, this pattern of environmental responsiveness is not limited to mouse lemurs; Wright (1999) observed that eight other species weaned their offspring by late March presumably to coincide with peak fruit and insect abundance. For female mouse lemurs that were still lactating in April-late in the reproductive season-the timing of important life-history events can be tight. The short schedule of sequential events was illustrated by one female at RNP. She was lactating in April and weighed 43 g. When she was captured one month later, she was no longer lactating and weighed 65 g. It seems that she was preparing for seasonal hibernation and had done so in a very short period of time.

There are broad differences among mouse lemur species in the timing of the reproductive season (Lahann et al., 2006; Blanco, 2007). Whereas seasonality in rainfall patterns as they affect resource availability may influence timing and length of the annual reproductive period, likely there are multiple factors that play a role in the variability exhibited both within and between populations. Thus, differences may be associated with variability in genetic, hormonal, ecological and social factors, as well as other external triggers such as photoperiod and climate. Detailed comparative studies await and could provide some answers to these important questions. Collaboration in applying similar methods of data collection and analyses among researchers set up in geographic locales across Madagascar would make for useful and reliable cross-species comparisons.

THE ADVANTAGES OF ESTROUS SYNCHRONY

A female's nursing ability is limited by the number of pairs of teats. In rodents, where this relationship has been investigated, the number of offspring produced is, on average, one-half as many as the species-typical number of available mammaries (Gilbert, 1986). Pup mortality was high when litter size exceeded mammary number (Gilbert, 1986). Mouse lemurs have four teats, and through this study, I discovered that female brown mouse lemurs typically gave birth to two offspring, supporting Gilbert's claim that this number would accord with mouse lemur optimal nursing ability. However, cooperative breeding of young, observed in grey mouse lemurs, may aid in successfully raising mouse lemur offspring when more than two are produced, as they sometimes are. Results from field research have revealed that seasonal breeding (with females presumably cycling synchronously) sets the stage for cooperative breeding in closely related female grey mouse lemurs (Eberle and Kappeler, 2003, 2007). Cooperative care of mouse lemur young included allogrooming and allonursing, especially when the female was the only mother in the nest, and even adoption of the young if a mother died before weaning was complete (Eberle and Kappeler, 2003, 2007). Communal rearing can also improve infant survival through social thermoregulation (Radespiel and Zimmermann, 2001b). Kin selection (enhancing one's own genetic fitness by increasing the fitness of kin), is likely the basis for the expression of cooperative care in these related females (Eberle and Kappeler, 2003, 2007). At RNP, studies are needed to explore whether estrus synchrony and seasonal breeding are associated with cooperative care of young.

Generally, in free-ranging populations, when females exhibited estrous synchrony, even dominant males were less likely to monopolize them (Radespiel 1998; Wright, 1999). In this respect, there may be benefits to relaxing the degree of estrous synchrony. In one captive population of grey mouse lemurs, a high degree of estrous synchrony occurred at the onset of the breeding season, weakening with succeeding estrous cycles (Radespiel and Zimmermann, 2001b). The researchers suggested that perhaps complete synchrony was avoided to increase the possibility of males finding a mate on the one or two nights of peak estrus, while simultaneously decreasing female–female competition (Radespiel and Zimmermann, 2001b).

In free-ranging populations it is not always possible to monitor estrous cycles so closely, but it is possible to determine peaks of estrus, gestation, and lactation. Thus, at RNP I found that brown mouse lemur females in estrus were captured over several months: a single female was captured in estrus in July, 100% of females captured in September were in estrus and a decreasing number of estrous females were captured for several months thereafter. This pattern of initial strong synchronous cycling was noted by Blanco (2007, in press) at RNP. This researcher also discovered that females that were simultaneously in estrus tended to cluster in particular sampling areas. However, as in my study, Blanco noted that there was an appreciable degree of intrapopulational variation in timing of estrus (Blanco, 2007, in press). Variability in the expression of estrus—tight and relaxed synchrony—within a population may offer multiple benefits, such as thermoregulatory advantages, enhanced survival of offspring if females are nesting communally, increased potential for males to locate females in estrus, and decreased female–female competition.

Photoperiod is likely to be the most important environmental factor triggering reproductive activity, but not the only one to affect breeding. In captivity, exposure to *constant* long-day length did not trigger sexual change in male grey mouse lemurs because in addition to exposure to day lengths greater than twelve hours (Perret, 1997), it was the seasonal change associated with *alternating* day lengths that was required to instigate male sexual activity (Perret and Aujard, 2001). In females, too, previous exposure to short day lengths was required for strong estrus synchronization, but other factors fine-tuned the manifestation of reproductive activity.

Lastly, in one population of grey mouse lemurs, resident males exhibited increase in testicular volume earlier than the nonresidents that were migrating into the area (Randrianambinina et al., 2003a,b). Also, heavier grey mouse lemur females cycled early (Randrianambinina et al., 2003a,b). In this same location, where *M. murinus* and *M. ravelobensis* occur in sympatry, females of the former entered estrus in August, and females of the latter exhibited estrus in November. These observations suggest the presence of a genetic basis for the differences shown by the two species in timing of estrus (Randrianambinina et al., 2003a,b).

POSTPARTUM ESTRUS

In grey mouse lemur, testicular volume was already reduced by January, yet females exhibited postpartum estrus from mid-February to March (Schmelting et al., 2000). Nine of eleven females conceived successfully while lactating, suggesting that grey mouse lemurs were able to experience two breeding peaks and two litters within one season (Schmelting et al., 2000). Additionally, *M. ravelobensis* females were still lactating as late as April (Schmelting et al., 2000), in *M. berthae*, a female was pregnant as late as April, five months after male testicular volume peaked (although male volume was still high in January) (Schwab, 2000). In these examples, a second breeding period was not confirmed, but the assumption would be that females underwent estrus later in the season, in January/February, and that males remained spermatogenic even as testicular volume decreased. The same assumption would apply for RNP females captured lactating in April.

Each year of my study, a single female was captured gestating after December and several females were lacating into the month of April (see Figure 6–1). Trap data were not sufficiently complete for these females to determine if they had previously gestated. F10 underwent one cycle while lactating in March 1993, but when she was recaptured, she showed no signs of a second pregnancy. While lactating the following February, she was recaptured with perforated vaginal skin, a condition not preceded by pre-estrus swelling, signaling an atypical estrus with no resultant pregnancy. Two other females experienced vulval activity while lactating in March and April 1993. In one, vulval activity resulted in full vaginal perforation, but because she was not recaptured, I could not confirm that a second pregnancy occurred. In the other, vulval activity may have been postparturition opening. Six other females, for whom trap data were continuous enough to detect vulval changes had they occurred during lactation, showed no signs of reproductive activity indicative of a postpartum estrus.

The question of whether females at RNP can have multiple successful births over an extended reproductive season remains open. Blanco (2007, in press) found some hints for postpartum estrus at RNP. Specifically, vaginal swelling in two females that had shown previous signs of vaginal opening and pregnancy suggested the occurrence of postpartum activity. Blanco, however, warns that the postpartum vaginal swelling experienced by the females may have followed an abortion or the perinatal death of the first litter. In my study, a second gestation, occurring after the gestation peak in November, was not positively confirmed for any female and there were only hints of postpartum estrus in a small number of females. Poor capture rates of all individuals in the population in December and January made it impossible to know if these particular females had lost their first litter, or were indeed able to raise two litters.

If the "window of optimal environmental conditions" is restricted, females giving birth outside the period of resource abundance could be at a disadvantage (Blanco, in press). A second litter in brown mouse lemurs might interrupt life-cycle events important toward survival of both the offspring and the mother (see Chapter 4). Observations on the timing of offspring independence suggested that weaning was timed so that subsequent stages in the life cycle, such as females accumulating fat when food was abundant, were not impeded. In general, athough they have been documented in some captive and field studies (Andriantsiferana et al., 1974; Schmelting et al., 2000; Wrogemann and Zimmermann, 2001; Lahann et al., 2006), for most mouse lemurs second litters may be relatively rare.

ATYPICAL ESTRUS

In both years of the study, there were females that showed atypical patterns of vulval activity. These patterns were manifested as superficial slits of the vulval skin, appearing between March and May. For three of these females, I was able to confirm that vulval activity never resulted in full vaginal opening. Possibly, the atypical vulval activity characterized some young females because in both years of the study, there was at least one individual whose low body mass and small size hinted that she was a new addition to the population from that year's breeding season.

In captivity, female mouse lemurs also exhibited differing patterns in vaginal morphology, which were associated with atypical estrus (Glatston, 1979; Buesching et al., 1998). Glatston (1979) discovered that some grey mouse lemur females had abnormally short estrous periods, which were associated with abnormal swelling patterns or with no swelling at all. In another captive study, the cycle of one female was characterized by several small swellings and one vaginal perforation, which was observed during what would have been the inactive period and was not correlated with the female's progesterone profile (Buesching et al., 1998). The cycle was the female's first, which may explain the atypical nature, an explanation that may apply to females at RNP. In captivity, atypical cycles were shown to be infertile (Glatston, 1979; Buesching et al., 1998), not associated with silent ovulation. Consequently, vaginal morphology alone may not be an indicator of hormonal cycling, and, wherever possible, ethological data should be used to confirm the occurrence of reproductive activity (Buesching et al., 1998).

MALE REPRODUCTIVE PATTERNS

At RNP, mouse lemurs evaded capture in December and January, estimated to be the period of birth and lactation for females that were gestating in November. Perhaps nursing females stayed closer to the nests and were less willing to venture away to be captured in traps while foraging. This hypothesis, while plausible for females, cannot explain the simultaneous disappearance of males from the traps. Sympatric *M. ravelobensis* and *M. murinus* in Ampijoroa, and *M. murinus* in Mandena also exhibited low trappability in the same period as mouse lemurs at RNP (Schmelting et al., 2000; Randrianambinina et al., 2003a,b; Lahann et al., 2006) (see Chapter 5). In the pair-bonded *C. medius*, males invested considerable parental care in raising offspring, even when the young were the result of extra-pair breeding (Fietz, 2003a; Fietz and Dausmann, 2003). Males stayed with the young during the first two weeks after birth. Without the male, females were unable to rear their offspring successfully (Fietz and Dausmann, 2003). Male mouse lemurs, however, are not likely to offer such assistance because field research has shown that they mate promiscuously (see Table 6–1). Thus, the whereabouts and activity of brown mouse lemur males following the period of mating requires some serious investigation as it can shed light on male–female social relationships. It is known that by the time that the majority of female mouse lemurs are giving birth and tending to offspring, male testicular volume had already decreased, often to prebreeding levels.

In captive and free-ranging grey and brown mouse lemurs and in free-ranging *M. berthae* and *M. ravelobensis* species, males exhibited increased testicular volume up to one month before females were in estrus, perhaps as part of precopulatory intrasexual competition for eventual access to fertile females (Schmelting et al., 2000; Schwab, 2000; Wrogemann et al., 2001) (see Table 6–1). As with other hibernating mammalian males (Bronson, 1989; Barnes 1996), the early launch in reproductive activity in male mouse lemurs may provide the additional time needed for spermatogenesis. Seasonally increasing testicular volume has been observed in all mouse lemur species studied to date, with highest testicular volume exhibited between August and October (*M. murinus*—Fietz, 1999c; *M. berthae*—Schwab, 2000; *M. ravelobensis*—Weidt et al., 2004; *M. rufus*—this study). Testicular volume below 200 mm³ was considered quiescent in *M. murinus* and *M. ravelobensis* (Schmelting et al., 2000), and at RNP, before August, male testicles were too small to obtain a useful measurement.

Large testicular volume coupled with the occurrence of sperm plugs and little or no sexual size dimorphism suggest that male mouse lemurs compete for females by producing large quantities of sperm (Kappeler, 1997b; Fietz, 1999c; Weidt et al., 2004). Furthermore, the evidence for mouse lemurs points to a promiscuous mating system, one within which males are unable to monopolize females through contest competition, implying that physical dominance is not related to reproductive success (see Chapter 5). Nevertheless, results from captive studies are conflicting: in one study there was no correlation between dominance and number of offspring produced (Radespiel et al., 2002); in another, male dominance increased priority access to females, but females exerted choice over their sexual partners (Andrès et al., 2003). Given that both contest competition and female choice surfaced as important determinants of reproductive outcome, the authors proposed an interesting alternative to the sperm competition theory to explain the large testicular size of male mouse lemurs. They suggested that males needed large amounts of sperm because of the short mating season. Indeed, at RNP and elsewhere, male testicular volume remained large only for a short interval (see Table 6–1). Estrus in females, despite some intrapopulational variability, also occurred within a tight period of time. The authors commented that in the wild, there were indications to support the claim of contest competition: heavier males were found closer to females during the mating season in one study, males were seen mate-guarding, and they frequently engaged in agonistic encounters (Petter et al., 1977; Pagès-Feuillade, 1988; Fietz, 1998, 1999c). Together, these observations suggest that precopulatory competition occurs and that female choice influences mating outcome. Yet, other factors such as the presence of multiple paternity within a litter indicate that sperm competition is part of how males compete.

In conclusion, alternative mating strategies may coexist depending on the availability and distribution of females and in association with specific social and ecological circumstances (Andrès et al., 2003) (see "Scramble and Contest Competition," Chapter 5).

YOUNG MOUSE LEMURS

If direct observation of a small-bodied, solitary, nocturnal forager in the rainforest was a challenge, catching a glimpse of an infant mouse lemur was an even greater one. Only on one occasion was I able to inspect infant mouse lemurs closely. In January and February, my team and I searched for nests to check on daytime sleeping associations. On one occasion, in mid-January, we chanced upon a nest that apparently had been knocked down to the forest floor by that morning's strong winds. Despite the night's windy turbulence, the nest had retained its spherical shape. Within the nest lay three infants: two female and one male. The mother, whom we recognized by her ear notch, had been captured nine weeks earlier, her vaginal area widely perforated. Assuming that time to be close to the conception and based on a 58-day gestation period from captive data, birth had occurred in the first week of January. At the time of our discovery, infants would have been approximately ten days old. The male weighed 13 g, and the three averaged 12.5 cm in length from tip of head to tip of tail. Toothcombs were erupted but not the upper canines and incisors. On the ground, the infants moved rapidly but they were slow on the vine, which they clutched tenaciously, waiting for their mother.

In captivity, infants attained 13 g when they were five days old (Glatston, 1979), suggesting that the RNP infant male was underweight compared to a captive individual or that he was younger than my estimate. The pelage color of the infants was a dullish grey dorsally, with a creamy underbelly, a coloration that differed distinctly from the bright reddish-brown that characterizes the adult fur. In these infants, only the area extending supraorbitally toward the ears was reddish. While we hid waiting to take pictures, we watched the mother return to retrieve each young, one by one, transferring them to a new nest located at a height of approximately 10 m. Using her teeth, the mother lifted one infant by the back of the head and ascended the tree. A second infant was lifted by the nape. The third remained almost completely immobile as it waited. The mother returned for this infant a full two hours later, perhaps in response to her infant's vocalizations because mothers are stimulated to retrieve by the calls of their young (Colas, 1999). The calls of the infant were inaudible to us, discernable only through the moving mouth. That we could not hear the infant's calls was not surprising as many mouse lemur vocalizations are too high-pitched for the human ear (Petter and Charles-Dominique, 1979). When the mother arrived, she picked up the infant with her teeth latching onto the middle of its back and carried the limp body to the new nest.

Roughly two months later, in March, when the mother was recaptured and her offspring would have been approximately two months old, she was no longer lactating. This observation is in line with other data regarding

(a)

(b)

Brown mouse lemur mother retrieves young
after nest was destroyed by a storm. Photo
taken in January in RNP.

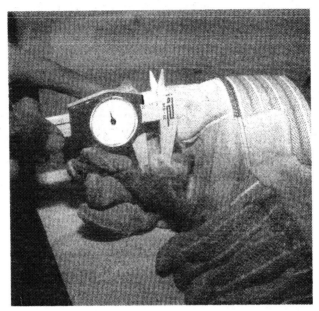

View of testicular measurement of brown mouse lemur during
the breading season in RNP

the short weaning time of young mouse lemurs. Observations on another
female confirmed that brown mouse lemur offspring reached independence at approximately two months of age. Indeed, first trappings of individuals that appeared to be newly independent young mouse lemurs
from the year's breeding season occurred in February, only a few months
after most females were captured gestating. Young females were captured
between February and May, whereas young males were captured between
April and May, but the reasons behind this differential appearance of the
sexes remained unclear.

FEMALE REPRODUCTIVE POTENTIAL

Several factors contribute to the high reproductive potential in mouse
lemurs. Mouse lemurs give birth in the first year of their life, habitually
producing litters. The young develop quickly; in captivity, infant grey
mouse lemurs reached 45% of adult body mass and 82% of adult size in
forty-five days (Colas, 1996). Gestation length was reported to be the shortest for any primate (approximately fifty-eight days in brown mouse lemurs,
sixty-two days in grey mouse lemurs, Glatston, 1979; Wrogemann et al.,
2001). Data from RNP suggested that females probably reproduced each
year although assessing female reproductive success in the wild is ham-
pered because postpartum survivorship of offspring is not guaranteed
and cannot be validated easily (Andriantsiferana et al., 1974; Glatston,

Close-up of spherical leaf nest of the brown mouse lemur in RNP.

1979; Wrogemann and Zimmermann, 2001). Reproductive potential may be further enhanced by the probable longevity of mouse lemurs, which in captivity can be twelve to fourteen years (Perret, 1996).

Experience with mothering further enhances production and survival of offspring. Captive grey mouse lemur females did not exhibit reduction in reproductive abilities with aging. Instead, even at an advanced age, they produced healthy large litters with improved newborn survival (Perret, 1996, 1997). Mature females produced three to four young as opposed to primiparous females that gave birth to two young (Colas, 1996). The offspring of mature females had more frequent access to their mother during lactation, achieving heavier body mass at weaning (Colas, 1996). Experience was quickly acquired; a single cycle was enough to achieve appropriate maternal behavior (Colas, 1996). Cooperative nursing and adoption of young are additional factors that can ensure survival of young, enhancing reproductive potential.

Finally, as alluded to earlier, the potentially high reproductive success in geographic locals where resources for mouse lemurs may be available over a greater temporal range may be manifested through increased number of litters per year (Lahann et al., 2006; Blanco in press), or perhaps even in the number of young produced per litter. If the availability of mouse lemur food resources is linked to rainfall, and if food abundance is the most likely reason behind increased reproductive productivity, then the brown mouse lemur at RNP, a location that can average over 4000 mm of annual rainfall (see Figure 2–1) should experience high reproduction, but this association between reproductive potential and resource reproductivity in the brown mouse remains to be supported.

Whereas certain life-history and ecological factors may enhance reproductive potential and offspring survival in mouse lemurs, other factors have a negative influence. In the wild, mouse lemurs suffer from high predation that is among the highest for any primate species (Goodman et al., 1991). And, whereas maximum lifespan can be extended in captivity, average longevity may encompass only five breeding seasons (Perret, 1996). However, even with restricted longevity and even if only one litter of two offspring is produced each year, a female that survives for only five seasons may produce up to ten offspring. This projection, less than 50% of the maximum known number of young produced in captivity (twenty-three offspring in eleven breeding seasons, Perret, 1996), is high given the slower reproductive rate of many other primate species. Coupled with the additional benefit that female susceptibility to predation may be less than that for males that are more active and that migrate (see Chapter 6), the reproductive output of female mouse lemurs is high. Nevertheless, despite the prolific nature of mouse lemurs, which could contribute to the rapid expansion of populations and may compensate for high predation rates, high rates of reproduction may not be able to outweigh the effects of diminishing natural habitat. Continued investigation into the ecology and reproductive patterns of brown mouse lemurs and other mouse lemur species in the wild is needed to benefit natural and captive populations.

SUMMARY

With habitat loss constituting a major threat to the survival of lemurs throughout Madagascar, an understanding of reproductive behavior is essential to their conservation. Sexually quiescent during the short days of the austral winter, mouse lemurs are long-day breeders, with seasonal onset of sexual activity associated with dramatic changes in genital appearance. The onset of the first breeding season at RNP was signaled by one female in mid-July that was captured with a perforated vulva. Male testicular volume peaked in September and was lowest in December. Seventy-one percent of gestating females captured were detected in mid- to late November. Lactating females were discovered from January and as late as April. Though the possibility cannot be excluded entirely, there are few indications that second litters are habitually produced by the brown mouse lemur at RNP. Individuals gave birth the first year of their lives producing one annual litter, typically comprised of two to three offspring.

At RNP, breeding in the brown mouse lemur occurred so that lactation and weaning coincided with the time of maximum food availability, toward the end of the rainy season. Captive studies have shown that photoperiod is the important cue for timing of annual cycles, but ecological cues and genetic differences may also drive the process. In *M. rufus* and other mouse lemurs that hibernate, there is the pressure to time reproductive events according to optimal seasonality, as many females are also preparing for seasonal torpor by increasing their body fat. At this time, young mouse lemurs attain independence from their mothers. Consequently, the seasonal regimen of reproductive activity, parturition, weaning of the young, fattening, and hibernation center on the period when food resources are at their most abundant. Seasonal control and synchronization of reproduction occurs in dry forest and rainforest mouse lemur species.

7

The Annual Cycle of the Brown Mouse Lemur

An Overview

A YEAR IN THE LIFE OF THE BROWN MOUSE LEMUR

The goal of this study was to investigate the behavior and ecology of the brown mouse lemur, *Microcebus rufus*. I hope that my study will serve as an impetus for additional inquiries into the many aspects of the behavior of this species that remain unknown. The Talatakely Research Station in Ranomafana National Park proved to be an ideal place for the study. At the time, amenities were basic but adequate—their simplicity added to the field experience. There were tents for sleeping, and water was carried from the river for all our needs. A crew of committed local people helped to manage the research cabin, cook food, and clean. Others became valuable research colleagues, offering their considerable knowledge of the rainforest to support the many studies that took place in the park.

Through a continuous long-term study, I focused on several aspects of the life history of the brown mouse lemur. Primarily, I aimed to investigate dietary behavior and seasonal fluctuations in body mass and activity levels. I hypothesized that mouse lemurs had dietary preferences and I predicted that specific plant and insect resources would be incorporated into the diet, irrespective of habitat wide resource availability. To monitor fluctuations in the quantity and quality of fruit and insects eaten, data on fruit and flower phenological cycles and on insect availability were related to feeding patterns. I also hypothesized that as part of the annual cycle, some mouse lemurs of both sexes would exhibit seasonal increase in body mass and subsequent reduction in activity during some part of the dry season. Body measurements were taken directly on captured individuals to monitor changes. Other indirect methods were used to shed light on mouse lemur behavior. Seasonal changes in activity levels were inferred from the presence or absence of mouse lemurs in traps. Diet was inferred from material (primarily seeds and chitin remains) found in fecal samples easily collected from trapped animals. Reproductive state was monitored through changes in testicular size and vulval activity in captured individuals. Litter size was inferred from ventral palpation of pregnant females. Information on nesting was collected by locating daytime nests and counting individuals that emerged. Social behavior was inferred, most frequently, from data on nest occupancy and home-range overlap. Occasionally, while in the forest, my guides and I observed mouse lemurs feeding. Generally, direct observations of individuals interacting were rare and all the more valuable when we noticed them. Below, I summarize the main findings of the study, described in detail in the previous chapters.

Results from the data suggested that the brown mouse lemur at RNP has strong solitary tendencies. At the same time, the trap data showed that a large number of individuals, up to nineteen, could be captured at a single trap location, pointing to a high degree of home-range overlap. Because of this high degree of overlap, it is likely that males could not maintain exclusive home ranges and therefore could not monopolize females. In all, existing evidence suggests that the brown mouse lemur is similar to other species of *Microcebus*, which have been shown to be non-gregarious and promiscuous and to live in multimale–multifemale social organizations characterized by dispersed spatial distribution.

I also found that brown mouse lemurs consumed a variety of fruits; twenty-four different kinds were identified taxonomically, whereas an additional forty to fifty-two remained unidentified. Mouse lemurs increased the quantity and diversity of fruit intake toward the end of the rainy season when fruit productivity was high. Mouse lemurs relied heavily on several varieties of the epiphytic semiparasite mistletoe, *Bakerella*. *Bakerella* was eaten year-round irrespective of the availability and abundance of other fruits. Other epiphytic plants were also part of the diet of these mouse lemurs.

Bakerella is high in fat, making this mistletoe an ideal staple resource, essential to mouse lemur survival. Mammalian dispersers of mistletoes are relatively rare. Therefore, the important discovery of an association between mistletoes and mouse lemurs leads to questions regarding the ecology of their relationship that require further investigation. Beetles, too, were consumed regularly year-round, suggesting that these insects, like *Bakerella*, served as another staple resource. Overall, the brown mouse lemur can broadly be described as a "frugivore–faunivore," with seasonal patterns in fruit intake. The range of food resources exploited by mouse lemurs may be an advantage to their successful survival, especially if they target rich resources such as high-lipid mistletoes and beetles. These and other foods are used by mouse lemurs to support seasonal fattening, which occurs before hibernating in the dry season.

In general, brown mouse lemurs at RNP, like other mouse lemur populations, follow photoperiodically driven rhythms in activity, metabolism, body temperatures, and body mass. These changes vary seasonally and are associated with food availability and social activity. The relationship between photoperiod and mouse lemur physiology has been studied extensively in captive mouse lemurs (e.g., Petter-Rousseaux, 1970, 1981; Perret, 1972, 1974, 1977, 1982, 1992). Such is the control of photoperiod over mouse lemur biological rhythms that when kept under an accelerated photoperiod schedule, individuals experienced significant reduction in maximum survival and lifespan (Perret, 1997). Perret, in particular, has studied in detail, the annual endocrinological cycle of grey mouse lemurs and its close synchronization with photoperiodic change. Perret (1974) found that immediately before the period of shortened day length, feeding activity by mouse lemurs increased, whereas the activity of the thyroid decreased, leading to fat storage. With endocrine functions decreasing, metabolism, body temperature, sexual activity, and overall activity were also decreased, and mouse lemurs became more socially tolerant, nesting together in large groups (Perret, 1972, 1992; Glatston, 1979). Normal endocrine functions resumed when day length began to increase, signaling the start of the reproductive season when mouse lemurs became sexually active. Male testicular development increased, female estrus commenced, and individual

Recently matured brown mouse lemur in Ranomafana National Park.

oxygen consumption became higher. In males, testicular development was sometimes accompanied by loss of body mass (Perret, 1977). At the end of the reproductive season, when day length began to shorten once again, the cycle began afresh.

To monitor these rhythms in a free-ranging population, I collected data on known mouse lemurs at RNP and monitored fluctuations in monthly climatic conditions and resource availability. Figure 7–1 provides a schematic that combines the cumulative results of the research as a way to highlight key events in the annual life cycle of the brown mouse lemur at RNP. Increased temperatures and precipitation signaled the onset of the wet season in December and resulted in the first spike in the diversity of available fruit. In mid-rainy season, between February and March, the diversity of fruiting trees and shrubs peaked, whereas March through May were characterized by peak fruit abundance. Between January and May, various important fruit sources for brown mouse lemurs were in high abundance, including *Bakerella*. January was also a month characterized by peak availability of insects. At this time of abundance, mouse lemurs increased fruit consumption in both the quantity and the variety eaten. The period of increased fruit intake was associated with the timing of two important events in the life cycle of the brown mouse lemur: the appearance of young mouse lemurs feeding independently and seasonal fattening in preparation for the dearth of the dry season.

Specifically, between April and June, as photoperiod decreased (short day length), a number of male and female mouse lemurs showed marked seasonal fattening. Population averages for body mass and tail circumference were higher than annual averages; some individuals weighed over 50 g. Fattening was followed by a decrease in activity during the dry season, when these mouse lemurs no longer entered traps presumably because they had entered a state of hibernation. The reduced metabolic activity allowed mouse lemurs to store and use fat over the course of the dry season when average rainfall, temperature, and resource abundance were at their minimum. Trap data suggested that animals remained inactive from six to twenty-five weeks. Torporing mouse lemurs resumed activity, as indicated by their reappearance in the traps, having lost the body fat that they metabolized during their period of absence.

Other males and females remained active throughout the dry season without appreciable changes in body mass. However, more males than females remained active, as reflected by the high male-biased sex ratio between June and September. Mouse lemurs born into the population from that year's breeding season made their appearance as independent individuals between February and May. Some of these new males may have remained active throughout the dry season as they dispersed from their natal ground. Females contributed more to population continuity than did males, which appeared to be the main dispersing sex. Indeed, females of

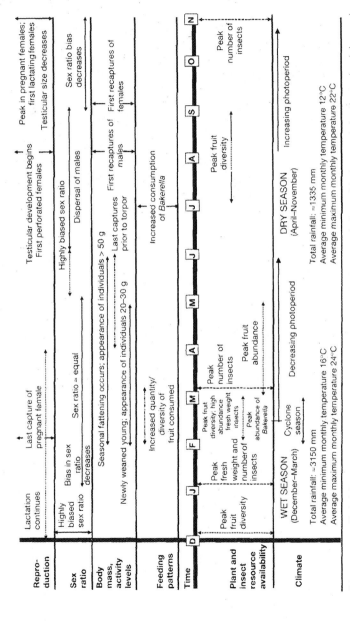

Figure 7–1 Rainfall, temperature, and resource seasonality in association with the reproductive schedule, and other milestones in the annual life cycle of *Microcebus rufus* at Talatakely, RNP. To follow the annual cycle, begin with the Time axis, moving from December (D) to November (N). Below the Time axis, there is information on Resource Availability, Climate, and Photoperiod. Above the Time axis are particular aspects of mouse lemur behavior and ecology: Feeding, Body Mass, and Activity Level changes, Sex Ratio, and Reproduction. Vertical arrows within each month represent events and behaviors that occur within the specified month only. Horizontal arrows are for events and behaviors that span several months. Different arrow styles differentiate the lines.

other mouse lemur species studied were found to be philopatric, forming spatially clustered matrilines, whereas the males dispersed.

In July, a month of relatively higher rainfall within the dry season, there was once again a peak in diversity of fruit availability, but mouse lemurs only increased consumption of *Bakerella*. In the period between August and October, previously torporing males and females resumed activity. Sexually quiescent during the short days of the austral winter, mouse lemurs are long-day breeders, with seasonal onset of sexual activity associated with dramatic changes in genital appearance. Therefore, as photoperiod increased (long day length) and mouse lemurs resumed activity, they became sexually active. Torporing females reappeared in September and October, ready for sexual activity, whereas males became active earlier, between August and September. The extra time may have been used for spermatogenesis and to establish sexual hierarchy before they gained access to females. All males showed signs of testicular development, whereas females exhibited vulval perforation. Testicular development continued and testicular volume was highest in September.

Both sexes resumed activity from seasonal torpor having lost body mass compared to their prehibernation states. In mouse lemurs, the timing of emergence from hibernation may influence availability for breeding opportunities. It may also influence survival itself because individuals prepare to breed at a time when resources are relatively scarce. The bias in sex ratio did not begin to decrease substantially until October, when members of both sexes came out of their seasonal hypothermic states and dispersal activity had either decreased or stopped.

In November, the last month of the dry season, testicular size began to decrease, returning to pre-reproductive size in December. Females that were gestating and females that were already lactating were first detected in mid-November. The end of November marked the peak time for pregnancies. The females that were examined carried one to three fetuses. Very few individuals were captured in December and January, perhaps as a result of females remaining closer to their young in the nests. The few animals that were captured were mostly male. At RNP, up to five individuals were found occupying single nests. In January and February, some nests were shared by adult and young individuals.

The annual cycle began afresh, with all mouse lemurs benefiting from available resources. The period of greatest fruit availability, between February and May, occurred at the same time as the appearance of lighter-weight individuals (20–30 g), presumably the newly weaned young of the season. Young were born at the beginning of the rainy season, which means that the period in which they began to feed independently coincided with the time of maximum food availability. Because maternal investment, from estrus to weaning, covers six to eight months, the mating season must occur as the days grow long so that young mouse lemurs are weaned in the austral summer months when food availability is expected to be high. There were few definite hints for the existence of postpartum estrum, but some lactating females were captured in April.

French (1988) emphasized that "time, like energy, is at a premium for hibernators." Hibernators must juggle the constraints of time—such as how long to stay dormant—with energy needs. However, seasonal reproductive schedules in Madagascar are not restricted to mouse lemurs. They commonly occur in other lemurs as a way for lactating mothers and developing young to have access to abundant resources (Pereira, 1993; Wright, 1999). The exact timing depends on species-specific length of gestation and postnatal development. For instance, births in the larger-bodied diurnal lemurs of the family Lemuridae are timed to occur just before the rainy season, allowing the young to grow surrounded by plenty of nutritious food (Pereira, 1993). In mouse lemurs, the young are born and grow to maturity almost entirely within the rainy season, leaving time for mothers to fatten in order to enter hibernation in the dry season. Although brown mouse lemurs can enter daily torpor to conserve energy, not all individuals experience an active and inactive period during the year. The active period includes behaviors associated with mating, gestation, lactation, emergence of young as independently feeding individuals, and prehibernatory fattening. Females that plan to hibernate have to complete these events of the life cycle during the active period. Young individuals, too, are time-constrained, as they need to grow before the dry season, and possibly to deposit fat in order to enter hibernation. Through a relatively fast developmental pace, mouse lemurs reach maturity before the dearth of the dry season (Radespiel, Ehresmann, et al., 2003).

LOCAL ECOLOGIES

Mouse lemurs from various regions of Madagascar face the stresses associated with seasonal changes in climate and resource availability. In the study at RNP, I discovered that brown mouse lemurs, a rainforest species, had similar feeding and activity patterns as those reported for grey mouse lemurs, a species found predominantly in dry forests. Seasonal fattening has been documented in mouse lemur populations in various regions of Madagascar, including in another population of brown mouse lemur in Mantadia National Park, a central eastern rainforest (Andriantsiferana and Rahandraha, 1973; Russell, 1975; Hladik et al., 1980; Petter-Rousseaux, 1980; Petter-Rousseaux and Hladik, 1980; Ortmann et al., 1996, 1997; Schmid, 1996; Atsalis, 1999b; Schmid et al., 2000; Randrianambinina et al., 2003b).

A primary function of annual cycles in mouse lemurs and other small mammals is to reduce exposure to stressful climatic and resource conditions. In the case of mouse lemurs, stressful conditions in Madagascar, which occur during the dry season, are thought to be intense in west coast dry deciduous forests. The marked dry season in the west coast was believed to have greater influence on the behavior of mouse lemur populations that reside there, than the influence that the presumably less severe conditions of the rainforest environment have on the brown mouse lemur. To evaluate this claim, I compare data from RNP with data from a long-term study on the climate and phenology of a dry deciduous forest in Morondava, located in western Madagascar (Sörg and Rohner, 1996). In this region, most of the annual precipitation fell between December and March, averaging 699 mm, whereas total rainfall between April and November averaged 100 mm (calculated from Table 1, Sörg and Rohner, 1996). This means that the area experienced a decline of approximately 85% in precipitation between rainy and dry seasons. In Ranomafana, the decline was less, at 57% (3149 mm in the rainy season versus 1334 mm in the dry season). Morondava experienced mean temperature of approximately 27°C during the rainy season and 23.5°C during the dry season, representing a decrease of approximately 14%. In Ranomafana, the decrease was approximately 17% (20.3°C in the wet season versus 16.8°C in the dry season). Thus, seasonally and annually, precipitation was higher in the rainforest than in the dry forest, and the rainforest exhibited a smaller decrease in rainfall during the dry season than did the dry forest. Nevertheless, rainfall at RNP was decreased by half in the dry season, and whereas the reduction in average temperatures was only slightly greater in the rainforest than in the dry forest, average temperatures in the rainforest were lower than those of the dry forest. Moreover, despite Ranomafana's higher precipitation in the dry season, there were marked changes in fruit and insect availability and abundance between wet and dry seasons. Given this information, it appears that mouse lemurs in the east coast rainforest, like their west coast congeners, are subject to seasonal climatic and resource stresses. These stresses have resulted in behavioral adaptations to reduce their effects.

Yet, differences in local habitats are pivotal in driving seasonal responses (Randrianambinina et al., 2003a,b) because as already mentioned, among mouse lemur species there is flexibility in the response to local ecologies. *Microcebus ravelobensis* and *M. berthae* were not observed to undergo seasonal hibernation (Ortmann et al., 1996, 1997; Schmid, 1996; Schmid et al., 2000; Randrianambinina et al., 2003a,b), and grey mouse lemurs in Ampijoroa, located in the northwest did not undergo seasonal hibernation even though they do hibernate in other regions (Schmelting et al., 2000; Lutermann and Zimmermann, 2001).

Perhaps the main conclusion here is that there is considerable flexibility in the expression of seasonal response in mouse lemurs, not just between species, but within a single species or population and even, as was suggested by this study on the brown mouse lemur, in the same individual from year to year. This flexibility may be an important advantage to aiding mouse lemurs in adapting when faced with changes in their native habitats.

MOUSE LEMURS AS SMALL MAMMALS

To study mouse lemurs is to study essential mammalian patterns of survival. Indeed, within the order Primates, where most species weigh more than 5 kg (Smith and Jungers, 1997) and are diurnal and social, the combination of small body size, nocturnality, and nongregarious behavior is relatively rare. Among mammals in general, however, small-bodied species under 5 kg constitute the majority in all orders combined (Bourlière, 1975; Fleming, 1979). Consequently, within the general context of small mammal ecology, mouse lemur behavior is far from unique. Although debate exists as to the degree to which life-history attributes are related directly to body size (Western, 1979) or to ecological factors (Promislow and Harvey, 1990; Kozlowski and Weiner, 1997; Purvis and Harvey, 1997), small body size undeniably creates a common set of ecological constraints (Golley et al., 1975) exerting a pervasive influence on species biology.

The study of small mammals offers many opportunities to explore the shared behavioral and ecological adaptations associated with size. Among other similarities, small mammals, including mouse lemurs, have high rates of predation, reproduction, metabolism, and growth, relative to large mammals (e.g., Kleiber, 1961; Western, 1979; McNab, 1980; Clutton-Brock and Harvey, 1983; Goodman et al., 1993). The relatively high metabolic rate of small mammals has a strong influence on survival so much so that when small mammals, both temperate and tropical species, are confronted with seasonally unfavorable conditions and diminishing food supplies, they face a strong challenge in maintaining a balanced physiological state, or homeostasis (Kleiber, 1961; Fleming, 1979). Under these circumstances, small mammals, including mouse lemurs, often respond by eating concentrated foods when available, storing body fat when food is abundant, and relying on hypothermia for varying lengths of time to decrease energy costs (Bourlière, 1975; Fleming, 1979). In most mammals, photoperiod is the most significant cue directing adaptation to seasonal environmental changes (Bartness and Wade, 1989; Kriegsfeld and Nelson, 1996; Goldman, 1999; Perret and Aujard, 2001), but among primates, only certain species of the family Cheirogaleidae are known to enter periods of photoperiod-driven hibernation after increasing their body fat stores. Upon emerging from hibernation, mouse lemurs and other small mammals, face additional challenges. In many small mammals that hibernate, the males emerge earlier than females having lost body mass. They may continue to lose mass as they establish home ranges, prepare for the production of high sperm volume, and compete for females that are synchronously in estrus. In females, weight loss probably occurs during lactation because of the high reproductive investment. Though many species rely on diverse environmental cues, photoperiod, again, is the main cue in timing annual events related to reproduction, which must occur so that the energetically costly activities of raising the young coincide with resources at their greatest abundance.

Compared with other prosimians of similar body size, mouse lemurs have shorter periods of gestation and development. As an example, *Galago demidovi*, at 60 g, gestates for a little less than four months, giving birth to one offspring that requires eight to ten months to develop (Bearder, 1999). Similarly sized mouse lemurs gestate for approximately two months with young developing in about two to three months. Nevertheless, even with all the traits that mouse lemurs have in common with other small nonprimate mammals and even though they are characterized by high fetal and postnatal growth rates compared to other primates, mouse lemurs do maintain primate life-history traits (Kappeler, 1996b). Compare, for instance, certain rodents that experience dormancy, the Heteromyidae, Sciuridae, and Zapodidae, with mouse lemurs. Among rodents, these taxa have the slowest reproductive rate, less than 2.3 litters per individual per season, and the longest life span, 7.5 to 12.5 months (French et al., 1975). Yet, the rodents exhibit faster reproductive rates than mouse lemurs that produce one or, rarely, two litters per year, usually with two offspring, and which typically survive to seven years of age (or double that in captivity; Perret, 1990).

In addition to relatively longer gestation, development, and lifespan, mouse lemurs and the other prosimians are characterized by large brain size to body size compared with other terrestrial mammalian groups (Bearder, 1999). These features of primate life history influence the process of socialization and the establishment of extensive social networks and long-term social ties (Pereira and Altmann, 1985; Shea, 1987). The origin and establishment of sociality has been linked to a reliance on plant resources, whose patchy and predictable distribution promotes information sharing (Müller and Soligo, 2001). Dependence on plant resources was documented in my study at RNP supporting this scenario for the origin of sociality in nongregarious primates. Indeed, whereas the social systems of nongregarious primates were thought to be primitive and asocial, this notion has been changing as more data accumulate. Capture data on the brown mouse lemur at RNP point to a high degree of spatial overlap of individual home ranges, suggesting a multimale–multifemale system. In fact, field data on many mouse lemur species have revealed that dispersed multimale–multifemale systems are the prevailing social organization (Müller and Thalmann, 2000). Mouse lemur species, however, differ in their specific expressions of social behavior despite significant similarities in general organization (Wimmer et al., 2002; Weidt et al., 2004). Additional research will reveal to us how mouse lemurs establish and maintain their nongregarious social networks and how the life-history cycles affect their social patterns. It follows that given their similarities to small nonprimate mammals, the extensive body of information available for many small mammal taxa can aid in our understanding of mouse lemur social behavior.

THE FUTURE

More than thirty years ago, Martin (1973) signaled the need for additional information on the behavior of mouse lemurs. He stressed that this was necessary not only because of the lack of data on nocturnal primates in general, but also to test the proposal that mouse lemurs along with bushbabies may be suitable analogs for the ancestral primate. Since then, the relevance of *Microcebus* as a model for the ancestral primate has been questioned (Gebo, 2004; Soligo and Martin, 2006), but the urgent need for further study on mouse lemurs and their relatives remains. Fortunately, there has been a proliferation of innovative field studies on various mouse lemur species by many dedicated researchers. Additional research is needed on mouse lemurs in their natural habitats, especially those in east coast rainforests where fewer studies have taken place. Information on basic ecology is needed to understand the requirements for sustaining mouse lemur populations. Given the challenge of studying a small nocturnal primate in the wild, especially in the rainforest, the recent interest in mouse lemurs found in diverse habitats suggests that the difficulties are not insurmountable.

Madagascar is home to more than 13% of the world's primates, a percentage that increases as new lemurs are discovered with startling frequency. Lemurs are among the most recognized primates by the general public. They also serve as flagship species for scientific research and conservation (Tuttle, 1998). In Madagascar, conservation threats are significant as habitat is lost to human activity. The obstacles to protecting lemurs and other animals in their natural environments are formidable, but the interest of students and researchers in animal behavior and ecology can constitute an important influence contributing to local conservation efforts. Their presence while doing field work discourages hunting and the destruction of habitat, but more importantly, provides an opportunity to open channels of communication between local people and the scientific community, and through them, the world at large (Tuttle, 1998). Therefore, contrary to some popular assertions, science is not an ivory tower: biologists in various fields are at the forefront of a battle that aspires to preserve rare species, local ecologies, and to establish secure connections with local people.

I return to the question posed in the first chapter, Are nocturnal primates destined to go "from obscurity to extinction" (Martin, 1995)? Certainly the many successful research studies from established field sites such as Kirindy and Ranomafana act to keep Madagascar and its unique inhabitants on the public and scientific radar. Among the most significant contributions of long-term field sites, in Madagascar and elsewhere, is the promotion of collaborative relationships between native and foreign peoples. Any researcher—native or foreign—can provide testimony to the importance of local people to research efforts. Local people are a wonderful source of knowledge on native fauna and flora that can enhance the research. I can state with conviction that without the tireless and uncomplaining assistance of several local field guides, the present project would have been much more limited in scope. Therefore, I cannot thank enough my RNP research team: Le Jean and Jean-Marie, Pierre and François. This source of support should be reassuring to new students of primate behavior who wish to undertake the challenge of studying a nocturnal species. Working side by side with local people makes the research possible. More importantly perhaps, the research itself makes possible our conservation efforts and promotes goodwill and friendship among the world's diverse cultures.

References

Allen, M. E. 1989. *Nutritional Aspects of Insectivory.* East Lansing: Michigan State University.

Altringham, J. D. 1996. *Bats: Biology and Behavior.* Oxford: Oxford University Press.

Amico, G., and M. A. Aizen. 2000. Mistletoe Seed Dispersal by a Marsupial. *Nature* 408: 929–930.

Andrès, M., H. Gachot-Neveu, and M. Perret. 2001. Genetic Determination of Paternity in Captive Grey Mouse Lemurs: Pre-Copulatory Sexual Competition Rather than Sperm Competition in a Nocturnal Prosimian? *Behaviour* 138 (8): 1047–1063.

Andrès, M., M. Solignac, and M. Perret. 2003. Mating System in Mouse Lemurs: Theories and Facts, Using Analysis of Paternity. *Folia Primatologica* 74 (5–6): 355–366.

Andriantsiferana, R., and T. Rahandraha. 1973. Contribution a L'étude de la Biologie de *Microcebus murinus* Elevé en Captivité. *Comptes Rendus de l'Academie des Sciences Paris, Series D* 277: 1787–1790.

Andriantsiferana, R., Y. Rarijaona, and A. Randrianaivo. 1974. Observations sur la Reproduction du Microcèbe (*Microcebus murinus*, Miller 1777) en captivité à Tananarive. *Mammalia* 38: 235–242.

Ankel-Simons, F. 1996. Deciduous Dentition of the Aye-Aye, *Daubentonia madagascariensis. American Journal of Primatology* 39: 87–97.

Armitage, K. B. 1998. Reproductive Strategies of Yellow-Bellied Marmots: Energy Conservation and Differences between the Sexes. *Journal of Mammalogy* 79: 385–393.

Arnold, W. 1990. The Evolution of Marmot Sociality: Costs and Benefits of Joint Hibernation. *Behavioral Ecology and Sociobiology* 27: 239–246.

Arnold, W. 1993. Energetics of Social Hibernation. In *Life in the Cold: Ecological, Physiological, and Molecular Mechanisms,* eds. C. Carey, G. L. Florant, B. A. Wunder, and B. Horwitz, 65–80. Boulder, Colorado: Westview Press.

Aslam, H., A. Schneiders, M. Perret, G. F. Weinbauer, and J. K. Hodges. 2002. Quantitative Assessment of Testicular Germ Cell Production and Kinematic and Morphometric Parameters of Ejaculated Spermatozoa in the Grey Mouse Lemur, *Microcebus murinus*. *Reproduction* 123: 323–332.

Atherton, R. G., and A. T. Haffenden. 1983. Long-Tailed Pygmy-Possums. In *Complete Book of Australian Mammals*, ed. R. Strahan, 166–167. Sydney: Angus and Robertson Publishers.

Atsalis, S. 1998. Feeding Ecology and Aspects of Life History in *Microcebus rufus* (Family Cheirogaleidae, Order Primates). Ph.D. dissertation, City University of New York.

Atsalis, S. 1999a. Diet of the Brown Mouse Lemur, *Microcebus rufus* (Family Cheirogaleidae), in Ranomafana National Park, Madagascar. *International Journal of Primatology* 20 (2): 193–229.

Atsalis, S. 1999b. Seasonal Fluctuations in Body Fat and Activity Levels in a Rainforest Species of Mouse Lemur, *Microcebus rufus*. *International Journal of Primatology* 20 (6): 883–909.

Atsalis, S. 2000. Spatial Distribution and Population Composition of the Brown Mouse Lemur (*Microcebus rufus*) in Ranomafana National Park, Madagascar, and Its Implications for Social Organization. *International Journal of Primatology* 51 (1): 61–78.

Atsalis, S., J. Schmid, and P. M. Kappeler. 1996. Metrical Comparisons of Three Species of Mouse Lemur. *Journal of Human Evolution* 31: 61–68.

Aujard, F., M. Perret, and G. Vannier. 1998. Thermoregulatory Responses to Variations of Photoperiod and Ambient Temperature in the Male Lesser Mouse Lemur: A Primitive or an Advanced Adaptive Character? *Journal of Comparative Physiology B: Biochemical, Systemic, and Environmental Physiology* 168 (7): 540–548.

Balko, E. 1997. *A Behaviorally Plastic Response to Forest Composition and Habitat Disturbance by* Varecia variegata variegata *in Ranomafana National Park, Madagascar.* Syracuse: State University of New York College of Environmental Science and Forestry.

Barclay, R. M. R. 1995. Does Energy or Calcium Availability Constrain Reproduction by Bats? *Symposia of the Zoological Society of London* 67: 245–258.

Barnes, B. M. 1989. Freeze Avoidance in a Mammal: Body Temperatures Below 0° in an Arctic Hibernator. *Science* 224: 1593–1595.

Barnes, B. M. 1996. Relationships between Hibernation and Reproduction in Male Ground Squirrels. In *Adaptations to the Cold: Tenth International Hibernation Symposium*, eds. F. Geiser, A. J. Hulbert, and S. C. Nicol, 71–80. Armidale, Australia: University of New England Press.

Barre, V., A. Levec, J. J. Petter, and R. Albignac. 1988. Etude du Microcèbe par Radio-Tracking dans la Forêt de L'Ankarafantsika. In *L'Equilibre des Ecosystèmes Forestiers à Madagascar,* 61–71. Gland, Switzerland: IUCN.

Bartness, T. J., and G. N. Wade. 1989. Photoperiodic Control of Seasonal Body Weight in Hamsters. *Neuroscience and Biobehavioral Reviews* 9: 599–612.

Bazzaz, F. A., and S. T. A. Pickett. 1980. Physiological Ecology of Tropical Succession, a Comprehensive Review. *Annual Review of Ecology and Systematics* 11: 287–310.

Bearder, S. K. 1987. Lorises, Bushbabies, and Tarsiers: Diverse Societies in Solitary Foragers. In *Primate Societies*, eds. B. B. Smuts, D. L. Cheney, R. M. Seyfarth, R. W. Wrangham, and T. T. Struhsaker, 14–24. Chicago, IL: University of Chicago Press.

Bearder, S. K. 1999. Physical and Social Diversity among Nocturnal Primates: A New View Based on Long Term Research. *Primates* 40 (1): 267–282.

Bearder, S. K., and G. A. Doyle. 1974. Ecology of Bushbabies *Galago senegalensis* and *Galago crassicaudatus* with Some Notes on Their Behaviour in the Field. In *Prosimian Biology*, eds. R. D. Martin, G. A. Doyle, and A. C. Walker, 109–130. London: Duckworth.

Bearder, S. K., and R. D. Martin. 1980. Acacia Gum and Its Use by Bushbabies, *Galago senegalensis* (Primates: Lorisidae). *International Journal of Primatology* 1: 103–128.

Bearder, S., K. Nekaris, and C. Buzzell. 2002. Dangers in the Night: Are Some Nocturnal Primates Afraid of the Dark? In *Eat or Be Eaten: Predator Sensitive Foraging among Primates*, ed. L. Miller, 21–43. Cambridge: Cambridge University Press.

Bercovitch, F. B. 1989. Body Size, Sperm Competition, and Determinants of Reproductive Success in Male Savanna Baboons. *Evolution* 43 (7): 1507–1521.

Blanco, M. B. in press. Reproductive Schedules of Brown Mouse Lemurs (*Microcebus rufus*) at Ranomafana National Park, Madagascar. *International Journal of Primatology.*

Blanco, M. B. 2007. Reproductive Schedules of Brown Mouse Lemurs (*Microcebus rufus*) at Ranomafana National Park, Madagascar. *American Journal of Physical Anthropology* (44): 75–76.

Blumstein, D. T., I. Soyeon, A. Nicodemus, and C. Zugmeyer. 2004. Yellow-Bellied Marmots (*Marmota flaviventris*) Hibernate Socially. *Journal of Mammalogy* 85 (1): 25–29.

Bordignon, M. O. 2006. Diet of the Fishing Bat *Noctilio leporinus* (Linnaeus) (Mammalia, Chiroptera) in a Mangrove Area of Southern Brazil. *Revista Brasileira de Zoologia* 23 (1): 256–260.

Borror, D. J., and R. E. White. 1970. *A Field Guide to Insects.* Boston, MA: Houghton Mifflin Company.

Borror, D. J., D. M. De Long, and C. A. Triplehorn. 1981. *An Introduction to the Study of Insects.* Philadelphia, PA: Saunders College Publishing.

Bourlière, F. 1975. Mammals, Small and Large: The Ecological Implications of Size. In *Small Mammals: Their Productivity and Population Dynamics*, eds. F. B. Golley, K. Petrusewicz, and L. Ryszowski, 1–8. Cambridge: Cambridge University Press.

Bourlière, F., and A. Petter-Rousseaux. 1966. Existence Probable d'un Rythme Métabolique Saisonnier Chez les Cheirogaleinae (Lemuroidea). *Folia Primatologica* 4: 249–256.

Branch, L. C., D. Villarreal, and G. S. Fowler. 1993. Recruitment, Dispersal, and Group Fusion in a Declining Population of the Plains Viscacha (*Lagostomus maximus;* Chinchillidae). *Journal of Mammalogy* 74 (1): 9–20.

Braune, P., S. Polenz, V. Zietemann, and E. Zimmermann. 2001. Species-Specific Signaling in Two Sympatrically Living Nocturnal Primates, the Grey and the Golden-Brown Mouse Lemur (*Microcebus murinus* and *Microcebus ravelobensis*), in Northwestern Madagascar. *Advances in Ethology* 36: 126.

Braune, P., S. Schmid, and E. Zimmermann. 2003. First Evidence for a Gathering Call in a Nocturnal Solitary Ranging Primate. *Folia Primatologica* 74 (4): 185.

Braune, P., S. Schmid, and E. Zimmermann. 2005. Spacing and Group Coordination in a Nocturnal Primate, the Golden Brown Mouse Lemur (*Microcebus ravelobensis*): the Role of Olfactory and Acoustic Signals. *Behavioral Ecology and Sociobiology* 58 (6): 587–596.

Bronson, F. H. 1989. Mammalian Reproductive Biology. Chicago, IL: University of Chicago Press.

Buesching, C. D., M. Heistermann, J. K. Hodges, and E. Zimmermann. 1998. Multimodal Oestrus Advertisement in a Small Nocturnal Prosimian, *Microcebus murinus. Folia Primatologica* 69 (Supplement 1): 295–308.

Bullock, S. H., and J. A. Solís-Magallanes. 1990. Phenology of Canopy Trees of a Tropical Deciduous Forest in México. *Biotropica* 22: 22–35.

Calder, D. M. 1983. Mistletoes in Focus: An Introduction. In *The Biology of Mistletoes*, eds. M. D. Calder and P. Bernhardt, 1–18. New York: Academic Press.

Carey, H. V. 2005. Gastrointestinal Responses to Fasting in Mammals: Lessons from Hibernators. In *Physiological and Ecological Adaptations to Feeding in Vertebrates*, eds. J. M. Starck and T. Wang, 229–254. Enfield, NH: Science Publishers.

Cartmill, M. 1990. Human Uniqueness and Theoretical Content in Paleoanthropology. *International Journal of Primatology* 11: 173–192.

Cartmill, M. 1992. New Views on Primate Origins. *Evolutionary Anthropology* 1 (3): 105–111.

Charles-Dominique, P. 1971. Eco-Ethologie des Prosimiens du Gabon. *Extrait de la revue Biologia Gabonica* 7 (2): 121–228.

Charles-Dominique, P. 1972. Ecologie et Vie Sociale de *Galago demidovii* Fischer 1808. *Zeitschrift fur Tierpsychologie* 9: 7–41.

Charles-Dominique, P. 1975. Nocturnality and Diurnality: An Ecological Interpretation of these Two Modes of Life by an Analysis of the Higher Vertebrate Fauna in Tropical Forest Ecosystems. In *Phylogeny of Primates: A Multidisciplinary Approach*, eds W. P. Luckett, F. S. Szalay, 69–88. New York: Plenum Press.

Charles-Dominique, P. 1977. *Ecology and Behaviour of Nocturnal Primates*. New York: Columbia University Press.

Charles-Dominique, P. 1978. Solitary and Gregarious Prosimians: Evolution of Social Structure in Primates. In *Recent Advances in Primatology*, eds. D. J. Chivers and K. A. Joysey, 139–149. New York: Academic Press.

Charles-Dominique, P., and R. D. Martin. 1970. Evolution of the Lorises and Lemurs. *Nature* 227: 257–260.

Charles-Dominique, P., and J. J. Petter. 1980. Ecology and Social Life of *Phaner furcifer*. In *Nocturnal Malagasy Primates, Ecology, Physiology, and Behavior*, eds. P. Charles-Dominique, H. M. Cooper, A. Hladik, C. M. Hladik, E. Pagès, G. F. Pariente, A. Petter-Rousseaux, and A. Schilling, 75–95. New York: Academic Press.

Charlot, S., and Perret, M. 2000. Effects of Social Environment on Daily Heterothermia in a Malagasy Primate: The Grey Mouse Lemur (*Microcebus murinus*). *Folia Primatologica* 71 (4): 254–255.

Claridge, M. F. 1986. Insect Assemblages—Diversity, Organization, and Evolution. In *Organization of Communities, Past and Present*, eds. J. H. R. Gee and P. S. Giller, 141–162. Oxford: Blackwell Scientific Publications.

Clark, A. B. 1978. Sex Ratio and Local Resource Competition in a Prosimian Primate. *Science* 201: 163–165.

Clark, A. B. 1985. Sociality in a Nocturnal "Solitary" Prosimian: *Galago crassicaudatus*. *International Journal of Primatology* 6: 581–600.

Clutton-Brock, T. H. 1989. Mammalian Mating Systems. *Proceedings of the Royal Society of London B* 236: 339–372.

Clutton-Brock, T. H., and P. H. Harvey. 1977a. Primate Ecology and Social Organization. *Journal of Zoology (London)* 183: 1–39.

Clutton-Brock, T. H., and P. H. Harvey. 1977b. Species Differences in Feeding and Ranging Behaviour in Primates. In *Primate Ecology*, ed. T. H. Clutton-Brock, 557–584. London: Academic Press.

Clutton-Brock, T. H., and P. H. Harvey. 1978. Mammals, Resources and Reproductive Strategies. *Nature* 273: 191–195.

Clutton-Brock, T. H., and P. H. Harvey. 1983. The Functional Significance of Variation in Body Size among Mammals. In *Advances in the Study of Mammalian Behavior*, eds. J. F. Eisenberg and D. G. Kleiman, 632–663. Shippensburg, PA: American Society of Mammalogists.

Coe, M. J. 1984. Primates: Their Niche Structure and Habitats. In *Food Acquisition and Processing in Primates*, eds. D. J. Chivers, B. A. Wood, and A. Bilsborough, 1–32. New York: Plenum.

Colas, S. 1996. Energetics and Behavioural Aspects of Maternal Investment in *Microcebus murinus*. *Folia Primatologica* 67 (2): 86–87.

Colas, S. 1999. Evidence for Sex-biased Behavioral Maternal Investment in the Gray Mouse Lemur (*Microcebus murinus*). *International Journal of Primatology* 20 (2): 911–926.

Corbin, G. D., and J. Schmid. 1995. Insect Secretions Determine Habitat Use Patterns by a Female Lesser Mouse Lemur (*Microcebus murinus*). *American Journal of Primatology* 37: 317–324.

Cork, S. J. 1994. The Digestive Constraints on Dietary Scope in Small and Moderately-Small Mammals, How Much Do We Really Understand? In

The Digestive System in Mammals, Food, Form and Function, eds. D. J. Chivers and P. Langer, 337–369. Cambridge: Cambridge University Press.

Coutts, R. A., M. B. Fenton, and E. Glen. 1973. Food Intake by Captive *Myotis lucifugus* and *Eptesicus fuscus* (Chiroptera: Vespertilionidae). *Journal of Mammalogy* 54: 985–990.

Craul, M., E. Zimmermann, and U. Radespiel. 2003. Experimental Evidence for Female Mate Choice in the Grey Mouse Lemur (*Microcebus murinus*). *Folia Primatologica* 74: 179–230.

Crook, J. H., and J. S. Gartlan. 1966. Evolution of Primate Societies. *Nature* 210: 1200–1203.

Dagosto, M. 1989. Locomotion of *Varecia variegata* and *Propithecus diadema* at Ranomafana National Park, Madagascar. *American Journal of Physical Anthropology* 78: 209.

Dammhahn, M., and P. M. Kappeler. 2003. The Social System of the World's Smallest Primate, the Pygmy Mouse Lemur (*Microcebus berthae*). *Folia Primatologica* 74: 188.

Dammhahn, M., and P. M. Kappeler. 2005. Social System of *Microcebus berthae*, the World's Smallest Primate. *International Journal of Primatology* 26 (2): 407–435.

Dammhahn, M., and P. M. Kappeler. 2006. Feeding Ecology and Activity Patterns of *Microcebus berthae* and sympatric *M. murinus* (Cheirogaleidae). *International Journal of Primatology* 27 (1): 44.

Dausmann, K. H., J. U. Ganzhorn, and G. Heldmaier. 2001. Why Does It Sleep So Well? The Physiological Basis of Hibernation in *Cheirogaleus medius*. *Folia Primatologica* 72 (3): 157.

Dausmann, K. H., J. Glos, J. U. Ganzhorn, and G. Heldmaier. 2004. Hibernation in a Tropical Primate—Even in the Wound-Down Hibernating State, this Lemur Can Warm up without Waking up. *Nature* 429 (6994): 825–826.

Davidar, P. 1983. Birds and Neotropical Mistletoes: Effects on Seedling Recruitment. *Oecologia* 60: 271–273.

Deppe, A. M. 2005. Visual Predator Recognition and Response in Wild Brown Mouse Lemurs (*Microcebus rufus*) in Ranomafana National Park, Madagascar. *American Journal of Primatology* 66 (1): 97–98.

Deppe, A. M. 2006. Visual Snake Recognition in Wild Brown Mouse Lemurs. *American Journal of Primatology* 68 (1): 34.

Deppe, A. M., M. Randriamiarisoa, A. Kasprak, P. C. Wright. in preparation. A Predation Event on a Small Nocturnal Primate, the Brown Mouse Lemur (*Microcebus rufus* by a Diurnal Carnivore, the Right-Tailed Mongoose (*Galidia elegans*).

Dew, J. L., and P. Wright. 1998. Frugivory and Seed Dispersal by Four Species of Primates in Madagascar's Eastern Rain Forest. *Biotropica* 30 (3): 425–437.

Di Fiore, A. 2003. Ranging Behavior and Foraging Ecology of Lowland Woolly Monkeys (*Lagothrix lagotricha poeppigii*) in Yasuni National Park, Ecuador. *American Journal of Primatology* 59: 47–66.

Dice, L. R. 1945. Measures of the Amount of Ecologic Association between Species. *Ecology* 26 (3): 297–302.

Dickman, C. R., and C. Huang. 1988. The Reliability of Fecal Analysis as a Method for Determining the Diet of Insectivorous Mammals. *Journal of Mammalogy* 69 (1): 108–113.

Donque, G. 1972. The Climatology of Madagascar. In *Biogeography and Ecology in Madagascar*, eds. R. Battistini and G. Richard-Vindard, 87–142. The Hague: Junk.

Doyle, G. A. 1974. The Behaviour of the Lesser Bushbaby *Galago senegalensis moholi*. In *Prosimian Biology*, eds. R. D. Martin, G. A. Doyle, and A. C. Walker, 213–231. London: Duckworth.

Duckworth, J. W., M. I. Evans, A. F. A. Hawkins, R. J. Safford, and R. J. Wilkinson. 1995. The Lemurs of Marojejy Strict Nature Reserve, Madagascar: A Status Overview with Notes on Ecology and Threats. *International Journal of Primatology* 16 (3): 545–559.

Dufils, J.-M. 2003. Forest Ecology. In *The Natural History of Madagascar*, eds. S. M. Goodman and J. P. Benstead, 88–96. Chicago, IL: University of Chicago Press.

Dunbar, R. I. M. 1988. *Primate Social Systems*. Ithaca, NY: Comstock/Cornell.

Durbin, J. C. 1999. Lemurs as Flagships for Conservation in Madagascar. In *New Directions in Lemur Studies*, eds. B. Rakotosamimanana, H. Rasamimanana, J. U. Ganzhorn, and S. M. Goodman, 269–281. New York: Kluwer Academic/Plenum Press.

Durham, D. L. 2003. *Variation in Responses to Forest Disturbance and the Risk of Local Extinction: A Comparative Study of Wild Eulemurs at Ranomafana National Park, Madagascar*. Davis: University of California.

Dutrillaux, B., and Y. Rumpler. 1995. Phylogenetic Relations among Prosimii with Special Reference to Lemuriformes and Malagasy Nocturnals. In *Creatures of the Dark: The Nocturnal Prosimians*, eds. L. Alterman, G. A. Doyle, and M. K. Izard, 141–150. New York: Plenum Press.

Eberle, M., and P. M. Kappeler. 2002. Cooperative Breeding in Grey Mouse Lemurs (*Microcebus murinus*). In *Caring for Primates. Abstracts of the XIXth Congress. The International Primatological Society*, 28. Beijing: Mammalogical Society in China.

Eberle, M., and P. M. Kappeler. 2003. Cooperative Breeding in Grey Mouse Lemurs (*Microcebus murinus*). *Folia Primatologica* 74 (5–6): 367.

Eberle, M., and P. M. Kappeler. 2007. The Family Insurance: Kin Selection and Cooperative Breeding in a Solitary Primate (*Microcebus murinus*). *American Journal of Primatology* 69 (1): 127.

Eisenberg, J. F. 1981. *The Mammalian Radiations: An Analysis of Trends in Evolution, Adaptation, and Behavior*. Chicago, IL: University of Chicago Press.

Eisenberg, J. F., and E. Gould. 1970. *The Tenrecs: A Study in Mammalian Behavior and Evolution*. Washington, DC: Smithsonian Institution Press.

Eisenberg, J. F., N. A. Muckenhirn, and R. Rudran. 1972. The Relations between Ecology and Social Structure in Primates. *Science* 176: 863–874.

Emlen, S. T., and L. W. Oring. 1977. Ecology, Sexual Selection and the Evolution of Mating Systems. *Science* 197: 215–223.

Emmons, L. H., J. Nais, and A. Briun. 1991. The Fruit and Consumers of *Rafflesia keithii* (Rafflesiaceae). *Biotropica* 23: 197–199.

Fairbairn, D. J. 1977. The Spring Decline in Deer Mice: Death or Dispersal? *Canadian Journal of Zoology* 55: 84–92.

Fenton, M. B., D. W. Thomas, and R. Sasseen. 1981. *Nycteris grandis* (Nycteridae), an African carnivorous bat. *Journal of Zoology (London)* 194: 461–465.

Fenton, M. B., D. H. M. Cumming, I. L. N. Rautenbach, S. G. Cumming, M. S. Cumming, F. Gavin, R. D. Taylor, C. V. Portfors, M. C. Kalcounis, and Z. Mahlanga. 1998. Bats and the Loss of Tree Canopy in African Woodlands. *Conservation Biology* 12 (2): 399–407.

Fietz, J. 1998. Body Mass in Wild *Microcebus murinus* over the Dry Season. *Folia Primatologica* 69: 183–190.

Fietz, J. 1999a. Monogamy as a Rule Rather than Exception in Nocturnal Lemurs: The Case of the Tat-Tailed Dwarf Lemur, *Cheirogaleus medius*. *Ethology* 105: 259–272.

Fietz, J. 1999b. Demography and Floating Males in a Population of *Cheirogaleus medius*. In *New Directions in Lemur Studies*, eds. B. Rakotosamimanana, H. Rasamimanana, J. Ganzhorn, and S. Goodman, 159–172. New York: Kluwer Academic/Plenum Press Publishers.

Fietz, J. 1999c. Mating System of *Microcebus murinus*. *American Journal of Primatology* 48: 127–133.

Fietz, J. 2003a. Pair Living and Mating Strategies in the Fat-Tailed Dwarf Lemur (*Cheirogaleus medius*). In *Monogamy: Mating Strategies and Partnerships in Birds, Humans and Other Mammals*, eds. U. H. Reichard and C. Boesch, 214–231. Cambridge: Cambridge University Press.

Fietz, J. 2003b. Primates: *Cheirogaleus*, Dwarf Lemurs or Fat-Tailed Lemurs. In *The Natural History of Madagascar*, eds. S. M. Goodman and J. P. Benstead, 1307–1309. Chicago, IL: University of Chicago Press.

Fietz, J., and K. H. Dausmann. 2003. Costs and Potential Benefits of Parental Care in the Nocturnal Fat-Tailed Dwarf Lemur (*Cheirogaleus medius*). *Folia Primatologica* 74 (5–6): 246–258.

Fietz, J., K. H. Dausmann, and F. Tataruch. 2001. Fat Accumulation and Composition in the Tropical Hibernator *Cheirogaleus medius*. *Folia Primatologica* 72 (3): 159.

Fietz, J., and J. U. Ganzhorn. 1999. Feeding Ecology of the Hibernating Primate *Cheirogaleus medius*: How Does it Get So Fat? *Oecologia* 121 (2): 157–164.

Fietz, J., H. Zischler, C. Schwiegk, J. Tomiuk, K. H. Dausmann, and J. U. Ganzhorn. 2000. High Rates of Extra-Pair Young in the Pair-Living Fat-Tailed Dwarf Lemur, *Cheirogaleus medius*. *Behavioral Ecology and Sociobiology* 49 (1): 8–17.

Fleagle, J. G. 1984. Primate Locomotion and Diet. In *Food Acquisition and Processing in Primates*, eds. D. J. Chivers, B. A. Wood, and A. Bilsborough, 105–117. New York: Plenum Press.

Fleagle, J. G. 1988. *Primate Adaptation and Evolution.* New York: Academic Press.

Fleagle, J. G. 1998. *Primate Adaptation and Evolution.* San Diego, CA: Academic Press.

Fleming, T. H. 1975. The Role of Small Mammals in Tropical Ecosystems. In *Small Mammals: Their Productivity and Population Dynamics*, eds. F. B. Golley, K. Petrusewicz, and L. Ryszkowski, 269–298. Cambridge: Cambridge University Press.

Fleming, T. H. 1979. Life History Strategies. In *Ecology of Small Mammals*, ed. D. M. Stoddart, 1–60. London: Chapman and Hall.

Fleming, T. H., R. Brirwisch, and G. H. Whitesides. 1987. Patterns of Tropical Vertebrate Frugivore Diversity. *Annual Review of Ecology and Systematics* 18: 91–109.

Fletcher, Q. E., R. J. Fisher, C. K. R. Willis, and R. M. Brigham. 2004. Free-Ranging Common Nighthawks Use Torpor. *Journal of Thermal Biology* 29: 9–14.

Florant, G. L. 1998. Lipid Metabolism in Hibernators: The Importance of Essential Fatty Acids. *American Zoologist* 38 (2): 331–340.

Florant, G. L., L. Hester, S. Ameenuddin, and D. A. Rintoul. 1993. The Effect of a Low Essential Fatty Acid Diet on Hibernation in Marmots. *American Journal of Physiology* 264: 747–753.

Foerg, R. 1982. Reproduction in *Cheirogaleus medius*. *Folia Primatologica* 39 (1–2): 49–62.

Foerg, R., and R. Hoffmann. 1982. Seasonal and Daily Activity Changes in Captive *Cheirogaleus medius*. *Folia Primatologica* 38: 259–268.

Foster, M. S., and R. W. McDiarmid. 1983. Nutritional Value of the Aril of *Trichilia cuneata*, a Bird-Dispersed Fruit. *Biotropica* 15: 26–31.

Fowler, P. A. 1988. Thermoregulation in the Female Hedgehog, *Erinaceus europaeus*, during the Breeding Season. *Journal of Reproduction and Fertility* 82: 285–292.

Frankie, G. W., H. G. Baker, and P. A. Opler. 1974. Comparative Phenological Studies of Trees in Tropical Wet and Dry Forests in the Lowlands of Costa Rica. *Journal of Ecology* 62: 881–919.

French, A. R. 1988. The Patterns of Mammalian Hibernation. *American Scientist* 76: 569–575.

French, A. R. 1992. Mammalian Dormancy. In *Mammalian Energetics: Interdisciplinary Views of Metabolism and Reproduction*, eds. T. E. Tomasi and T. H. Horton, 105–121. Ithaca, NY: Comstock Publishing Associates.

French, N. R., D. M. Stoddart, and B. Bobek. 1975. Patterns of Demography in Small Mammal Populations. In *Small Mammals: Their Productivity and Population Dynamics*, eds. F. B. Golley, K. Petrusewicz, and L. Ryszkowski, 73–102. Cambridge: Cambridge University Press.

Gaines, M. S., and M. L. Johnson. 1987. Phenotypic and Genotypic Mechanisms for Dispersal in *Microtus* Populations and the Role of Dispersal in Population Regulation. In *Mammalian Dispersal Patterns: The Effects of Social Structure on Population Genetics*, eds. B. D. Chepko-Sade and Z. T. Halpin, 162–179. Chicago, IL: University of Chicago Press.

Gaines, M. S., and L. R. J. McClenaghan. 1980. Dispersal in Small Mammals. *Annual Review of Ecology and Systematics* 11: 163–196.

Ganzhorn, J. U. 1988. Food Partitioning among Malagasy Primates. *Oecologia* 75: 436–450.

Ganzhorn, J. U. 1989a. Niche Separation of Seven Lemur Species in the Eastern Rainforest of Madagascar. *Oecologia* 79: 279–286.

Ganzhorn, J. U. 1989b. Primate Species Separation in Relation to Secondary Plant Chemicals. *Human Evolution* 4 (2): 125–132.

Ganzhorn, J. U., and P. M. Kappeler. 1996. Lemurs of the Kirindy Forest. *Primate Report* 46 (1): 257–274.

Garber, P. A. 1984. Proposed Nutritional Importance of Plant Exudates in the Diet of the Panamanian Tamarin, *Saguinus oedipus geoffroyi*. *International Journal of Primatology* 5: 1–5.

Garber, P. A. 1987. Foraging Strategies among Living Primates. *Annual Review of Anthropology* 16: 339–364.

Gaulin, S. J. C. 1979. A Jarman/Bell Model of Primate Feeding Niches. *Human Ecology* 7: 1–21.

Gautier-Hion, A., J.-M. Duplantier, R. Quris, F. Feer, C. Sourd, J.-P. Decoux, G. Dubost, L. Emmons, C. Erard, P. Hecketsweiler, A. Moungazi, C. Roussilhon, and J.-M. Thiollay. 1985. Fruit Characters as a Basis of Fruit Choice and Seed Dispersal in a Tropical Forest Vertebrate Community. *Oecologia* 65 (3): 324–337.

Gebo, D. L. 1987. Locomotor Diversity in Prosimian Primates. *American Journal of Primatology* 13: 271–281.

Gebo, D. L. 2004. A Shrew-Sized Origin for Primates. *Yearbook of Physical Anthropology* 47: 40–62.

Geiser, F. 1986. Thermoregulation and Torpor in the Kultarr, *Antechinomys laniger* (Marsupalia: Dasyuridae). *Journal of Comparative Physiology B: Biochemical, Systemic, and Environmental Physiology* 156: 751–757.

Geiser, F., and R. V. Baudinette 1987. Seasonality of Torpor and Thermoregulation in Three Dasyurid Marsupials. *Journal of Comparative Physiology B: Biochemical, Systemic, and Environmental Physiology* 157: 335–344.

Geiser, F., and G. J. Kenagy. 1993. Dietary Fats and Torpor Patterns in Hibernating Ground Squirrels. *Canadian Journal of Zoology* 71: 1182–1186.

Génin, F. 2000. Food Restriction Enhances Deep Torpor Bouts in the Grey Mouse Lemur. *Folia Primatologica* 71 (4): 258–259.

Génin, F. 2001. Gumnivory in Mouse Lemurs during the Dry Season in Madagascar. *Folia Primatologica* 72 (3): 119–120.

Génin, F., and M. Perret. 2000. Photoperiod-Induced Changes in Energy Balance in Gray Mouse Lemurs. *Physiology and Behavior* 71 (3–4): 315–321.

Génin, F., and M. Perret. 2003. Daily Hypothermia in Captive Grey Mouse Lemurs (*Microcebus murinus*): Effects of Photoperiod and Food Restriction. *Comparative Biochemistry and Physiology Part B* 136 (1): 71–81.

Genoud, M. 2002. Comparative Studies of Basal Rate of Metabolism in Primates. *Evolutionary Anthropology* 11 (Supplement 1): 108–111.

Gilbert, A. N. 1986. Mammary Number and Litter Size in Rodentia: The "One-Half Rule". *Proceedings of the National Academy of Sciences of the United States of America* 83: 4828–4830.

Gillies, A. C., G. T. H. Ellison, and J. D. Skinner. 1991. The Effect of Seasonal Food Restriction on Activity, Metabolism and Torpor in the South African Hedgehog (*Atelerix frontalis*). *Journal of Zoology (London)* 223: 117–130.

Gingerich, P. D. 1975. Dentition of *Adapis parisiensis* and the Evolution of Lemuriform Primates. In *Lemur Biology*, eds. I. Tattersall and R. W. Sussman, 65–80. New York: Plenum Press.

Glander, K. E., P. C. Wright, P. S. Daniels, and A. M. Merenlender. 1992. Morphometrics and Testicle Size of Rain Forest Lemur Species from Southeastern Madagascar. *Journal of Human Evolution* 22: 117.

Glatston, A. R. H. 1979. *Reproduction and Behaviour of the Lesser Mouse Lemur (Microcebus murinus, Miller 1777) in Captivity*. London: University College, University of London.

Glaw, F., and M. Vences. 2003. Introduction to Amphibians. In *The Natural History of Madagascar*, eds. S. M. Goodman and J. P. Benstead, 883–898. Chicago, IL: University of Chicago Press.

Godfrey, L. R., W. L. Jungers, E. L. Simons, P. S. Chatrath, and B. Rakotosamimanana. 1999. Past and Present Distributions of Lemurs in Madagascar. In *New Directions in Lemur Studies*, eds. B. Rakotosamimanana, H. Rasamimanana, J. U. Ganzhorn, and S. M. Goodman, 19–53. New York: Kluwer Academic/Plenum Press.

Godin, A. J. 1977. *Order Rodentia: Wild Mammals of New England*. Baltimore, MD: Johns Hopkins University Press.

Godschalk, S. K. B. 1983a. The Morphology of Some South African Mistletoe Fruits. *South African Journal of Botany* 2 (1): 52–56.

Godschalk, S. K. B. 1983b. A Biochemical Analysis of the Fruit of *Tapinanthus leendertziae*. *South African Journal of Biology* 2 (1): 42–45.

Godschalk, S. K. B. 1983c. Mistletoe Dispersal by Birds in South Africa. In *The Biology of Mistletoes*, eds. M. D. Calder and P. Bernhardt, 117–128. New York: Academic Press.

Godschalk, S. K. B. 1985. Feeding Behavior of Avian Dispersers of Mistletoe Fruit in the Loskop Dam Nature Reserve, South Africa. *South African Journal of Zoology* 20 (3): 136–146.

Goldman, B. D. 1999. The Circadian Timing System and Reproduction in Mammals. *Steroids* 64: 679–685.

Golley, F. B., K. Petrusewicz, and L. Ryszkowski. 1975. *Small Mammals: Their Productivity and Population Dynamics.* Cambridge: Cambridge University Press.

Goodman, S. M. 2003. Predation on Lemurs. In *The Natural History of Madagascar*, eds. S. M. Goodman and J. P. Benstead, 1221–1228. Chicago, IL: University of Chicago Press.

Goodman, S. M., and J. P. Benstead, eds. 2003. *The Natural History of Madagascar.* Chicago, IL: University of Chicago Press.

Goodman, S. M., and J. P. Benstead. 2005. Updated Estimates of Biotic Diversity and Endemism for Madagascar. *Oryx* 39 (1): 73–77.

Goodman, S. M., G. K. Creighton, and C. Raxworthy. 1991. The Food Habits of the Madagascar Long-Eared Owl *Asio madagascariensis* in Southeastern Madagascar. *Bonner Zoologische Beitraege* 42: 21–26.

Goodman, S. M., J. U. Ganzhorn, and D. Rakotondravony. 2003. Introduction to the Mammals. In *The Natural History of Madagascar*, eds. S. M. Goodman and J. P. Benstead, 1159–1186. Chicago, IL: University of Chicago Press.

Goodman, S. M., J. U. Ganzhorn, and L. Wilmé. 1997. Observations at a *Ficus* Tree in Malagasy Humid Forest. *Biotropica* 29 (4): 480–488.

Goodman, S. M., S. O'Conner, and O. Langrand. 1993. A Review of Predation on Lemurs: Implications for the Evolution of Social Behavior in Small, Nocturnal Primates. In *Lemur Social Systems and Their Ecological Basis*, eds. P. M. Kappeler and J. U. Ganzhorn, 51–66. New York: Plenum Press.

Gosset, D., and J. J. Roeder. 2000. Colour and Shape Discrimination in Black Lemurs (*Eulemur macacao*). *Folia Primatologica* 71: 173–176.

Grassi, C. 2001. *The Behavioral Ecology of Hapalemur griseus griseus: The Influences of Microhabitat and Population Density on this Small-Bodied Prosimian Folivore.* Austin: University of Texas at Austin.

Greenwood, P. J. 1980. Mating Systems, Philopatry and Dispersal in Birds and Mammals. *Animal Behaviour* 28: 1140–1162.

Groeneveld, L. F., R. M. Rasoloarison, A. D. Yoder, C. H. Roos, and P. M. Kappeler. 2006. Diversity of Mouse and Dwarf Lemurs. *International Journal of Primatology* 27 (1): 444.

Groves, C. P. 2000. The Genus *Cheirogaleus:* Unrecognized Biodiversity in Dwarf Lemurs. *International Journal of Primatology* 21: 943–962.

Groves, C. P. 2005. Order Primates. In *Mammal Species of the World: A Taxonomic and Geographic Reference*, eds. D. E. Wilson and D. M. Reeder, 111–184. Baltimore, MD: Johns Hopkins University Press.

Gür, H., and M. K. Gür. 2005. Annual Cycle of Activity, Reproduction, and Body Mass of Anatolian Ground Squirrels (*Spermophilus xanthoprymnus*) in Turkey. *Journal of Mammalogy* 86 (1): 7–14.

Gursky, S. 1995. Group Size and Composition in the Spectral Tarsier, *Tarsius spectrum*, Sulawesi, Indonesia: Implications for Social Organization. *Tropical Biodiversity* 3 (1): 57–62.

Gursky, S. 1997. *Modeling Maternal Time Budgets: The Impact of Lactation and Gestation on the Behavior of the Spectral Tarsier,* Tarsius spectrum. Stony Brook: SUNY-Stony Brook.

Gursky, S. 2000. Effect of Seasonality on the Behavior of an Insectivorous Primate, *Tarsius spectrum. International Journal of Primatology* 24 (1): 477–495.

Gursky, S. 2002a. The Behavioral Ecology of the Spectral Tarsier, *Tarsius spectrum. Evolutionary Anthropology* 11: 226–234.

Gursky, S. 2002b. Determinants of Gregariousness in the Spectral Tarsier (Prosimian: *Tarsius spectrum*). *Journal of Zoology* 256: 1–10.

Gursky, S. 2003. Lunar Philia in a Nocturnal Primate. *International Journal of Primatology* 24 (2): 351–367.

Hafen, T., H. Neveu, Y. Rumpler, I. Wilden, and E. Zimmermann. 1998. Acoustically Dimorphic Advertisement Calls Separate Morphologically and Genetically Homogenous Populations of the Grey Mouse Lemur (*Microcebus murinus*). *Folia Primatologica* 69 (1): 342–356.

Halle, S., and N. C. Stenseth, eds. 2000. *Activity Patterns in Small Mammals: An Ecological Approach.* New York: Springer. 320 p.

Hanski, I. 2004. *Biology of an Old Adaptive Radiation: Evolutionary Community Ecology of the Beetles Canthonini and Helictopleurini in Madagascar.* Helsinki: University of Helsinki.

Hapke, A., J. Fietz, S. D. Nash, D. Rakotondravony, B. Rakotosamimanana, J. B. Ramanamanjato, G. F. N. Randria, and H. Zischler. 2005. Biogeography of Dwarf Lemurs: Genetic Evidence for Unexpected Patterns in Southeastern Madagascar. *International Journal of Primatology* 26 (4): 873–901.

Harborne, J. B. 1972. *Phytochemical Ecology.* London: Academic Press.

Harcourt, C. 1986. Seasonal Variation in the Diet of South African Galagos. *International Journal of Primatology* 7: 491–506.

Harcourt, C. 1987. Brief Trap/Retrap Study of the Brown Mouse Lemur (*Microcebus rufus*). *Folia Primatologica* 49: 209–211.

Harcourt, C. 1991. Diet and Behaviour of a Nocturnal Lemur, *Avahi laniger,* in the Wild. *Journal of Zoology (London)* 223: 667–674.

Harcourt, C., and S. K. Bearder. 1989. A Comparison of *Galago moholi* in South Africa with *Galago zanzibaricus. International Journal of Primatology* 10: 35–45.

Harcourt, C., and L. T. Nash. 1986a. Species Differences in Substrate Use and Diet between Sympatric Galagos in Two Kenyan Coastal Forests. *Primates* 27: 41–52.

Harcourt, C., and L. T. Nash. 1986b. Social Organization of Galagos in Kenyan Coastal Forests: I. *Galago zanzibaricus. American Journal of Primatology* 10: 339–355.

Harcourt, C., and J. Thornback. 1990. *Lemurs of Madagascar and the Comoros: The IUCN Red Data Book.* Gland, Switzerland: IUCN.

Harcourt, A. H., P. H. Harvey, S. G. Larson, and R. V. Short. 1981. Testis Weight, Body Weight, and Breeding System in Primates. *Nature* 293: 55–57.

Harder, B. 2007. Perchance to Hibernate: Can We Tap a Dormant Capacity to Downshift our Metabolism? *Science News* 171 (4): 49–64.

Harding, R. S. O. 1981. An Order of Omnivores, Non-Human Primate Diets in the Wild. In *Omnivorous Primates, Gathering and Hunting in Human Evolution*, eds. R. S. O. Harding and G. Teleki, 191–214. New York: Columbia University Press.

Harste, L. V. 1993. Feeding Behavior in *Microcebus rufus*. B.A. honors thesis, State University of New York at Stony Brook.

Harste, L. V., P. C. Wright, and J. Jernvall. 1997. *Microcebus rufus* Feeding Behaviour in the South-Eastern Rain Forest of Madagascar. *Primate Eye* 62: 6–7.

Harvey, P. H., and A. H. Harcourt. 1984. Sperm Competition, Testes Size, and Breeding Systems in Primates. In *Sperm Competition and the Evolution of Animal Mating Systems*, ed. R. L. Smith, 589–600. Orlando, FL: Academic Press.

Hawkins, A. F. A., and S. M. Goodman. 2003. Introduction to the Birds. In *The Natural History of Madagascar*, eds. S. M. Goodman and J. P. Benstead, 1019–1044. Chicago, IL: University of Chicago Press.

Hawksworth, F. G. 1983. Mistletoes as Forest Parasites. In *The Biology of Mistletoes*, eds. M. Calder and P. Bernhardt, 317–328. Sidney: Academic Press.

Heckman, E. L. 2005. *Mouse Lemur* (Microcebus) *Species Diversity: A Multilocus Perspective*. Evanston, IL: Northwestern University.

Heldmaier, G., S. Ortmann, and R. Elvert. 2004. Natural Hypometabolism during Hibernation and Daily Torpor in Mammals. *Respiratory Physiology and Neurobiology* 141: 317–329.

Hemingway, C. A. 1995. *Feeding and Reproductive Strategies of the Milne-Edwards' sifaka*, Propithecus diadema edwardsi. Durham, NC: Duke University.

Hemingway, C. A. 1996. Morphology and Phenology of Seeds and Whole Fruit Eaten by Milne-Edwards' Sifaka, *Propithecus diadema edwardsi*, in Ranomafana National Park, Madagascar. *International Journal of Primatology* 17 (5): 637–659.

Herbst, L. H. 1986. The Role of Nitrogen from Fruit Pulp in the Nutrition of the Frugivorous Bat *Carollia perspicillata*. *Biotropica* 18: 39–44.

Hill, W. C. O. 1953. Primates: Comparative Anatomy and Taxonomy. I. Strepsirhini. A Monograph. Edinburgh: University Press.

Hladik, C. M. 1979. Diet and Ecology of Prosimians. In *The Study of Prosimian Behavior*, eds. G. A. Doyle and R. D. Martin, 307–357. New York: Academic Press.

Hladik, C. M. 1981. Diet and the Evolution of Feeding Strategies among Forest Primates. In *Omnivorous Primates, Gathering and Hunting in Human Evolution*, eds. R. S. O. Harding and G. Teleki, 215–254. New York: Columbia University Press.

Hladik, C. M., P. Charles-Dominique, and J. J. Petter. 1980. Feeding Strategies of Five Nocturnal Prosimians in the Dry Forest of the West Coast of Madagascar. In *Nocturnal Malagasy Primates: Ecology, Physiology, and Behavior*, eds. P. Charles-Dominique, H. M. Cooper, A. Hladik, C. M. Hladik, E. Pagès, G. F. Pariente, A. Petter-Rousseaux, and A. Schilling, 41–73. New York: Academic Press.

Hoffmann, K. 1981. Photoperiodism in Vertebrates. In *Biological Rhythms*, ed. J. Aschoff, 449–473. New York: Plenum Press.

Honess, P., and S. Bearder. 2006. Creatures of the Dark Revealed; A Reassessment of Diversity and Taxonomic Tools in Nocturnal Primates. *International Journal of Primatology* 27 (1): 439.

Honess, P., C. Roos, and T. Olson. 2006. The Impact of New Taxonomic Tools on the Recognition of Diversity in Nocturnal Primates. *International Journal of Primatology* 27 (1): 440.

Howe, H. F., and G. F. Estabrook. 1977. On Intra-Specific Competition for Avian Dispersers in Tropical Trees. *American Naturalist* 111: 817–832.

Howell, D. J. 1974. Bats and Pollen: Physiological Aspects of the Syndrome of Chiropterophily. *Comparative Biochemistry and Physiology Part A* 48: 263–276.

Hudson, J. W. 1965. Temperature Regulation and Torpidity in the Pygmy Mouse, *Baiomys taylori*. *Physiological Zoology* 38: 243–254.

Jacobs, G. H., and J. F. Deegan. 1993. Photopigments Underlying Color Vision in Ringtail Lemurs (*Lemur catta*) and Brown Lemurs (*Eulemur fulvus*). *American Journal of Primatology* 30 (3): 243–256.

Johnson, C. N. 1988. Dispersal and the Sex Ratio at Birth in Primates. *Nature* 332: 726–728.

Kappeler, P. M. 1991. Patterns of Sexual Dimorphism in Body Weight among Prosimian Primates. *Folia Primatologica* 57: 132–146.

Kappeler, P. M. 1995. Life History Variation among Nocturnal Prosimians. In *Creatures of the Dark: The Nocturnal Prosimians*, eds. L. Alterman, G. A. Doyle, and M. K. Izard, 75–92. New York: Plenum Press.

Kappeler, P. M. 1996a. Intrasexual Selection and Phylogenetic Constraints in the Evolution of Sexual Canine Dimorphism in Strepsirhine Primates. *Journal of Evolutionary Biology* 9: 43–65.

Kappeler, P. M. 1996b. Causes and Consequences of Life-History Variation among Strepsirhine Primates. *American Naturalist* 148 (5): 868–891.

Kappeler, P. M. 1997a. Intrasexual Selection in *Mirza coquereli*: Evidence for Scramble Competition in a Solitary Primate. *Behavioral Ecology and Sociobiology* 45: 115–127.

Kappeler, P. M. 1997b. Intrasexual Selection and Testis Size in Strepsirhine Primates. *Behavioral Ecology* 8 (1): 10–19.

Kappeler, P. M. 1997c. Determinants of Primate Social Organization: Comparative Evidence and New Insights from Malagasy Lemurs. *Biological Reviews of the Cambridge Philosophical Society* 72 (1): 111–151.

Kappeler, P. M. 1998. Nests, Tree Holes, and the Evolution of Primate Life Histories. *American Journal of Primatology* 46: 7–33.

Kappeler, P. M. 2000. Lemur Origins: Rafting by Groups of Hibernators? *Folia Primatologica* 71 (6): 422–425.

Kappeler, P. M. 2003. *Mirza coquereli*, Coquereli's Dwarf Lemur. In *The Natural History of Madagascar*, eds. S. M. Goodman and J. P. Benstead, 1316–1318. Chicago, IL: University of Chicago Press.

Kappeler, P. M., and A. Dill. 2000. The Lemurs of Kirindy. *Natual History* 109 (7): 58–65.

Kappeler, P. M., and R. M. Rasoloarison. 2003. *Microcebus*, Mouse Lemurs, Tsidy. In *The Natural History of Madagascar*, eds. S. M. Goodman and J. P. Benstead, 1310–1315. Chicago, IL: University of Chicago Press.

Kappeler, P. M., R. M. Rasoloarison, L. Razafimanantsoa, L. Walter, and C. Roos. 2005. Morphology, Behaviour and Molecular Evolution of Giant Mouse Lemurs (*Mirza* spp) Gray, 1870, with Description of a New Species. *Primate Report* 71 (July): 3–26.

Kappeler, P. M., B. Wimmer, and D. Tautz. 2001. Genetic and Social Structure of a Polygynous Nocturnal Lemur (*Mirza coquereli*, Primates: Cheirogaleidae). *Zoology* 103 (Supplement): 44.

Kappeler, P. M., B. Wimmer, D. Zinner, and D. Tautz. 2002. The Hidden Matrilineal Structure of a Solitary Lemur: Implications for Primate Social Evolution. *Proceedings of the Royal Society of London B* 269 (1502): 1755–1763.

Kaufman, G. A., and D. W. Kaufman. 1994. Changes in Body Mass Related to Capture in the Prairie Deer Mouse (*Peromyscus maniculatus*). *Journal of Mammalogy* 75: 681–691.

Kay, R. F. 1984. On the Use of Anatomical Features to Infer Foraging Behavior in Extinct Primates. In *Adaptations for Foraging in Nonhuman Primates: Contributions to an Organismal Biology of Prosimians, Monkeys and Apes*, eds. P. S. Rodman and J. G. H. Cant, 21–53. New York: Columbia University Press.

Kenagy, G. J. 1973. Daily and Seasonal Patterns of Activity and Energetics in a Heteromyid Rodent Community. *Ecology* 54: 1201–1219.

Kleiber, M. 1961. *The Fire of Life: An Introduction to Animal Energetics*. New York: John Wiley and Sons.

Knight, R. S., and W. R. Siegfried. 1983. Inter-Relationships between Type, Size and Colour of Fruits and Dispersal in Southern African Trees. *Oecologia* 56: 405–412.

Kocsard-Varo, G. 2000. Role of the Pineal Gland in Hibernators: A Concept Proposed to Clarify Why Hibernators Have to Leave Torpor and Sleep. *Medical Hypotheses* 54 (4): 645–647.

Koenig, A., C. Borries, M. K. Chalise, and P. Winkler. 1997. Ecology, Nutrition, and Timing of Reproductive Events in an Asian Primate, the Hanuman Langur (*Presbytis entellus*). *Journal of Zoology* 243 (2): 215–235.

Korschgen, L. J. 1969. Procedures for Food-Habits Analysis. In *Wildlife Management Techniques*, ed. R. H. J. Giles, 233–250. Washington, DC: The Wildlife Society.

Kozlowski, J., and J. Weiner. 1997. Interspecific Allometries Are By-Products of Body Size Optimization. *American Naturalist* 149: 352–380.

Krause, D. W., J. H. Hartman, and N. A. Wells. 1997. Late Cretaceous Vertebrates from Madagascar: Implications for Biotic Change in Deep Time. In *Natural Change and Human Impact in Madagascar*, eds. S. M. Goodman and B. D. Patterson, 3–43. Washington, DC: Smithsonian Institution Press.

Kricher, J. 1997. *A Neotropical Companion. An Introduction to the Animals, Plants, and Ecosystems of the New World Tropics.* Princeton, NJ: Princeton University Press.

Kriegsfeld, L. J., and R. J. Nelson. 1996. Gonadal and Photoperiodic Influences of Body Mass Regulation in Adult Male and Female Prairie Voles. *American Journal of Physiology* 270: R1013–R1018.

Kuijt, J. 1969. *The Biology of Parasitic Flowering Plants.* Los Angeles: University of California Press.

Kunz, T. H., and J. O. Whitaker. 1983. An Evaluation of Fecal Analysis for Determining Food Habits of Insectivorous Bats. *Canadian Journal of Zoology* 61: 1317–1321.

Kurland, J. A., and J. D. Pearson. 1986. Ecological Significance of Hypometabolism in Non-Human Primates: Allometry, Adaptation, and Deviant Diets. *American Journal of Physical Anthropology* 71: 445–457.

Lahann, P. 2007. Feeding Ecology and Seed Dispersal of Sympatric Cheirogaleid Lemurs (*Microcebus murinus, Cheirogaleus medius, Cheirogaleus major*) in the Littoral Rainforest of South-east Madagascar. *Journal of Zoology* 271: 88–98.

Lahann, P., J. Schmid, and J. Ganzhorn. 2006. Geographic Variation in Populations of *Microcebus murinus* in Madagascar: Resource Seasonality or Bergmann's Rule. *International Journal of Primatology* 27 (4): 983–999.

Langrand, O. 1990. *Guide to the Birds of Madagascar.* New Haven, CT: Yale University Press.

Larson, D. L. 1996. Seed Dispersal by Specialist versus Generalist Foragers: The Plant's Perspective. *Oikos* 76: 113–120.

Lebec, A. 1984. *Relations Entre Le Comportement Agressif du Mâle Microcèbe, Les Autres Comportements de La Physiologie, Sexuelle.* Facteurs Déterminants. Paris: University of Paris-VI.

Lehman, S. M., A. Rajaonson, and S. Day. 2006. Edge Effects and their Influence on Lemur Density and Distribution in Southeast Madagascar. *American Journal of Physical Anthroplogy* 129: 232–241.

Leipoldt, M., J. Tomiuk, L. Bachmann, S. Atsalis, P. M. Kappeler, J. Schmid, and J. U. Ganzhorn. 1998. The Impact of Genetics on the Conservation of Malagasy Lemur Species. *Folia Primatologica* 69: 121–126.

Lewis, R. J., and P. M. Kappeler. 2005. Seasonality, Body Condition, and Timing of Reproduction in Propithecus verreauxi verreauxi in the Kirindy Forestq. *American Journal of Primatology* 67 (3): 347–364.

Lidicker, W. Z., Jr. 1985. Dispersal. In *Biology of New World Microtus*, ed. R. H. Tamarin, 420–454. Shippensburg, PA: The American Society of Mammalogists.

Liman, E. R., and H. Innan. 2003. Relaxed Selective Pressure on an Essential Component of Pheromone Transduction in Primate Evolution. *Proceedings of the National Academy of Sciences of the United States of America* 100: 3328–3332.

Louis, E. E., Jr., M. S. Coles, R. Andriantompohavana, J. A. Sommer, S. E. Engberg, J. R. Zaonarivelo, M. I. Mayor, and R. A. Brenneman. 2006. Revision of the Mouse Lemurs (*Microcebus*) of Eastern Madagascar. *International Journal of Primatology* 27 (2): 347–389.

Lutermann, H., and E. Zimmermann. 2001. Nesting and Resting in a Small Nocturnal Primate: Behavioural Ecology of Inactivity from a Female Perspective. *Folia Primatologica* 72 (3): 172.

Lyman, C. P. 1963. Hibernation in Mammals and Birds. *American Scientist* 51: 127–138.

Lyman, C. P. 1982a. Entering Hibernation. In *Hibernation and Torpor in Mammals and Birds*, eds. C. P. Lyman, J. S. Willis, A. Malan, and L. C. H. Wang, 37–53. New York: Academic Press.

Lyman, C. P. 1982b. The Hibernating State. In *Hibernation and Torpor in Mammals and Birds*, eds. C. P. Lyman, J. S. Willis, A. Malan, and L. C. H. Wang, 54–76. New York: Academic Press.

Lyman, C. P. 1982c. Who Is Who among the Hibernators. In *Hibernation and Torpor in Mammals and Birds*, eds. C. P. Lyman, J. S. Willis, A. Malan, and L. C. H. Wang, 12–36. New York: Academic Press.

Lyman, C. P., J. S. Willis, A. Malan, and L. C. H. Wang. 1982. *Hibernation and Torpor in Mammals and Birds*. New York: Academic Press.

Mabberley, D. J. 1987. *The Plant-Book: A Portable Dictionary of the Higher Plants.* Cambridge: Cambridge University Press.

MacFarland Symington, M. 1987. Sex Ratio and Maternal Rank in Wild Spider Monkeys: When Daughters Disperse. *Behavioral Ecology and Sociobiology* 20: 421–425.

MacKinnon, J., and K. MacKinnon. 1980. The Behavior of Wild Spectral Tarsiers. *International Journal of Primatology* 1: 361–379.

Malan, A. 1996. The Origins of Hibernation: A Reappraisal. In *Adaptations to the Cold: Tenth International Hibernation Symposium*, eds. F. Geiser, A. J. Hulbert, and S. C. Nicol, 1–6. Armidale, Australia: University of New England Press.

Martin, R. D. 1972a. Adaptive Radiation and Behaviour of the Malagasy Lemurs. *Philosophical Transactions of the Royal Society of London B* 264: 295–352.

Martin, R. D. 1972b. A Preliminary Field Study of the Lesser Mouse Lemur (*Microcebus murinus* J. F. Miller 1777). *Zeitschrift fur Tierpsychologie Suppl* 9: 43–89.

Martin, R. D. 1972c. A Laboratory Breeding Colony of the Lesser Mouse Lemur. In *Breeding Primates*, ed. W. I. B. Beveridge, 161–171. Basel, Switzerland: Karger.

Martin, R. D. 1973. A Review of the Behaviour and Ecology of the Lesser Mouse Lemur (*Microcebus murinus* J. F. Miller 1777). In *Comparative Ecology and Behaviour of Primates*, eds. R. P. Michael and J. H. Crook, 1–68. London: Academic Press.

Martin, R. D. 1990. *Primate Origins and Evolution: A Phylogenetic Reconstruction.* London: Chapman and Hall.

Martin, R. D. 1995. Prosimians: From Obscurity to Extinction? In *Creatures of the Dark: The Nocturnal Prosimians*, eds. L. Alterman, G. A. Doyle, and M. K. Izard, 535–563. New York: Plenum Press.

Martin, R. D. 2000. Origins, Diversity and Relationship of Lemurs. *International Journal of Primatology* 21 (6): 1021–1049.

Martin, R. D. 2002. Primatology as an Essential Basis for Biological Anthropology. *Evolutionary Anthropology* 11 (Supplement 1): 3–6.

Martin, R. D., and S. K. Bearder. 1979. Radio Bush Baby. *Natural History* 88 (8): 76–81.

Martínez del Rio, C. 1994. Nutritional Ecology of Fruit-Eating and Flower-Visiting Birds and Bats. In *The Digestive System in Mammals, Food, Form and Function*, eds. D. J. Chivers and P. Langer, 103–127. Cambridge: Cambridge University Press.

Martínez del Rio, C., A. Silva, R. Medel, and M. Hourdequin. 1996. Seed Dispersers as Disease Vectors: Bird Transmission of Mistletoe Seeds to Plant Hosts. *Ecology* 77 (3): 912–921.

McCormick, S. A. 1981. Oxygen Consumption and Torpor in the Fat-Tailed Dwarf Lemur (*Cheirogaleus medius*): Rethinking Prosimian Metabolism. *Comparative Biochemistry and Physiology Part A* 68: 605–610.

McGavin, G. C. 2002. *Insects: Spiders and Other Terrestrial Arthropods*. New York: Dorling Kindersley. 255 p.

McKey, D. 1975. The Ecology of Coevolved Seed Dispersal Systems. In *Coevolution of Animals and Plants*, eds. L. E. Gilbert and P. H. Raven, 151–191. Austin: University of Texas Press.

McNab, B. K. 1980. Food Habits, Energetics, and the Population Biology of Mammals. *American Naturalist* 116: 106–124.

McNab, B. K. 1986. The Influence of Food Habits on the Energetics of Eutherian Mammals. *Ecological Monographs* 56: 1–19.

Meier, B., and R. Albignac. 1991. Rediscovery of *Allocebus trichotis* Gunter 1875 (Primates) in North East Madagascar. *Folia Primatologica* 56: 57–63.

Merenlender, A. 1993. *The Effects of Sociality on the Demography and Genetic Structure of* Lemur fulvus rufus *(Polygamous) and* Lemur rubriventer *(Monogamous) and the Conservation Implications*. Rochester, NY: University of Rochester.

Meyers, D. M. 1993. *The Effects of Resource Seasonality on Behavior and Reproduction in the Golden-Crowned Sifaka* (Propithecus tattersalli, Simons 1988) *in Three Malagasy Forests*. Durham, NC: Duke University.

Meyers, D. M., and P. C. Wright. 1993. Resource Tracking: Food Availability and *Propithecus* Seasonal Reproduction. In *Lemur Social Systems and Their Ecological Basis*, eds. P. M. Kappeler and J. U. Ganzhorn, 179–192. New York: Plenum Press.

Michener, G. R. 2004. Hibernation. In *Encyclopedia of Animal Behavior*, ed. M. Bekoff, 621–624. Wesport, CT: Greenwood Press.

Milton, K., and F. R. Dintzis. 1981. Nitrogen-to-Protein Conversion Factors for Tropical Plant Samples. *Biotropica* 13: 17.

Mittermeier, R. A., J. F. Oates, A. E. Eudey, and J. Thornback. 1986. Primate Conservation. In *Behavior, Conservation, and Ecology*, eds. G. Mitchell and J. Erwin, 3–72. New York: Alan R. Liss.

Mittermeier, R. A., I. Tattersall, W. R. Konstant, D. M. Meyers, and R. B. Mast. 1994. *Lemurs of Madagascar.* Washington, DC: Conservation International.

Moraes, P. L. R., O. Carvalho Jr., and K. B. Strier. 1998. Population Variation in Patch and Party Size in Muriquis (*Brachyteles arachnoides*). *International Journal of Primatology* 19: 325–337.

Moreno-Black, G. 1978. The Use of Scat Samples in Primate Diet Analysis. *Primates* 19: 215–221.

Morland, H. S. 1993. Seasonal Behavioral Variation and Its Relationship to Thermoregulation in Ruffed Lemurs (*Varecia variegata variegata*). In *Lemur Social Systems and Their Ecological Basis*, eds. P. M. Kappeler and J. U. Ganzhorn, 193–203. New York: Plenum Press.

Mrosovsky, N. 1977. Hibernation and Body Weight in Dormice: A New Type of Endogenous Cycle. *Science* 196: 902–903.

Muchlinski, A. E. 1978. Photoperiod as a Possible Stimulus for Preparation and Initiation of Hibernation in *Zapus hudsonius*. *Journal of Thermal Biology* 3: 87.

Müller, A. E. 1998. A Preliminary Report on the Social Organization of *Cheirogaleus medius* (Cheirogaleidae, Primates) in North-West Madagascar. *Folia Primatologica* 69: 160–166.

Müller, A. E. 1999a. Aspects of Social Life in the Fat-Tailed Dwarf Lemur (*Cheirogaleus medius*): Inferences from Body Weights and Trapping Data. *American Journal of Primatology* 49 (3): 265–280.

Müller, A. E. 1999b. Social Organization of the Fat-Tailed Dwarf Lemur (*Cheirogaleus medius*) in Northwestern Madagascar. In *New Directions in Lemur Studies*, eds. H. Rasamimanana, B. Rakotosamimanana, J. U. Ganzhorn, and S. M. Goodman, 139–158. New York: Plenum Press.

Müller, A. E. 1999c. Paternal Investment in the Monogamous Fat-Tailed Dwarf Lemur (*Cheirogaleus medius*) in Northwestern Madagascar. *American Journal of Physical Anthropology Suppl* 28: 207.

Müller, A. E., and C. Soligo. 2001. Why Are Primates Social? *Folia Primatologica* 72 (3): 173–174.

Müller, A. E., and U. Thalmann. 2000. Origin and Evolution of Primate Social Organisation: A Reconstruction. *Biological Reviews of the Cambridge Philosophical Society* 75 (3): 405–435.

Müller, E. F. 1985. Basal Metabolic Rates in Primates: The Possible Role of Phylogenetic and Ecological Factors. *Comparative Biochemistry and Physiology* 81A (4): 707–711.

Musto, N., A. M. Deppe, L. Randrianasolo, and P. C. Wright. 2005. Predation Avoidance May Affect Habitat Preference of the Brown Mouse Lemur (*Microcebus rufus*) in Ranomafana National Park, Madagascar. *American Journal of Primatology* 66 (1): 87.

Mutschler, T., and C. L. Tan. 2003. Hpalemur, Bamboo or Gentle Lemurs. In *The Natural History of Madagascar*, eds. S. M. Goodman and J. P. Benstead, 1324–1329. Chicago, IL: University of Chicago.

Nadkarni, N. M. 1981. Canopy Roots, Convergent Evolution in Rainforest Nutrient Cycles. *Science* 214: 1023–1024.

Nadkarni, N. M. 1983. The Effects of Epiphytes on Nutrient Cycles within Temperate and Tropical Rainforest Tree Canopies. Ph.D. dissertation, University of Washington.

Nadkarni, N. M. 1984. Epiphyte Biomass and Nutrient Capital of a Neotropical Elfin Forest. *Biotropica* 16: 249–256.

Nash, L. T. 1986. Influence of Moonlight Level on Travelling and Calling Patterns in Two Sympatric Species of *Galago* in Kenya. In *Current Perspectives in Primate Social Dynamics*, eds. F. A. King and D. Taub, 357–367. New York: Van Nostrand Reinhold Co.

Nash, L. T., and C. S. Harcourt. 1986. Social Organization of Galagos in Kenyan Coastal Forests: II. *Galago garnetti. American Journal of Primatology* 10: 357–369.

Nekaris, K. A., and S. K. Bearder. 2007. The Lorisiform Primates of Asia and Mainland Africa: Diversity Shrouded in Darkness. In *Primates in Perspective*, eds. C. J. Campbell, A. Fuentes, K. C. MacKinnon, M. Panger, and S. K. Bearder, 24–25. New York: Oxford University Press.

Nekaris, K. A. I. 2000. The Socioecology of the Mysore Slender Loris (*Loris tradigradus lydekkerianus*) in Dindigul, Tamil Nadu, South India. Ph.D. dissertation, Washington University at St. Louis.

Nekaris, K. A. I. 2001. Activity Budget and Positional Behavior of the Mysore Slender Loris (*Loris tardigradus lydekkerianus*): Implications for Slow Climbing Locomotion. *Folia Primatologica* 72 (4): 228–241.

Nekaris, K. A. I. 2003. Spacing System of the Mysore Slender Loris (*Loris lydekkerianus lydekkerianus*). *American Journal of Physical Anthropology* 121: 86–96.

Nekaris, K. A. I., and D. T. Rasmussen. 2001. The Bug-Eyed Slender Loris: Insect Predation and Its Implications for Primate Origins. *American Journal of Physical Anthropology* 32 (Supplement): 112.

Nekaris, K. A. I., and D. T. Rasmussen. 2003. Diet and Feeding Behavior of Mysore Slender Lorises. *International Journal of Primatology* 24 (1): 33–46.

Nestler, J. R., G. P. Dieter, and B. G. Klokeid. 1996. Changes in Total Body Fat during Daily Torpor in Deer Mice (*Peromyscus maniculatus*). *Journal of Mammalogy* 77 (1): 147–154.

Neveu, H., T. Hafen, E. Zimmermann, and Y. Rumpler. 1998. Comparison of the Genetic Diversity of Wild and Captive Groups of *Microcebus murinus* Using the Random Amplified Polymorphic DNA Method. *Folia Primatologica* 69 (Supplement 1): 127–135.

Nickrent, D. L. 2002. Plantas Parásitas en la Mundo. In *Plantas Parásitas de la Península Ibérica e Islas Baleares*, eds. J. A. López-Sáez, P. Catalán, and L. Sáez, 7–27. Madrid: Mundi-Prensa.

Nicol, S., and N. A. Andersen. 2002. The Timing of Hibernation in Tasmanian Echidnas: Why Do they Do it When they Do? *Comparative Biochemistry and Physiology Part B* 131: 603–611.

Niemitz, C. 1984. Synecological Relationships and Feeding Behaviour of the Genus *Tarsius*. In *The Biology of Tarsiers*, ed. C. Niemtz, 59–76. New York: Gustav Fishcer Verlag.

Nietfeld, M. T., M. W. Barrett, and N Silvy. 1994. Wildlife Marking Techniques. In *Research and Management Techniques for Wildlife and Habitats*, ed. T. A. Bookhout, 140–168. Bethesda, MD: The Wildlife Society.

Nietsch, A., and C. Niemitz. 1992. *Indication for Facultative Polygamy in Free-Ranging* Tarsius spectrum *Supported by Morphometric Data*. Strasbourg: International Primatological Society, 318 p.

Nomakwezi, M., and B. G. Lovegrove. 2002. Reproductive Activity Influences Thermoregulation and Torpor in Pouched Mice, *Saccostomus campestris*. *Journal of Comparative Physiology B: Biochemical, Systemic, and Environmental Physiology* 172 (1): 7–16.

Nowak, R. M. 1991. *Walker's Mammals of the World*. Baltimore, MD: Johns Hopkins University Press.

O'Farrell, M. J., W. A. Clark, F. H. Emmeson, S. M. Juarez, F. R. Kay, T. M. O'Farrell, and T. Y. Goodlet. 1994. Use of a Mesh Live Trap for Small Mammals: Are Results from Sherman Live Traps Deceptive? *Journal of Mammalogy* 75 (3): 692–699.

Olivieri, G. L., K. Guschanski, U. Radespiel. 2006. Conservation Genetics of Mouse Lemurs (*Microcebus* spp.) in North-Western Madagascar. *International Journal of Madagascar* 27 (1): 57.

Olupot, W., C. A. Chapman, P. M. Waser, and G. Isabirye-Basuta. 1997. Mangabey (*Cercocebusalbigena*) Ranging Patterns in Relation to Fruit Availability and the Risk of Parasite Infection in Kibale National Park, Uganda. *American Journal of Primatology* 43 (1): 65–78.

Ortmann, S., G. Heldmaier, J. Schmid, and J. U. Ganzhorn. 1997. Spontaneous Daily Torpor in Malagasy Mouse Lemurs. *Naturwissenschaften* 84: 28–32.

Ortmann, S., J. Schmid, J. U. Ganzhorn, and G. Heldmaier. 1996. Body Temperature and Torpor in a Malagasy Small Primate, the Mouse Lemur. In *Adaptations to the Cold: Tenth International Hibernation Symposium*, eds. F. Geiser, A. J. Hulbert, and S. C. Nicol, 55–61. Armidale, Australia: University of New England Press.

Ostfeld, R. S. 1990. The Ecology of Territoriality in Small Mammals. *Trends in Ecology and Evolution* 5 (12): 411–414.

Overdorff, D. 1991. *Ecological Correlates to Social Structure in Two Prosimian Primates in Madagascar:* Eulemur fulvus rufus *and* Eulemur rubriventer. Durham, NC: Duke University.

Overdorff, D. 1993. Similarities, Differences, and Seasonal Patterns in the Diets of *Eulemur rubriventer* and *Eulemur fulvus rufus* in the Ranomafana National Park, Madagascar. *International Journal of Primatology* 14: 721–753.

Overdorff, D. J. 1996. Ecological Correlates to Social Structure in Two Lemur Species in Madagascar. *American Journal of Physical Anthropology* 100: 443–466.

Overdorff, D. J., and S. G. Strait. 1998. Seed Handling by Three Prosimian Primates in Southeastern Madagascar: Implications for Seed Dispersal. *American Journal of Primatology* 45 (1): 69–82.

Pagès, E. 1978. Home Range, Behaviour and Tactile Communication in a Nocturnal Malagasy Lemur *Microcebus coquereli*. In *Recent Advances in Primatology*, eds. D. J. Chivers and K. A. Joysey, 171–177. London: Academic Press.

Pagès, E. 1980. Ethoecology of *Microcebus coquereli* during the Dry Season. In *Nocturnal Malagasy Primates: Ecology, Physiology and Behavior*, eds. P. Charles-Dominique, H. M. Cooper, A. Hladik, C. M. Hladik, E. Pagès, G. F. Pariente, A. Petter-Rousseaux, and A. Schilling, 97–116. New York: Academic Press.

Pagès-Feuillade, E. 1988. Modalités de L'occupation de L'espace et Relation Inter-Individuelles chez un Prosimien Nocturne Malgache (*Microcebus murinus*). *Folia Primatologica* 50: 204–220.

Paine, R. T. 1971. The Measurements and Applications of the Calorie to Ecological Problems. *Annual Review of Ecology and Systematics* 2: 145–164.

Pariente, G. 1979. The Role of Vision in Prosimian Behavior. In *The Study of Prosimian Behavior*, eds. G. A. Doyle and R. D. Martin, 411–459. New York: Academic Press.

Pastorini, J., R. D. Martin, P. Ehresmann, E. Zimmermann, and M. R. J. Forstner. 2001. Molecular Phylogeny of the Lemur Family Cheirogaleidae (Primates) Based on Mitoochondrial DNA Sequences. *Molecular Phylogenetics and Evolution* 19: 45–56.

Pastorini, J., U. Thalmann, and R. D. Martin. 2003. A Molecular Approach to Comparative Phylogeography of Extant Malagasy Lemurs. *Proceedings of the National Academy of Sciences of the United States of America* 100 (10): 5879–5884.

Paul, A., and D. Thommen. 1984. Timing of Birth, Female Reproductive Success and Infant Sex Ratio in Semifree-ranging Barbary Macaques (*Macaca sylvanus*). *Folia Primatologica* 42 (1): 2–16.

Paulian, R., and P. Viette. 2003. An Introduction to Terrestrial and Freshwater Invertebrates. In *The Natural History of Madagascar*, eds. S. M. Goodman and J. P. Benstead, 503–511. Chicago, IL: University of Chicago Press.

Pereira, M. E. 1993. Seasonal Adjustment of Growth Rate and Adult Body Weight in Ringtailed Lemurs. In *Lemur Social Systems and Their Ecological Basis*, eds. P. M. Kappeler and J. U. Ganzhorn, 205–221. New York: Plenum Press.

Pereira, M. E., J. Aines, and J. L. Scheckter. 2002. Tactics of Heterothermy in Eastern Gray Squirrels (*Sciurus carolinensis*). *Journal of Mammalogy* 83 (2): 467–477.

Pereira, M. E., and J. Altmann. 1985. Development of Social Behavior in Free-Ranging Nonhuman Primates. In *Nonhuman Primate Models for Human Growth and Development*, ed. E. Watts, 217–309. New York: Alan R. Liss.

Pereira, M. E., R. A. Strohecker, S. A. Cavigelli, C. L. Hughes, and D. D. Pearson. 1999. Metabolic Strategy and Social Behavior in Lemuridae. In *New Directions in Lemur Studies*, eds. B. Rakotosamimanana, H. Rasamimanana, J. U. Ganzhorn, and S. M. Goodman, 93–118. New York: Kluwer Academic/ Plenum Press.

Perret, M. 1972. Recherches sur les Variations des Glandes Endocrines, et en Particulier de L'hypophyse, au Cours du Cycle Annuel, chez un Lemurién Malgache, *Microcebus murinus* (Miller 1777). *Mammalia* 36: 482–516.

Perret, M. 1974. Variations of the Endocrine Glands in *Microcebus murinus* (Miller, 1777). In *Prosimian Biology*, eds. R. D. Martin, G. A. Doyle, and A. C. Walker, 357–367. London: Duckworth.

Perret, M. 1977. Influence du Groupement Social sur L'activation Sexuelle Saisonniére Chez le Male de *Microcebus murinus* (Miller 1777). *Zeitschrift fur Tierpsychologie* 43: 159–179.

Perret, M. 1982. Influence of Social Grouping on the Reproductive Biology of the Female *Microcebus murinus* (Miller, 1777). *Zeitschrift Fuer Tierpsychologie* 60 (1): 47–65.

Perret, M. 1985. Influence of Social Factors on Seasonal Variations in Plasma Testosterone Levels of *Microcebus murinus. Zeitschrift fur Tierpsychologie* 69: 265–280.

Perret, M. 1990. Influence of Social Factors on Sex Ratio at Birth, Maternal Investment and Young Survival in a Prosimian Primate. *Behavioral Ecology and Sociobiology* 27: 447–454.

Perret, M. 1992. Environmental and Social Determinants of Sexual Function in the Male Lesser Mouse Lemur (*Microcebus murinus*). *Folia Primatologica* 59: 1–25.

Perret, M. 1995. Chemocommunication in the Reproductive Function of Mouse Lemurs. In *Creatures of the Dark: The Nocturnal Prosimians*, eds. L. Alterman, G. A. Doyle, and M. K. Izard, 377–392. New York: Plenum Press.

Perret, M. 1996. Age-Related Changes in Fertility in Female Lesser Mouse Lemurs (*Microcebus murinus*, Cheirogaleidae, Primates). *Folia Primatologica* 67 (2): 102.

Perret, M. 1997. Change in Photoperiodic Cycle Affects Life Span in a Prosimian Primate (*Microcebus murinus*). *Journal of Biological Rhythms* 12 (2): 136–145.

Perret, M. 1998. Energetic Advantage of Nest-Sharing in a Solitary Primate, the Lesser Mouse Lemur (*Microcebus murinus*). *Journal of Mammalogy* 79 (4): 1093–1102.

Perret, M., and F. Aujard. 2001. Regulation by Photoperiod of Seasonal Changes in Body Mass and Reproductive Function in Gray Mouse Lemurs (*Microcebus murinus*): Differential Responses by Sex. *International Journal of Primatology* 22 (1): 5–24.

Perret, M., and J. Predine. 1984. Effects of Long-Term Grouping on Serum Cortisol levels in *Microcebus murinus* (Prosimii). *Hormones and Behavior* 18 (3): 346–358.

Perret, M., and A. Schilling. 1995. Sexual Responses to Urinary Chemosignals Depend on Photoperiod in a Male Primate. *Physiology and Behavior* 58 (4): 633–639.

Perrin, M. R., and E. J. Richardson. 2004. Factors Affecting the Induction of Torpor and Body Mass in the Fat Mice, *Steatomys pratensis. Journal of Thermal Biology* 29: 133–139.

Peters, W. C. H. 1852. *Naturwissenschaftliche Reise nach Mosambique.* Berlin: Georg Reimer.

Petter, J. J. 1962. Recherches sur L'Ecologie et L'Ethologie des Lemuriens Malgaches. *Mémoires de Museum National D'Histoire Naturelle* A27: 1–146.

Petter, J. J. 1977. The Aye-Aye. In *Primate Conservation,* eds. P. Rainier and G. H. Bourne, 37–57. New York: Academic Press.

Petter, J. J. 1978. Ecological and Physiological Adaptations of Five Sympatric Nocturnal Lemurs to Seasonal Variations in Food Production. In *Recent Advances in Primatology,* eds. D. J. Chivers and J. Herbert, 211–223. London: Academic Press.

Petter, J. J., R. Albignac, and Y. Rumpler. 1977. *Mammifères Lemuriéns (Primates, Prosimiens). Faunes de Madagascar.* Paris: ORSTOM/CNRS.

Petter, J. J., and P. Charles-Dominique. 1979. Vocal Communication in Prosimians. In *The Study of Prosimian Behavior,* eds. G. A. Doyle and R. D. Martin, 247–305. New York: Academic Press.

Petterborg, L. J. 1978. Effect of Photoperiod on Body Weight in the Vole, *Microtus montanus. Canadian Journal of Zoology* 56: 431–435.

Petter-Rousseaux, A. 1964. Reproductive Physiology and Behavior of the Lemuroidea. In *Evolutionary and Genetic Biology of Primates,* ed. J. Buettner-Janusch, 91–132. New York: Academic Press.

Petter-Rousseaux, A. 1970. Observations sur L'Influence de la Photopériode sur L'Activité Sexuelle chez *Microcebus murinus* (Miller, 1777) en Captivité. *Annals of Biology, Animal Biochemisty and Biophysiology* 10: 203–220.

Petter-Rousseaux, A. 1974. Photoperiod, Sexual Activity and Body Weight Variation of *Microcebus murinus* (Miller 1777). In *Prosimian Biology,* eds. R. D. Martin, G. A. Doyle, and A. C. Walker, 365–373. London: Duckworth.

Petter-Rousseaux, A. 1980. Seasonal Activity Rhythms, Reproduction, and Body Weight Variations in Five Sympatric Nocturnal Prosimians, in Simulated Light and Climatic Conditions. In *Nocturnal Malagasy Primates: Ecology, Physiology and Behavior,* eds. P. Charles-Dominique, H. M. Cooper, A. Hladik, C. M. Hladik, E. Pagès, G. F. Pariente, A. Petter-Rousseaux, J. J. Petter, and A. Schilling, 137–152. New York: Academic Press.

Petter-Rousseaux, A. 1981. Activité Sexuelle de *Microcebus murinus* (Miller 1777) Soumis á des Régimes Photopériodiques Experimentaux. *Annals of Biology, Animal Biochemisty and Biophysiology* 15: 503–508.

Petter-Rousseaux, A., and C. M. Hladik. 1980. A Comparative Study of Food Intake in Five Nocturnal Prosimians in Simulated Climatic Conditions.

In *Nocturnal Malagasy Primates: Ecology, Physiology and Behavior*, eds. P. Charles-Dominique, H. M. Cooper, A. Hladik, C. M. Hladik, E. Pagès, G. F. Pariente, A. Petter-Rousseaux, J. J. Petter, and A. Schilling, 169–179. New York: Academic Press.

Pimley, E., S. Bearder, and A. Dixson. 2002. Patterns of Ranging and Social Interactions in Pottos (*Perodicticus potto edwardsi*) in Cameroon. In *Caring for Primates: Abstracts of the XIXth Congress of the International Society*, 32. Beijing: Mammalogical Society of China.

Pimley, E. R., S. K. Bearder, and A. F. Dixoson. 2005. Social Organization of the Milne-Edward's Potto. *American Journal of Primatology* 66 (4): 317–330.

Polhill, R., and D. Wiens. 1998. *Mistletoes of Africa.* Richmond-Surrey, UK: Royal Botanic Gardens Kew Publishing.

Power, M. L. 1996. The Other Side of Callitrichine Gummmivory; Digestibility and Nutritional Value. In *Adaptive Radiations of Neotropical Primates*, eds. M. A. Norconk, A. L. Rosenberger, and P. A. Garber, 97–110. New York: Plenum Press.

Promislow, D. E. L., and P. H. Harvey. 1990. Living Fast and Dying Young: A Comparative Analysis of Life-History Variation among Mammals. *Journal of Zoology (London)* 220: 417–437.

Pullen, S. L., S. K. Bearder, and A. F. Dixson. 2000. Preliminary Observations on Sexual Behavior and the Mating System in Free-Ranging Lesser Galagos (*Galago moholi*). *American Journal of Primatology* 51 (1): 79–88.

Purvis, A. 1995. A Composite Estimate of Primate Phylogeny. *Philosophical Transactions of the Royal Society of London B* 348 (1326): 405–421.

Purvis, A., and P. H. Harvey. 1997. The Right Size for a Mammal. *Nature* 386: 332–333.

Pusey, A. E., and C. Packer. 1987. Dispersal and Philopatry. In *Primate Societies*, eds. B. B. Smuts, D. L. Cheney, R. M. Seyfarth, R. W. Wrangham, and T. T. Struhsaker, 250–266. Chicago, IL: University of Chicago Press.

Rabinowitz, P. D., M. F. Coffin, and D. Falvey. 1983. The Separation of Madagascar and Africa. *Science* 220: 67–69.

Radespiel, U. 1998. The Social Organisation of the Grey Mouse Lemur (*Microcebus murinus*, J. F. Miller 1777). *Primate Eye* 65: 31–32.

Radespiel, U. 2000. Sociality in the Gray Mouse Lemur (*Microcebus murinus*) in Northwestern Madagascar. *American Journal of Primatology* 51: 21–40.

Radespiel, U., S. Cepok, E. Zimmermann, and V. Zietemann. 1998. Sex-Specific Usage Patterns of Sleeping Sites in Grey Mouse Lemurs (*Microcebus murinus*) in Northwestern Madagascar. *American Journal of Primatology* 46: 77–84.

Radespiel, U., V. Dal Secco, C. Drogemuller, P. Braune, E. Labes, and E. Zimmermann. 2002. Sexual Selection, Multiple Mating and Paternity in Grey Mouse Lemurs, *Microcebus murinus*. *Animal Behaviour* 63 (2): 259–268.

Radespiel, U., P. Ehresmann, and E. Zimmermann. 2001. Contest Versus Scramble Competition for Mates: The Composition and Spatial Structure of a Population of Gray Mouse Lemurs (*Microcebus murinus*) in North-West Madagascar. *Primates* 42 (3): 207–220.

Radespiel, U., P. Ehresmann, and E. Zimmermann. 2003. Species-Specific Usage of Sleeping Sites in Two Sympatric Mouse Lemur Species (*Microcebus murinus* and *M. ravelobensis*) in Northwestern Madagascar. *American Journal of Primatology* 59: 139–151.

Radespiel, U., H. Lutermann, B. Schmelting, M. W. Bruford, and E. Zimmermann. 2003. Patterns and Dynamics of Sex-Biased Dispersal in a Nocturnal Primate, the Grey Mouse Lemur, *Microcebus murinus*. *Animal Behaviour* 65 (4): 709–719.

Radespiel, U., Z. Sarikaya, E. Zimmermann, and M. W. Bruford. 2001. Sociogenetic Structure in a Free-Living Nocturnal Primate Population: Sex-Specific Differences in the Grey Mouse Lemur (*Microcebus murinus*). *Behavioral Ecology and Sociobiology* 50 (6): 493–502.

Radespiel, U., W. Reimann, M. Rahelinirina, and E. Zimmermann. 2006. Feeding Ecology of Sympatric Mouse Lemur Species in Northwestern Madagascar. *International Journal of Primatology* 27 (1): 311–321.

Radespiel, U., and E. Zimmermann. 2001a. Female Dominance in Captive Gray Mouse Lemurs (*Microcebus murinus*). *American Journal of Primatology* 54 (4): 181–192.

Radespiel, U., and E. Zimmermann. 2001b. Dynamics of Estrous Synchrony in Captive Gray Mouse Lemurs (*Microcebus murinus*). *International Journal of Primatology* 22 (1): 71–90.

Rakotoarison, N., H. Zimmermann, and E. Zimmermann. 1997. First Discovery of the Hairy-Eared Dwarf Lemur (*Allocebus trichotis*) in a Highland Rain Forest of Eastern Madagascar. *Folia Primatologica* 68 (2): 86–94.

Randrianambinina, B., D. Rakotondravony, U. Radespiel, and E. Zimmermann. 2003a. Diverging Annual Rhythms of Closely Related Nocturnal Primates: A Comparison of Golden Brown and Brown Mouse Lemurs. *Folia Primatologica* 74: 214.

Randrianambinina, B., D. Rakotondravony, U. Radespiel, and E. Zimmermann. 2003b. Seasonal Changes in General Activity, Body Mass and Reproduction of Two Small Nocturnal Primates: A Comparison of the Golden Brown Mouse Lemur (*Microcebus ravelobensis*) in Northwestern Madagascar and the Brown Mouse Lemur (*Microcebus rufus*) in Eastern Madagascar. *Primates* 44 (4): 321–331.

Rasmussen, D. T. 1990. Primate Origins: Lessons from a Neotropical Marsupial. *American Journal of Primatology* 22 (4): 263–277.

Rasmussen, D. T., and M. K. Izard. 1988. Scaling of Growth and Life History Traits Relative to Body Size and Metabolic Rate in Lorises and Galagos (Lorisidae, Primates). *American Journal of Physical Anthropology* 75: 357–367.

Rasmussen, D. T., and K. A. Nekaris. 1998. Evolutionary History of Lorisiform Primates. *Folia Primatologica* 69 (1): 250–285.

Rasmussen, D. T., and R. W. Sussman. 2007. Parallelisms among Primates and Possums. In *Primate Origins, Adaptations and Evolution*, eds. M. Ravosa and M. Dagosto, 775–803. New York: Springer.

Rasoazanabary, E. 1999. Do Male Mouse Lemurs (*Microcebus murinus*) Face a Trade Off between Survival and Reproduction during the Dry Season? *Primate Report* 54 (1): 27.

Rasoazanabary, E. 2006. Male and Female Activity Patterns in *Microcebus murinus* during the Dry Season at Kirindy Forest, Western Madagascar. *International Journal of Primatology* 27 (2): 437–464.

Rasoloarison, R. M., S. M. Goodman, and J. U. Ganzhorn. 2000. Taxonomic Revision of Mouse Lemurs (*Microcebus*) in the Western Portions of Madagascar. *International Journal of Primatology* 21 (6): 963–1019.

Raxworthy, C. J. 2003. Introduction to the Reptiles. In *The Natural History of Madagascar*, eds. S. M. Goodman and J. P. Benstead, 934–949. Chicago, IL: University of Chicago Press.

Razafindratsita, V. R. 1995. *Etude Biologique et Ecologique de Philepitta castanea (Muller, 1776) Son rôle dans la Régénération du Sous-Bois Forestier du Parc National de Ranomafana.* Université d'Antananarivo in Madagascar.

Reid, N. 1989. Dispersal of Mistletoes by Honeyeaters and Flowerpeckers: Components of Seed Dispersal Quality. *Ecology* 70 (1): 137–145.

Reid, N. 1990. Mutalistic Interdependence between Mistletoes (*Amyema quandang*), and Spiny-Cheeked Honeyeaters and Mistletoebirds in and Arid Woodland. *Australian Journal of Ecology* 15: 175–190.

Reid, N. 1991. Coevolution of Mistletoes and Frugivorous Birds? *Australian Journal of Ecology* 16: 457–469.

Reid, N., M. Stafford Smith, and Z. Yan. 1995. Ecology and Population Biology of Mistletoes. In *Forest Canopies*, eds. M. D. Lowman and N. M. Nadkarni, 285–310. London: Academic Press.

Reimann, W., U. Radespeil, and E. Zimmermann. 2003. Feeding Regimes of Two Sympatric Mouse Lemurs in North-Western Madagascar (*Microcebus murinus* and *M. ravelobensis*): No Clear Evidence for Niche Separation. *Folia Primatologica* 74: 215.

Remis, M. J. 1994. Feeding Ecology and Positional Behavior of Lowland Gorillas. Ph.D. dissertation, Yale University.

Rendigs, A., U. Radespiel, D. Wrogemann, and E. Zimmermann. 2003. Relationship between Microhabitat Structure and Distribution of Mouse Lemurs (*Microcebus spp.*) in Northwestern Madagascar. *International Journal of Primatology* 24 (1): 47–64.

Rice, W. R. 1989. Analyzing Tables of Statistical Tests. *Evolution* 43: 223–225.

Richard, A. F. 1985. *Primates in Nature*. New York: Freeman and Company.

Richard, A. F., and R. E. Dewar. 1991. Lemur Ecology. *Annual Review of Ecology and Systematics* 22: 145–175.

Richards, P. W. 1952. *The Tropical Rain Forest*. Cambridge: Cambridge University Press.

Ripley, S. 1984. Environmental Grain, Niche Diversification and Feeding Behavior in Primates. In *Food Acquisition and Processing in Primates*, eds. D. J. Chivers, B. A. Wood, and A. Bilsborough, 33–72. New York: Plenum Press.

Rosenberger, A. L. 1992. Evolution of Feeding Niches in New World Monkeys. *American Journal of Physical Anthropology* 88: 525–562.

Ross, C. 1992. Basal Metabolic Rate, Body Weight and Diet in Primates: An Evaluation of the Evidence. *Folia Primatologica* 58: 7–23.

Roth, O. 1996. *Ecology and Social Behavior of* Avahi laniger. Basel, Switzerland: Universitäte Basel.

Rouquier, S., A. Blancher, and D. Giorgi. 2000. The Olfactory Receptor Gene Repertoire in Primates and Mouse: Evidence for Reduction of the Functional Fraction in Primates. *Proceedings of the National Academy of Sciences of the United States of America* 97: 2870–2874.

Rowe, N. 1996. *The Pictorial Guide to the Living Primates*. New York: Pagonias Press.

Rowe, N. 2008. *All the World's Primates*. Rhode Island: Pogonias Press.

Rumpler, Y., S. Crovella, and D. Montagnon. 1994. Systematic Relationships among Cheirogaleidae (Primates, Strepsirhini) Determined from Analysis of Highly Repeated DNA. *Folia Primatologica* 63 (3): 149–155.

Rusak, B. 1981. Vertebrate Behavioral Rhythms. In *Biological Rhythms*, ed. J. Aschoff, 183–213. New York: Plenum Press.

Russell, R. J. 1975. Body Temperatures and Behavior of Captive Cheirogaleids. In *Lemur Biology*, eds. I. Tattersall and R. W. Sussman, 193–206. New York: Plenum Press.

Sauther, M. L. 1992. The Effect of Reproductive State, Social Rank and Group Size on Resource Use among Free-Ranging Ringtailed Lemurs (*Lemur catta*) of Madagascar. Ph.D. dissertation, Washington University at St. Louis.

Schatz, G. E. 2001. *Generic Tree Flora of Madagascar*. Kew, UK: Royal Botanic Gardens.

Schilling, A. 1980. The Possible Role of Urine in Territoriality of Some Nocturnal Prosimians. *Symposia of the Zoological Society of London* 43: 165–193.

Schmelting, B., P. Ehresmann, H. Lutermann, B. Randrianambinina, and E. Zimmermann. 2000. Reproduction of Two Sympatric Mouse Lemur Species (*Microcebus murinus* and *M. ravelobensis*) in North-West Madagascar: First Results of a Long Term Study. In *Diversite et Endemisme a Madagascar*, eds. W. R. Lourenco and S. M. Goodman, 165–175. Paris: Mémoires de la Societé de Biogéographie.

Schmid, J. 1996. Oxygen Consumption and Torpor in Mouse Lemurs (*Microcebus murinus* and *M. myoxinus*): Preliminary Results of a Study in Western Madagascar. In *Adaptations to the Cold: Tenth International Hibernation Symposium*, eds. F. Geiser, A. J. Hulbert, and S. C. Nicol, 47–54. Armidale, Australia: University of New England Press.

Schmid, J. 1998. Tree Holes Used for Resting by Gray Mouse Lemurs (*Microcebus murinus*) in Madagascar: Insulation Capacities and Energetic Consequences. *International Journal of Primatology* 19 (5): 797–809.

Schmid, J. 1999. Sex-Specific Differences in Activity Patterns and Fattening in the Gray Mouse Lemur (*Microcebus murinus*) in Madagascar. *Journal of Mammalogy* 80 (3): 749–757.

Schmid, J. 2000. Daily Torpor in the Gray Mouse Lemur (*Microcebus murinus*) in Madagascar: Energetic Consequences and Biological Significance. *Oecologia* 123: 175–183.

Schmid, J., and P. M. Kappeler. 1994. Sympatric Mouse Lemurs (*Microcebus* spp.) in Western Madagascar. *Folia Primatologica* 63: 162–170.

Schmid, J., and P. M. Kappeler. 1998. Fluctuating Sexual Dimorphism and Differential Hibernation by Sex in a Primate, the Gray Mouse Lemur (*Microcebus murinus*). *Behavioral Ecology and Sociobiology* 43: 125–132.

Schmid, J., T. Ruf, and G. Heldmaier. 2000. Metabolism and Temperature Regulation during Daily Torpor in the Smallest Primate, the Pygmy Mouse Lemur (*Microcebus myoxinus*) in Madagascar. *Journal of Comparative Physiology B: Biochemical, Systemic, and Environmental Physiology* 170: 59–68.

Schmid, J., and J. R. Speakman. 2000. Daily Energy Expenditure of the Grey Mouse Lemur (*Microcebus murinus*): A Small Primate that Uses Torpor. *Journal of Comparative Physiology B: Biochemical, Systemic, and Environmental Physiology* 170 (8): 633–641.

Schmid, J., and P. J. Stephenson. 2003. Physiological Adaptations of Malagasy Mammals: Lemurs and Tenrecs Compared. In *The Natural History of Madagascar*, eds. S. M. Goodman and J. P. Benstead, 1198–1203. Chicago, IL: University of Chicago Press.

Schmidt-Nielsen, K. 1984. *Scaling: Why Is Animal Size So Important?* Cambridge: Cambridge University Press.

Schmidt-Nielsen, K. 1998. *Animal Physiology*. Englewood Cliffs, NJ: Prentice-Hall.

Schülke, O. 2003. *Phaner furcifer*, Fork-Marked Lemur, Vakihandry, Tanta. In *The Natural History of Madagascar*, eds. S. M. Goodman and J. P. Benstead, 1318–1320. Chicago, IL: University of Chicago Press.

Schülke, O. 2005. Evolution of Pair-Living in *Phaner furcifer*. *International Journal of Primatology* 26 (4): 903–919.

Schupp, E. W. 1993. Quantity, Quality, and the Effectiveness of Seed Dispersal by Animals. *Vegetatio* 107/108: 15–29.

Schwab, D. 2000. A Preliminary Study of Spatial Distribution and Mating System of Pygmy Mouse Lemur (*Microcebus cf. myoxinus*). *American Journal of Primatology* 51: 41–60.

Schwab, D., and J. U. Ganzhorn. 2004. Distribution, Population Structure and Habitat use of *Microcebus berthae* Compared to those of Other Sympatric Cheirogalids. *International Journal of Primatology* 25 (2): 307–330.

Schwartz, J. H., and I. Tattersall. 1985. Evolutionary Relationships of Living Lemurs and Lorises (Mammalia, Primates) and Their Potential Affinities with European Eocene Adapidae. *Anthropological Papers of the American Museum of Natural History* 60: 1–100.

Seamans, M. E., and R. J. Gutiérrez. 1995. Breeding Habitat of the Mexican Spotted Owl in the Tularosa Mountains, New Mexico. *The Condor* 97: 944–952.

Shea, B. T. 1987. Reproductive Strategies, Body Size, and Encephalization in Primate Evolution. *International Journal of Primatology* 8: 139–156.

Siegel, S., and N. J. Castellan Jr. 1988. *Non-Parametric Statistics for the Behavioral Sciences*. New York: McGraw-Hill.

Siemers, B. M., J. B. Ramanamajato, and J. U. Ganzhorn. 2003. Sensory Ecology of Prey Detection in Free-Living Grey Mouse Lemurs (*Microcebus murinus*). *Folia Primatologica* 74 (4): 221.

Smith, A. C. 2000. Composition and Proposed Nutritional Importance of Exudates Eaten by Saddleback (*Saguinus fuscicollis*) and mustached (*Saguinus mystax*) Tamarins. *International Journal of Primatology* 21: 415–429.

Smith, A. P. 1997. Deforestation, Fragmentation and Reserve Design in Western Madagascar. In *Tropical Forest Remnants: Ecology, Management, and Conservation of Fragmented Communities*, eds. W. F. Laurance and R. O. Bierregaard, 415–441. Chicago, IL: University of Chicago Press.

Smith, A. P., and J. U. Ganzhorn. 1996. Convergence in Community Structure and Dietary Adaptation in Australian Possums and Gliders and Malagasy Lemurs. *Australian Journal of Ecology* 21 (2): 31–46.

Smith, R. J, and W. L. Jungers. 1997. Body Mass in Comparative Primatology. *Journal of Human Evolution* 32: 523–559.

Smythe, N. 1982. The Seasonal Abundance of Night-Flying Insects in a Neotropical Forest. In *The Ecology of a Tropical Forest, Seasonal Rhythms and Long-Term Changes*, eds. E. G. J. Leigh, A. S. Rand, and D. M. Windsor, 309–318. Washington, DC: Smithsonian Institution Press.

Snyder, R. L., D. E. Davis, and J. J. Christian. 1961. Seasonal Changes in the Weights of Woodchucks. *Journal of Mammalogy* 42: 297–312.

Soligo, C., and R. D. Martin. 2006. Adaptive Origins of Primates Revisited. *Journal of Human Evolution* 50: 414–430.

Sörg, J. P., and U. Rohner. 1996. Climate and Tree Phenology of the Dry Deciduous Forest of the Kirindy Forest. *Primate Report* 46: 57–80.

Stanger, K. F., B. S. Coffman, and M. K. Izard. 1995. Reproduction in Coquerel's Dwarf Lemur (*Mirza coquereli*). *American Journal of Primatology* 36 (3): 223–237.

Sterling, E. 1992. Timing of Reproduction in Aye-Ayes in Madagascar (*Daubentonia madagascariensis*). *American Journal of Primatology* 27 (1): 59–60.

Sterling, E. 2003. *Daubentonia madagascariensis*, Aye-Aye. In *The Natural History of Madagascar*, eds. S. M. Goodman and J. P. Benstead, 1348–1351. Chicago, IL: University of Chicago Press.

Sterling, E. J. 1993a. Behavioral Ecology of the Aye-Aye (*Daubentonia madagascariensis*) on Nosy Mangabe, Madagascar. Ph.D. dissertation, Yale University.

Sterling, E. J. 1993b. Patterns of Range Use and Social Organization in Aye-Ayes *Daubentonia madagascariensis* on Nosy Mangabe. In *Lemur Social Systems and Their Ecological Basis*, eds. P. M. Kappeler and J. Ganzhorn, 1–10. New York: Plenum Press.

Sterling, E. J., E. S. Dierenfeld, C. J. Ashbourne, and A. T. Feistner. 1994. Dietary Intake, Food Composition and Nutrient Intake in Wild and Captive Populations of *Daubentonia madagascariensis*. *Folia Primatologica* 62 (1–3): 115–124.

Sterling, E. J., and A. F. Richard. 1995. Social Organization in the Aye-Aye *Daubentonia madagascariensis* and the Perceived Distinctiveness of Nocturnal Primates. In *Creatures of the Dark: The Nocturnal Prosimians*, eds. L. Alterman, G. A. Doyle, and M. K. Izard, 439–451. New York: Plenum Press.

Stiles, E. W. 1993. The Influence of Pulp Lipids on Fruit Preference by Birds. *Vegatatio* 107/108: 227–235.

Stokes, M. K., N. A. Slade, and S. M. Blair. 2001. Influences of Weather and Moonlight on Activity Patterns of Small Mammals: A Biogeographical Perspective. *Canadian Journal of Zoology* 79: 966–972.

Storey, M. 1995. Timing of Hot Spot-Related Volcanism and the Breakup of Madagascar and India. *Science* 267: 852–855.

Strait, S. G. 1993. Differences in Occlusal Morphology and Molar Size in Frugivores and Faunivores. *Journal of Human Evolution* 25: 471–484.

Studier, E. H., and S. H. Sevick. 1992. Live Mass, Water Content, Nitrogen and Mineral Levels in Some Insects from South-Central Lower Michigan. *Comparative Biochemistry and Physiology Part A* 103: 579–595.

Studier, E. H., S. H. Sevick, J. O. Keeler, and R. A. Schenck. 1994a. Nutrient Levels in Guano from Maternity Colonies of Big Brown Bats. *Journal of Mammalogy* 75: 71–83.

Studier, E. H., S. H. Sevick, D. M. Ridley, and D. E. Wilson. 1994b. Mineral and Nitrogen Concentrations in Feces of Some Neotropical Bats. *Journal of Mammalogy* 75: 674–680.

Suazo, A. A., A. T. Delong, A. A. Bard, and D. M. Oddy. 2005. Repeated Capture of Beach Mice (*Peromyscus polionotus phasma* and *P. p. niveiventris*) Reduces Body Mass. *Journal of Mammalogy* 86 (3): 520–523.

Sussman, R. W. 1991. Primate Origins and the Evolution of Angiosperms. *American Journal of Primatology* 23 (4): 209–223.

Sussman, R. W. 1995. How Primates Invented the Rainforest and Vice Versa. In *Creatures of the Dark: The Nocturnal Prosimians*, eds. L. Alterman, G. A. Doyle, and M. K. Izard, 1–10. New York: Plenum Press.

Sussman, R. W., and W. G. Kinzey. 1984. The Ecological Role of the Callitrichidae: A Review. *American Journal of Physical Anthropology* 64: 419–449.

Symington, M. M. 1990. Fission-Fusion Social Organization in *Ateles* and Pan. *International Journal of Primatology* 11: 47–61.

Tan, C. L. 2000. *Behavior and Ecology of Three Sympatric Bamboo Lemur Species (genus Hapalemur) in Ranomafana National Park, Madagascar.* Stony Brook: State University of New York.

Tan, Y., A. D. Yoder, N. Yamashita, and L. Wen-Hsiung. 2005. Evidence from Opsin Genes Rejects Nocturnality in Ancestral Primates. *Proceedings of the National Academy of Sciences of the United States of America* 102 (41): 14712–14716.

Tattersall, I. 1982. *The Primates of Madagascar.* New York: Columbia University Press.

Tattersall, I. 2007. Madagascar's Lemurs: Cryptic Diversity or Taxonomic Inflation. *Evolutionary Anthropology* 16: 12–23.

Tattersall, I., and R. W. Sussman. 1989. Ecology and Behavior of the Malagasy Primates. In *Perspectives in Primate Biology,* eds. P. K. Seth and S. Seth, 61–69. New Delhi, India: Today and Tomorrow's Printers and Publishers.

Tavaré, S., C. R. Marshall, O. Will, C. Soligo, and R. D. Martin. 2002. Using the Fossil Record to Estimate the Age of the Last Common Ancestor of Extant Primates. *Nature* 416 (6882): 726–729.

Terborgh, J., and C. H. Janson. 1986. The Socioecology of Primates. *Annual Review of Ecology and Systematics* 17: 111.

Thalmann, U. 2001. Food Resource Characteristics in Two Nocturnal Lemurs with Different Social Behavior: *Avahi occidentalis* and *Lepilemur edwardsi. International Journal of Primatology* 22: 287–324.

Thalmann, U., and J. U. Ganzhorn. 2003. Lepilemur, Sportive Lemur. In *The Natural History of Madagascar,* eds. S. M. Goodman and J. P. Benstead, 1336–1340. Chicago, IL: University of Chicago Press.

Tremble, M., Y. Muskita, J. Supriatna. 1993. Field Observations of *Tarsius dianae* at Lore Lindu National Park, Central Sulawesi, Indonesia. *Tropical Biodiversity* 1 (2): 67–76.

Trivers, R. L. 1972. Parental Investment and Sexual Selection. In *Sexual Selection and the Descent of Man,* ed. B. Campbell, 136–179. Chicago, IL: Aldine.

Turk, D. 1995. *A Guide to Trees of Ranomafana National Park and Central Eastern Madagascar, Tsimbazaza Botanical and Zoological Garden and Missouri Botanical Garden.* Antananarivo, Madagascar: USAID.

Tutin, C. E. G., and M. Fernandez. 1993. Faecal Analysis as a Method of Describing Diets of Apes, Examples from Sympatric Gorillas and Chimpanzees at Lopé, Gabon. *Tropics* 2: 189–197.

Tutin, C. E. G., M. Fernandez, M. E. Rogers, E. A. Williamson, and W. C. McGrew. 1991. Foraging Profiles of Sympatric Lowland Gorillas and Chimpanzees in the Lopé Reserve, Gabon. *Philosophical Transactions of the Royal Society of London B* 334: 179–186.

Tuttle, R. H. 1998. Global Primatology in a New Millennium. *International Journal of Primatology* 19 (1): 1–12.

van der Pijl, L. 1982. *Principles of Dispersal in Higher Plants*. Berlin: Springer.

van Hooff, J. A. R. A. M., and C. P. van Schaik. 1992. Cooperation in Competition: The Ecology of Primate Bonds. In *Coalitions and Alliances in Humans and Other Animals*, eds. A. H. Harcourt and F. B. M. de Waal, 357–389. New York: Oxford University Press.

van Horn, R. N., and G. G. Eaton. 1979. Reproductive Physiology and Behavior in Prosimians. In *The Study of Prosimian Behavior*, eds. G. A. Doyle and R. D. Martin, 79–122. New York: Academic Press.

van Leeuwen, W. M. D. 1954. On the Biology of Some Javanese Loranthaceae and the Role Birds Play in Their Life Historie. *Beaufortia* 41: 103–207.

van Ommeren, R. J., and T. G. Whitman. 2002. Changes in Interactions between Juniper and Mistletoe Mediated by Shared Avian Frugivores: Parasitism to Potential Mutualism. *Oecologia* 130: 281–288.

van Schaik, C. P., J. W. Terborgh, and S. J. Wright. 1993. The Phenology of Tropical Forests: Adaptive Significance and Consequences for Primary Consumers. *Annual Review of Ecology and Systematics* 24: 353–377.

van Schaik, C. P., and J. A. R. A. M van Hooff. 1983. On the Ultimate Causes of Primate Social Systems. *Behaviour* 85 (1–2): 91–117.

Vaughan, T. A., J. M. Ryan, and N. J. Czaplewski. 2000. *Mammalogy*. New York: Saunders College Publishing.

Walsberg, G. E. 1975. Digestive Adaptations of *Phainopepla nitens* Associated with the Eating of Mistletoe Berries. *The Condor* 77: 169–174.

Warren, R. 1994. *Lazy Leapers: A Study of the Locomotor Ecology of Two Species of a Saltatory Nocturnal Lemur in Sympatry at Ampijoroa, Madagascar.* Liverpool, UK: University of Liverpool.

Waser, P. M., and W. T. Jones. 1983. Natal Philopatry among Solitary Mammals. *The Quarterly Review of Biology* 58: 355–390.

Waterman, P. G. 1984. Food Acquisition and Processing as a Function of Plant Chemistry. In *Food Acquisition and Processing in Primates*, eds. D. J. Chivers, B. Wood, and A. Bilsborough, 177–211. New York: Plenum Press.

Weidt, A., N. Hagenah, B. Randrianambinina, U. Radespiel, and E. Zimmermann. 2004. Social Organization of the Golden Brown Mouse Lemur (*Microcebus ravelobensis*). *American Journal of Physical Anthropology* 123 (1): 40–51.

Western, D. 1979. Size, Life History and Ecology in Mammals. *African Journal of Ecology* 17: 185–204.

Whitaker, J. O., Jr. 1988. Food Habits Analysis of Insectivorous Bats. In *Ecological and Behavioral Methods for the Study of Bats*, ed. T. H. Kunz, 177–189. Washington, DC: Smithsonian Institution Press.

White, F. J., D. J. Overdorff, E. A. Balko, and P. C. Wright. 1995. Distribution of Ruffed Lemurs (*Varecia variegata*) in Ranomafana National Park. *Folia Primatologica* 64 (3): 124–131.

Wiegand, K., F. Jeltsch, and D. Ward. 1999. Analysis of the Population Dynamics of Acacia Trees in the Negev Desert, Israel with a Spatially-Explicit Computer Simulation Model. *Ecological Modelling* 117: 203–224.

Wiens, F., and A. Zitzmann. 2003. Social Structure of the Solitary Slow Loris *Nycticebus coucang* (Lorisidae). *Journal of Zoology* 261 (1): 35–46.

Williamson, E. A., C. E. G Tutin, and M. E. Rogers. 1990. Composition of the Diet of Lowland Gorillas at Lopé in Gabon. *American Journal of Primatology* 21: 265–277.

Wilson, F., A. K. Irvine, and N. G. Walsh. 1989. Vertebrate Dispersal Syndromes in Some Australian and New Zealand Plant Communities, with Geographic Comparisons. *Biotropica* 21: 133–147.

Wimmer, B., D. Tautz, and P. M. Kappeler. 2002. The Genetic Population Structure of the Gray Mouse Lemur (*Microcebus murinus*), a Basal Primate from Madagascar. *Behavioral Ecology and Sociobiology* 52 (2): 166–175.

Wolfe, J., and C. Summerlin. 1989. The Influence of Lunar Light on Nocturnal Activity of the Old Field Mouse. *Animal Behaviour* 37: 410–414.

Worthington, A. H. 1989. Adaptations for Avian Frugivory, Assimilation Efficiency and Gut Transit Time of *Manacus vitellinus and Pipra mentalis*. *Oecologia* 80: 381–389.

Wrangham, R. W. 1980. An ecological Model of Female-Bonded Primate Groups. *Behaviour* 75: 262–300.

Wrangham, R. W. 1987. Evolution of Social Structure. In *Primate Societies*, eds. B. B. Smuts, D. L. Cheney, R. M. Seyfarth, R. W. Wrangham, and T. T. Struhsaker, 282–298. Chicago, IL: University of Chicago Press.

Wright, H. T., and J. A. Rakotoarisoa. 2003. The Rise of Malagasy Societies: New Developments in the Archaeology of Madagascar. In *The Natural History of Madagascar*, eds. S. M. Goodman and J. P. Benstead, 112–119. Chicago, IL: University of Chicago Press.

Wright, P. C. 1985. The Costs and Benefits of Nocturnality for *Aotus trivirgatus* (the Night Monkey). Ph.D. dissertation, City University of New York.

Wright, P. C. 1992. Primate Ecology, Rainforest Conservation, and Economic Development: Building a National Park in Madagascar. *Evolutionary Anthropology* 1: 25–33.

Wright, P. C. 1995. Demography and Life History of Free-Fanging *Propithecus diadema edwardsi* in Ranomafana National Park, Madagascar. *International Journal of Primatology* 16: 835–854.

Wright, P. C. 1997. The Future of Biodiversity in Madagascar: A View from Ranomafana National Park. In *Natural Change and Human Impact in Madagascar*, eds. S. M. Goodman and B. D. Patterson, 381–405. Washington, DC: Smithsonian Institution Press.

Wright, P. C. 1998. Impact of Predation Risk on the Behaviour of *Propithecus diadema edwardsi* in the rain forest of Madagascar. *Behaviour* 135 (4): 483–512.

Wright, P. C. 1999. Lemur Traits and Madagascar Ecology: Coping with an Island Environment. *Yearbook of Physical Anthropology* 42: 31–72.

Wright, P. C., S. K. Heckscher, and A. E. Dunham. 1997. Predation on Milne-Edwards' Sifaka (*Propithecus diadema edwardsi*) by the Fossa (*Cryptoprocta ferox*) in the Rainforest of Southeastern Madagascar. *Folia Primatologica* 68: 34–43.

Wright, P. C., and L. B. Martin. 1995. Predation, Pollination and Torpor in Two Nocturnal Prosimians (*Cheirogaleus major* and *Microcebus rufus*) in the Rain Forest of Madagascar. In *Creatures of the Dark: The Nocturnal Prosimians*, eds. L. Alterman, G. A. Doyle, and M. K. Izard, 45–60. New York: Plenum Press.

Wright, P. C., V. R. Razafindratsita, S. T. Pochran, and J. Jernvall. 2005. The Key to Madagascar Frugivores. In *Tropical Fruits and Frugivores: The Search for Strong Interactors*, eds. J. L. Dew and J. P. Boubli, 121–138. The Netherlands: Springer.

Wrogemann, D., U. Radespiel, and E. Zimmermann. 2001. Comparison of Reproductive Characteristics and Changes in Body Weight between Captive Populations of Rufous and Gray Mouse Lemurs. *International Journal of Primatology* 22 (1): 91–108.

Wrogemann, D., and E. Zimmermann. 2001. Aspects of Reproduction in the Eastern Rufous Mouse Lemur (*Microcebus rufus*) and Their Implications for Captive Management. *Zoo Biology* 20 (3): 157–167.

Yamagiwa, J., T. Yumoto, T. Maruhashi, and N. Mwanza. 1993. Field Methodology for Analyzing Diets of Eastern Lowland Gorillas in Kahuzi-Biega National Park, Zaire. *Tropics* 2: 209–218.

Yamashita, N. 1996. Seasonality and Site Specificity of Mechanical Dietary Patterns in Two Malagasy Lemur Families (Lemuridae and Indriidae). *International Journal of Primatology* 17: 355–387.

Yoder, A. D. 2003. Phylogeny of the Lemurs. In *The Natural History of Madagascar*, eds. S. M. Goodman and J. P. Benstead, 1242–1247. Chicago, IL: University of Chicago Press.

Yoder, A. D., M. M. Burns, and F. Génin. 2002. Molecular Evidence of Reproductive Isolation in Sympatric Sibling Species of Mouse Lemurs. *International Journal of Primatology* 23 (6): 1335–1343.

Yoder, A. D., M. Cartmill, M. Ruvolo, K. Smith, and R. Vilgalys. 1996. Ancient Single Origin for Malagasy Primates. *Proceedings of the National Academy of Sciences of the United States of America* 93: 5122–5126.

Yoder, A. D., R. M. Rasoloarison, S. M. Goodman, J. A. Irwin, S. Atsalis, M. J. Ravosa, and J. U. Ganzhorn. 2000. Remarkable Species Diversity in Malagasy Mouse Lemurs (Primates, *Microcebus*). *Proceedings of the National Academy of Sciences of the United States of America* 97: 11325–11330.

Zimmermann, E. 1995a. Acoustic Communication in Nocturnal Prosimians. In *Creatures of the Dark: The Nocturnal Prosimians*, eds. L. Alterman, G. A. Doyle, and M. K. Izard, 311–330. New York: Plenum Press.

Zimmermann, E. 1995b. Loud Calls in Nocturnal Prosimians: Structure, Evolution and Ontogeny. In *Current Topics in Primate Vocal Communication*, eds. E. Zimmermann, J. D. Newman, and U. Jürgens, 47–72. New York: Plenum Press.

Zimmermann, E., S. Cepok, N. Rakotoarison, V. Zietemann, and U. Radespiel. 1998. Sympatric Mouse Lemurs in North-West Madagascar: A New Rufous Mouse Lemur Species (*Microcebus ravelobensis*). *Folia Primatologica* 69: 106–114.

Zimmermann, E., and C. Lerch. 1993. The Complex Acoustic Design of an Advertisement Call in Male Mouse Lemurs (*Microcebus murinus*, Prosimii, Primates) and Sources of Its Variation. *Ethology* 93: 211–224.

Index

A

Alberta humblotii, 50, 61 (table)
Allocebus trichotis, 5
Ampijoroa Forestry Reserve, 13, 74, 86, 105, 111, 120, 137, 162, 167, 182
Anatolian ground squirrel, 109–110
Animal prey, availability of, 60, 62–63
Annual cycle (Brown mouse lemur), 175–181, 179 (figure)
Atypical estrus, 155, 166–167

B

Bakerella, 49, 50 (table), 51–55, 57, 58 (figure), 59 (figure), 66, 176
Beetles as food for mouse lemurs, 55–56, 72–73
Behavioral thermoregulation, 110
Belding ground squirrels, 106–107, 109
Berthe's mouse lemur, see *Microcebus berthae*
Body mass:
    changes during gestation, 160 (table)
    changes during hibernation, 93 (table)
    monthly mean, 89 (table)
    population-level and, 98 (table)
    seasonal fluctuations and, 95 (table), 97 (table)

Bonding:
    Allocebus trichotis, 5–6
    Mirza coquereli, 5
    Phaner furcifer, 5, 119
Brown mouse lemur, see *Microcebus rufus*

C

Cantilevering, 64
Cheirogaleid species, 10–12, 42, 67, 75, 84–85, 113
Cheirogaleidae, 5–6
    communication, 17
    metabolic rates, 17–18
    seasonal behavioral cycle in, 84
    seasonal fluctuations in, 83–87
    size, 16
    social networks, 16
    thermoregulatory capacity, 17
Cheirogaleus, 5, 11, 43, 75, 84–85, 86, 105, 107
    social ties, 118
Chitin, 31, 45, 46, 72, 77, 176
Climatic and resource fluctuations:
    Cheirogaleidae, 83–87
    investigation in brown mouse lemurs, 87–91
    response of small mammals, 81–82
Coleoptera, 33, 56, 65, 74, 80
Contest competition, 143–145, 168

D

Daubentonia madagascariensis, 4, 22, 116, 153
Diet of mouse lemurs, 41–44
  beetles, 72–73
  diet comparison, 73–74
  mistletoes, 65–72
Diet investigation (brown mouse lemurs), 44–45
  animal prey resource, 60–63
  Bakerella, 51–55
  beetles, 55–57
  biochemical analysis, 46–47
  fecal sampling – to study diet, 77–78
  frugivory, 47–51
  fruit resource, 56–60
  MNI-F, 45
  MNI-I, 46
  NFT, 46
  observations, 63–65
  organic matter in feces, 56
  phytochemical analysis, 60
  TFT, 46
  VS, 46
Distribution of mouse lemur, 12–16
Dormancy, 82
Dwarf lemurs, see *Cheirogaleus*

E

Eastern rufous mouse lemur, see *Microcebus rufus*
Estrus:
  atypical, 155, 166–167
  postpartum, 165–166
Estrous cycle, 158, 164
Estrous synchrony, 163–165

F

Fattening and hibernation, 91–96
Fattening analysis:
  female pattern, 91, 94, 96
  male pattern, 91, 94, 96
Fecal analysis:
  advantages of, 77
  MNI-F, 45, 47
  MNI-I, 46, 55, 62

NFT, 46, 47–48, 56
  SEM, 77
  shortcomings of, 78
  TFT, 46, 48
  VS, 46, 62
Fecal samples, 47 (figure), 50 (table), 53 (table)
  for diet study, 77–78
Feeding, 63–65
Female brown mouse lemur:
  dispersal of, 141
  fattening analysis in, 91, 94, 96
  reproductive activity in, 155, 157 (figure), 162, 171–173
First recapture data, 89
Fork-crowned lemurs, see *Phaner*
Frugivory, 47–51
Fruits, 48 (table)
  availability of, 56–57
  measurements of, 52 (table)
  phytochemical analysis of, 60, 61 (table)

G

Giant mouse lemurs, see *Mirza*
Gestation, 155, 158, 159, 160 (table), 171
Golden brown mouse lemur, see *Microcebus ravelobensis*
Goodman's mouse lemur, see *Microcebus lehilahytsara*
Grey mouse lemur, see *Microcebus murinus*
Gums:
  as high energy food, 42–43
  as problematic food, 74

H

Hairy-eared dwarf lemur, see *Allocebus trichotis*
Haplorhini, 4
Hibernation, 93 (table)
  body mass changes, 93 (table)
  Cheirogaleus medius, 5
  definition of, 81–82
  emerging from, 108–110
  factors triggering, 82–83

Microcebus, 6–7
    small mammals and, 83
High-ranking males, 119, 144
Homeothermy, 81

J

Jolly's mouse lemur, see *Microcebus jollyae*

K

Kin selection, 164
Kirindy Forest, 108, 111, 127, 141,
    150 (table)
Kjeldahl technique, 60, 61 (table)

L

Last capture data, 89
Lemurs, 3, see also *individual entries*
    as recognized primates, 185
    researching lemurs, see
        Ranomafana National Park

M

Madagascar, 6, 69, 105, 150–151
    (table)
    ecological zones, 10
    flora and fauna, 2–3
    geography, 12–16, 14 (map), 105
    habitat for nocturnal primates, 2
Male-biased trap sex ratio, 87
Male brown mouse lemurs:
    dispersal of, 140, 141
    fattening analysis in, 91, 94, 96
    reproductive activity in, 154, 155,
        158 (figure), 167–168
Male reproductive patterns, 167–168
Mantadia National Park, 13, 103,
    107–108, 151 (table)
Mating patterns, 150–151 (table)
Medinilla, 30, 49, 50 (table), 59 (figure)
Microcebus, see also Cheirogaleidae;
        Young mouse lemurs
    Anatolian ground squirrel and,
        109–110
    annual cycle, 175–181, 179 (figure)
    Belding ground squirrels and,
        106–107

body size/diet requirements, 42
body temperature, 86
capturing, 87–88
characteristics, 1, 152
dietary diversity, 9, 43–44
distribution, 12–16
ecology of, 181–183
fattening and hibernation,
    91–96, 104
feeding patterns monitoring, 45–47
geographic distribution, 12–16
hibernation, 6
identification techniques, 8–9
feeding, 63–65
future, 185–186
lethargic, 85, 103
live-trapping, 35–37
living conditions, 6–7
local ecologies, 181–183
mating, 6–7
mistletoes and, 65–72
as model for ancestral primate, 185
observing, 38–39
omnivorous animals, 18–19
predators of, 22–23
primate origins and, 75–77
reproductive patterns of, 149–154
residents of, 142–143
seasonal responses of, 107–108
size, 1, 7
as small mammals, 183–185
social organization, 7
social status, 104–105
solitary, 126–129
species, 10–12, see also *individual species*
young, 90, 169–171
Microcebus berthae, 11, 162, 165
    body temperature, 86
    feeding patterns, 43, 75
    habitat, 13
    male dispersal, 140
    male reproductive patterns,
        167–168
    mating, 120
    smallest living primate, 10, 145
    social patterns, 119, 127
    torpor, 86

Microcebus griseorufus, 11, 13
Microcebus jollyae, 11, 13
Microcebus lehilahytsara, 11, 13
Microcebus mittermeieri, 11, 13
Microcebus murinus, 15, 73, 165, 167,
    see also *Microcebus rufus*
    body mass of, 85
    captive study, 107
    diet, 43
    fruit as principal diet, 10
    male-biased sex ratios, 105
    mating behavior, 152
    model of species geographic
        variation, 15
Microcebus myoxinus, 10, 11, 12, 15
Microcebus ravelobensis, 10, 11
    feeding patterns, 43, 74–75, 127
    gathering call, 147
    habitat, 13
    lack of seasonal response, 105
    male reproductive patterns,
        167–168
    mating season, 126, 161–162
    social patterns, 119–120, 127
    torpor, 86
Microcebus rufus, see also *Microcebus*
    murinus
    capturing, 8
    diet, 44
    insect as principal diet, 10
    investigation of diet, 44–47
    lethargy periods, 85
    life cycle of, 175–181, 179 (figure)
    as omnivorous animals, 9, 18–19
    population fluctuations in, 96–100
    reproduction in, 154–156
    seasonal fluctuations in, 87–91
    size, 7
    sleeping nests of, 110–112
    social interactions of, 124–126
    social organization of, 121–124
    trap sex ratio for, 103
Microcebus sambiranensis, 11, 15
Microcebus simmonsi, 11, 13
Microcebus tavaratra, 11, 15
Minimum number of individual
    fruit per fecal sample (MNI-F),
    45, 47

Minimum number of individual
    invertebrates found per sample
    (MNI-I), 45, 55, 62
Mirza, 5
Mirza coquereli, 119, 153
Mistletoes, 65–72
    Bakerella, 66, 67
    dispersal of, 70–71
    feeding ecology and, 68
    nutritional value of, 67–68
    Viscum, 66
Mittermeier's mouse lemur, see
    Microcebus mittermeieri
Mouse lemurs, see *Microcebus*
Mouse lemur species, see also
    individual species
    seasonal responses comparison,
        107–108
    diet comparison, 73–75

N

Nest associations, 125–126
Nocturnal primates:
    African, 118
    characteristics of, 127
    extinction threats, 2
    features of, 16–19
    study of, 1–2
    social life, 116–117
Nocturnal Strepsirrhines, sociality
    in, 115
    non-uniformity in social behavior,
        116–117
    research, 116
    social patterns, 115–116
Northern rufous mouse lemur, see
    Microcebus tavaratra
Number of fruit types per fecal
    sample (NFT), 46, 47–48, 56

O

Organic matter, fecal samples, 56

P

Petite phenologie, 25, 29, 58
Phaner, 5, 119
    social ties, 119

Phytochemical analysis of, 60,
    61 (table)
Population:
    changes in composition, 131–135
    continuity, 138–142
    female, 141
    male, 140, 141
Population composition, changes,
    131–135
Population fluctuations, brown
    mouse lemur, 96–100
Population nuclei, 7
Postpartum estrus, 155, 165–166
Predation, brown mouse lemur,
    139–140
Primate evolution and mouse
    lemurs, 75–77
Primates:
    mouse lemur, 75–77
    social life of nocturnal, 116
Prosimian, 4, 146, 184
Pygmy mouse lemur, see *Microcebus
    myoxinus*

R

Ranomafana National Park:
    flowering patterns in, 25–26, 27
        (figure), 28 (figure)
    fruiting patterns in, 26–30, 27
        (figure), 28 (figure)
    insects in, 30–34, 35 (figure)
    leaf nests at, 110–111
    live-trapping mouse lemurs
        in, 35–37
    location of, 21
    phenological monitoring, 24–25
    rainfall and temperature in, 23, 24
        (figure)
    richness of, 21–22
Red and grey mouse lemur, see
    Microcebus griseorufus
Red mouse lemur, see *Microcebus rufus*
Reproductive activity:
    female, 155, 156, 157 (figure), 162,
        171–173
    male, 154, 155, 158 (figure), 167–168
    photoperiod, 165

Reproductive patterns of brown
    mouse lemur, 154–156
    atypical estrus, 166–167
    births, 161
    estrous cycles, 156
    estrous synchrony, 163–165
    female reproductive potential,
        171–173
    gestation, 158–161
    male reproductive patterns,
        167–168
    postpartum estrus, 165–166
    reproductive seasonality, 161–163
    testicular enlargement, 156
Reproductive seasonality, 161–163
Residents, mouse lemur, 142–143

S

Sambirano mouse lemur, see
    Microcebus sambiranensis
Scanning electron microscopy
    (SEM), 77
Scramble competition, 144–145
Seasonal fluctuations:
    brown mouse lemur, 87–91
    Cheirogaleidae, 83–87
    response of small mammals,
        81–83
    spatial use, 137
    trap sex ratio, 135–138
Seasonal fluctuations (brown
    mouse lemur):
    activity levels, 96–100
    body mass, 88–89, 90, 94 (figure),
        95 (table), 97 (table)
    fattening and hibernation, 91–96
    population-level differences, 89–90
    seasonal response differences,
        100–107
    tail circumference, 88–89, 94
        (figure), 95 (table), 97 (table)
Seasonal hibernation, 85
Seasonal responses:
    differences in, 100–107
    species comparison, 107–108
Simmons's mouse lemur, see
    Microcebus simmonsi

Sleeping nests:
    hollows of dead trees, 111
    leaf nests, 110–111
    tree holes, 111
Social interactions, brown mouse
        lemur, 124–126
Social organization, 115
    Cheirogaleidae, 16
    Microcebus berthae, 119, 127
    Microcebus ravelobensis, 119–120, 127
    Microcebus rufus, 121–126
    nocturnal primates, 116–117
Social organization, investigation
        of (Brown mouse lemur), 121
    changes in population composition,
        131–135
    migration patterns and population
        continuity, 138–142
    population residents, 142–143
    scramble and contest competition,
        143–145
    seasonal fluctuations in trap sex
        ratio, 135–138
    social interactions, 124–126
    solitary mouse lemur, 126–129
    spatial distribution comparison, 122
    spatial overlap between sexes,
        121–122
    understanding spatial distribution,
        129–131
Social structure, definition, 115
Social thermoregulation, 128
Solitary mouse lemur, 126–129
Spatial distribution:
    male and female, 122
    trap data, 129–131
Spherical leaf nests, 110–111
Strepsirrhini, 3–4
    characteristics of mammals, 4

characteristics of primates, 4
sociality in nocturnal, 115–121, 128
Strong contest competition, 144–145

T

Tail circumference:
    fluctuations during hibernation,
        92 (table)
    population-level, 98 (table)
    seasonal fluctuations, 95 (table),
        97 (table)
Tapetum lucidum, 4
Testicle, enlargement, 155,
    156, 168
Tongolahy, see *Bakerella*
Torpor, 82, 83–84, 85
Total number of different fruit types
    (TFT), 46, 48
Trap sex ratio:
    male-biased, 87
    seasonal fluctuations, 135–138
Trap sites, of brown mouse lemur,
    130 (figure), 131 (figure)
Trapping:
    effects of, 112
    results of, 130 (table), 133 (figure)

V

Viscum, 66; see also Mistletoes
Volumetric score per sample (VS),
    46, 62

Y

Young mouse lemurs, 90
    characteristics of, 169
    size of, 169
    social behavior, 169–171